D0914996

Praise for The Challenge Culture

"Business and politics have become ever more competitive and unpredictable. In order to succeed in this environment, Travis introduces *The Challenge Culture* where employees are encouraged and are sufficiently self-confident to push back, engage in debate, and, along with their leaders, search intensively for the best answer to critical issues. A must-read for all people leading organizations in these turbulent times!"

—LARRY BOSSIDY, retired chairman and CEO of Honeywell International, coauthor of *Execution: The Discipline of Getting Things Done*

"A culture built on open dialogue and honesty will deliver collective positive outcomes for customers and team members."

—CATHERINE D'AMATO, president and CEO, The Greater Boston Food Bank

"What a wonderful read, with terrific, memorable thoughts, and a powerful theme: what is essential for a successful business is the ability to question the leadership and ask 'why?'. There are more lessons to be learned than offered by any Harvard MBA."

—JACK COWIN, chairman and managing director, Competitive Foods Australia Ltd.

"Nigel understands the intricacies of everything. And, even better, he knows how to put them together to make a business run the way it should. This book not only takes you inside his businesses, but inside the mind that challenged them to thrive. If you can use 20 percent of what he's suggesting, you'll be ahead of the game. Use 40 percent and you can blow the doors off."

—MARK GOLDSTEIN, former chief marketing officer, BBDO Worldwide

"*The Challenge Culture* is a must-read for those wanting to improve their leadership skills in light of a fast changing social and political workplace environment. Nigel implores all of us to foster an open and engaging culture of challenge. For over three decades, Nigel has been at the helm of internationally recognizable organizations, and the insights of *The Challenge Culture* provide a powerful playbook for people across the business world."

—SAM KENNEDY, president and CEO of the Boston Red Sox

"We all know that America *runs* on Dunkin', but have you ever wondered how Dunkin' runs? Dunkin' Brands chairman and CEO Nigel Travis has experience running some of the nation's largest franchises and shares his insight on the importance of creating a challenge culture, one that questions the status quo, encourages internal pushback, and helps companies be nimble enough to adapt to change. *The Challenge Culture* is a must-read for employers and employees alike, and promises to get ideas for long-term success percolating."

—ROBERT KRAFT, chairman and CEO of the Kraft Group and the New England Patriots

"Nigel Travis has been at the top of major maverick enterprises which missed moments for vital re-invention as well as those which seized the moment for needed transformation. I knew Bill Rosenberg, the visionary founder of Dunkin' Donuts, well and he'd have loved the challenge culture Travis helped inspire there today. Dissent is not disloyalty but can be the spark for innovation and the safeguard for integrity. Firms from the governance financial frauds of Enron and Worldcom to the privacy and gender 'bro cultures' at today's tech titans would have benefited from Travis' leadership lessons. Conformity kills creativity and subverts justice and *The Challenge Culture* is the antidote to a contagion of conformity across sectors."

—JEFFREY A. SONNENFELD, senior associate dean for Leadership Studies and Lester Crown Professor of Leadership Practice, Yale School of Management

THE
CHALLENGE
CULTURE

THE
CHALLENGE
CULTURE

*Why the Most Successful
Organizations Run on Pushback*

NIGEL TRAVIS

Chairman, Dunkin' Brands

PUBLICAFFAIRS

New York

PublicAffairs
Hachette Book Group
1290 Avenue of the Americas
New York, NY 10104

www.publicaffairsbooks.com
@Public_Affairs

Printed in the United States of America

First Edition: September 2018

Published by PublicAffairs, an imprint of Perseus Books, LLC, a subsidiary of Hachette Book Group, Inc. The PublicAffairs name and logo is a trademark of the Hachette Book Group.

The Hachette Speakers Bureau provides a wide range of authors for speaking events. To find out more, go to www.hachettespeakersbureau.com or call (866) 376-6591.

The publisher is not responsible for websites (or their content) that are not owned by the publisher.

PRINT BOOK INTERIOR DESIGN BY JEFF WILLIAMS.

Library of Congress Cataloging-in-Publication Data.

Names: Travis, Nigel, author.
Title: The challenge culture : why the most successful organizations run on
     pushback / Nigel Travis, Chairman, Dunkin Brands.
Description: First edition. | New York : PublicAffairs, [2018] | Includes
     bibliographical references and index.
Identifiers: LCCN 2018010002| ISBN 9781541762145 (hardcover : alk. paper) |
     ISBN 9781541762152 (ebook : alk. paper)
Subjects: LCSH: Corporate culture. | Travis, Nigel. | Businessmen--United
     States—Biography.
Classification: LCC HD58.7 .T734 2018 | DDC 658—dc23
LC record available at https://lccn.loc.gov/2018010002

ISBNs: 978-1-5417-6214-5 (hardcover); 978-1-5417-6215-2 (ebook); 978-1-5417-3610-8 (international edition)

LSC-C

10 9 8 7 6 5 4 3 2 1

Dedicated to my family, who continue to inspire me in every way—Joanna, David, Ian, and Brooke

Contents

The Fundamental Why

Joanna's Question

I had been thinking about the ideas in this book for almost four decades but never with the intention of writing them down. Then, a couple of years ago, a number of factors came together that made a book seem not only relevant but also useful, even necessary.

Most significant, the business environment had grown increasingly intense. The combined stresses of technology change, competitive pressure, and customer demand had a curious effect on some companies. They seemed to become rigid, authoritarian, intent on achieving control in what looked like an uncontrollable environment. Challenged from without, they responded by squelching challenge from within. In my role as chairman and CEO of Dunkin' Brands (which comprises both Dunkin' Donuts and Baskin-Robbins), we were subject to the same business pressures, but I strongly believed we had to respond differently by becoming more flexible, more egalitarian, and more able to adapt. The only way to do that was to embrace challenge and encourage pushback rather than reject them. How else will you hear new ideas and improve existing practices?

The political environment had become just as intense. The 2016 presidential campaign was raucous, and the first year of the Trump administration was full of ups and downs, twists and turns. It was very hard for people to get their heads around Trump's leadership style. Did he have the right management skills to be president? Could he listen? Would he engage in civil discourse? Was he able to tolerate challenge and questioning and pushback? These questions made me think harder about my own leadership approach and what I thought was really needed in our society today.

Finally, I found that pushback was becoming increasingly important in my personal life, as well. My two younger kids, then ten and twelve, were ferocious question askers (and still are). They push back constantly and challenge everything, and I saw that was how they were learning and growing and that it was strengthening and enriching our family life. In coaching youth soccer, I found that pushback and challenge were essential to learning skills and creating motivated teams. In the boards I sat on, I realized that questioning is an incredibly valuable skill, and pushback could save companies from making life-threatening mistakes.

The final impetus came from my wife, Joanna. One evening we were enjoying dinner at a favorite restaurant, one of the few times we had had a chance to spend time together, just the two of us, without kids or guests or business colleagues. At some point in the evening, probably after the second glass of wine, I told her that I was thinking about writing a book.

I don't remember how I expected her to react. Probably I was hoping she'd say, "What a fantastic idea!" or "Nigel, it'll be a runaway best seller!"

Joanna is a lawyer, trained in courtroom procedure, as well as an experienced nonprofit board director. After my pronouncement, she looked at me carefully for a moment, and I could see the very polished wheels turning in her head.

"OK, but what do you have to say? What's your message?"

She asked the question in a neutral way. Not sarcastic or disbelieving, nor gushy and encouraging. She was asking a question in search of gaining information she did not have. What would the book contribute to the conversation? What did I uniquely have to say that others did not?

That question continued to ring in my ears for some time. It's the kind of "why" question that is not asked enough in the business environment. Why are we pursuing this initiative? Why are we hiring this person? Why are we following this strategy? It was a *purposeful* question. I greatly value Joanna's ability to ask such questions because they keep me, and the family, grounded.

The answer to Joanna's question is this: the ability to create a culture of challenge in your organization—business, not-for-profit, governmental, academic—is essential to survival and sustainability in today's chaotic world. Only through questioning, pushback, challenge, and debate will you be able to stay relevant, respond to customers' needs, and sustain yourself. Not only do I understand the truth of this as CEO of Dunkin' but I have also learned it the hard way, in my experience as president and chief operating officer of Blockbuster, the now-defunct video retailer. As it did at Blockbuster, the lack of a challenge culture can contribute to a company's demise. It's an existential issue.

A challenge culture is particularly effective in times of change, and I think we'd all argue that we live in times of unending change. In a challenge culture, people are expected to question the status quo, push back on long-held assumptions, and examine and discuss new ideas and proposals, always looking for more and better information, refinements, and more exceptional initiatives. To do all this, people must be encouraged to challenge one another in every direction within the organization: up, down, or sideways. They must not be afraid to speak up, to question their bosses, their peers, and their board—despite the perceived difficulty of doing so—and they should be confident they won't face unfair repercussions if and when they do.

In a challenge culture, questioning is always meant to be positive and discourse is civil. Challenge, as we'll see, is different from confrontation. It does not involve attack, intimidation, bullying, demeaning, personal assault, badgering, or insult. Questioning is directed toward issues, not personalities or groups. Even when the process of challenge heats up or gets passionate, it doesn't turn nasty. Questioning, pushback, discourse, and challenge are meant to generate learning, stimulate ideas, foster innovation and creativity, and build healthy and respectful relationships.

The challenge culture is *not* a gladiatorial arena. It is not a 24/7 version of *Survivor*. As part of learning how to behave in a challenge culture, people have to understand what to challenge, how to challenge, and when to challenge. They pick their issues. They look for the right time and best place. They don't contend everything. They don't always pick up the cudgels when challenged.

The challenge culture has enabled us to achieve positive results at Dunkin' Brands. From a company with a management style not known for its transparency, we have become much more open to all kinds of conversations and that has enabled us to become more consistent in our execution, more nimble in embracing new technologies, and more attentive to our relationships both inside and outside the company. It is not easy to create a challenge culture, for many reasons. Corporate cultures seem to have a natural tendency to progress from the open to the authoritarian as the companies grow and gain dominance—as we've seen with old-line companies like GE.

Further, people are not necessarily trained in the essential challenge skills: purposeful questioning, positive pushback, and civil debate. Some management teams simply do not buy in to the importance of challenge and prefer to carry on the command-and-control style. But, as I'll discuss, many companies have found that approach rarely sustains itself. Even the military, where command-and-control management originated, has embraced questioning and challenge of its processes and practices in noncombat situations.

Throughout my career, I have refined the ideas that constitute the challenge culture and tried my best to put them successfully into practice. I have, at last, reached the point where I believe I understand the issues well enough to help others create and maintain a challenge culture in their own organizations. That is why I decided to write this book.

And that, my darling Joanna, is my long answer to your challenging question. Thank you for asking.

CHAPTER ONE

Challenge Starts with a Spark

Questioning the Status Quo

One of my most memorable moments of challenge featured Donald Trump—if indirectly.

In December 2004, I became president and CEO of Papa John's Pizza, after having spent the previous decade of my career as president and COO of Blockbuster, the video rental chain. My wife, Joanna, and I were living in Dallas at the time, where Blockbuster was headquartered. Joanna was expecting our first child in February, so I made a deal with John Schnatter, the chairman and founder of Papa John's, that I would work part-time until the baby was born. I'd shuttle between Dallas and Louisville, where Papa John's was based.

Of course, there really is no such thing as a part-time CEO. So, by the time our son, Ian, was born in February, I was going full steam with my new company. In March, I flew to Orlando to attend my first big convention of Papa John's franchisees. This was my moment to introduce myself, provide a glimpse of my management style, get to know the Papa John's people, and set a tone for my tenure as CEO. So, on the morning of the opening day, March 2005, John brought me on stage, and I made my presentation to a packed house. It went well enough. Applause and laughter and attention came at the right places. After the talk, I met a lot of people. Still, I ended the session feeling that something was missing. The status quo felt heavy around me. I felt we needed some kind of spark, an action to rally around, a challenge to the standard way of doing things.

In the afternoon session the audience got a treat. One of my colleagues had said he had learned about a big internal meeting held by our archrival, Domino's Pizza. One of the Domino's executives had made a speech to his troops in which he declared that Papa John's was their enemy number one. That got a big rise—hoots and guffaws—out of our audience. The Papa John's people are not only competitive by nature but they are also rather fanatical about their own beloved brand.

When the afternoon session concluded, I went back to my room to prepare for another presentation I would be making that evening. I was still thinking about the reaction the story about the Domino's meeting had gotten from the audience. How could we leverage and build on that? I flipped on the TV as I was getting changed. I was only half listening when I heard the word *Domino's*. I glanced at the TV and saw an ad for an upcoming episode of a very popular TV show of the time called *The Apprentice*, starring none other than our eventual forty-fifth president and sponsored by Domino's Pizza.

As you may remember, *The Apprentice* was a kind of *Survivor* for businesspeople. The contestants, all with business experience but known as apprentices on the show, formed into two competing "corporations." Each week, Trump, as the host and head judge, presented the teams with a task to carry out, such as managing a Planet Hollywood restaurant or raising money for a charity. At the end of the show, one team was declared the winner, the other the loser. And, in what became the show's signature moment, one of the individual contestants was identified as the weakest performer. Trump turned to that poor unfortunate soul and uttered, with great relish, the now immortal words, "You're fired!" The ultimate winner of the season got a one-year contract to lead one of Trump's companies at a starting salary of $250,000.

As the show gained popularity, it increasingly linked its tasks to specific, real companies that were eager to participate for the publicity, and that's where Domino's came in. As I learned from the promo, the task for the contestants on the upcoming March 31 episode, sponsored by Domino's, would be to come up with a new pizza flavor for the chain. Not only would Domino's get a ton of exposure from its participation, but the company also planned to use the show as a platform to launch its own, real new pizza specialty, the American Classic Cheeseburger Pizza. Trump himself would appear in the spots, and true to form, he hyped his endorsement well in advance of the airing, saying that the new Domino's American Classic flavor combined his "two favorite foods—pizza and cheeseburgers." (Oy.)

The premise was completely absurd to me. Corporate contestants with no expertise developing a specialty pizza? Trump, a known junk food eater, as an expert on taste? Teams competing, rather than collaborating, to create a successful product? It went counter to everything Papa John's stood for: a company "family," a passion for pizza, a devotion to quality, and a belief in long-term relationships with customers and partners.

That's when I had the brainstorm.

What if Papa John's got in on the act? What if we ran our own ad on that March 31 *Apprentice* episode, throwing down a challenge to the Domino's Pizza style and to Trump and his you're-fired approach? I wasn't sure how we would do it or if we could get it done in time, but I felt in my bones that it would be the kind of challenge moment that could make a statement to our own franchisees about how we wanted to operate. It might be the spark that could ignite the company.

I called John and caught him in his room.

"John, look," I said. "I have a crazy idea."

"OK." John didn't know me very well yet, but he had shown he was willing to listen to out-there ideas and would throw his full support behind them if he thought they had merit.

"I just saw on TV that Domino's is sponsoring an upcoming episode of *The Apprentice*," I told him.

"OK."

"The two competing teams will have to develop a new pizza variety on the show."

"Hah!"

"And Domino's will be introducing their own new pizza in the commercials."

"OK. So what's the idea?"

"What if we run our own Papa John's ad right in the middle of the show?" I said. "You'll be the judge. You'll make fun of the whole concept. And you'll fire Domino's."

"Ha!" John laughed. "I love it."

"OK, the show airs March 31," I said, "so we've only got a couple of weeks."

"Can we pull it off?" John asked. He was already saying "we," so that was a good sign.

"I don't know yet," I said. "I'll call our advertising people right now and see what they say."

"Go for it," John said.

Then I had a flash realization. "Hang on a tick," I said to John. "You know, this idea will only have the impact on the company that we want if the franchisees are in on the plan from the start. We need them to buy in, to support and approve the idea, before we go ahead." In a way, the idea was really about challenging us, as a company, even more than it was about challenging Domino's as a competitor.

"Agreed," he said.

"So, if the agency people think we can make it happen," I said to John, "what if I present the idea tonight to the franchisees and see what they think?"

"Great," John said. "Do it."

My next call was to Jordan Zimmerman, founder and chairman of Zimmerman Advertising, our ad agency. I ran the *Apprentice* idea by him.

"What do you think?" I asked.

"It's brilliant," Jordan said. (At least that's how I remember it.)

"But can we get it done to run by March 31?" I asked.

"We can do it," Jordan assured me.

I hung up and scribbled a few notes for my talk. That evening I got up before the assembled crowd. I was excited and feeling like this could be the spark, the public challenge, the explicit statement of intent that we needed: the challenge to Domino's and to our own status quo.

"Good evening, everyone!" I began. "Does everybody remember the story we heard this afternoon of the Domino's meeting?"

Up went a howl and some boos from the audience. They remembered.

"Well, I'm sure we'd all like to respond somehow, wouldn't we?" I asked. "Am I right?"

A cheer of assent.

"Well, I have a kind of crazy idea to do just that," I said. "But it's no good unless you're all behind it. I want to run the idea by you and see what you think of it. Is that OK? Are you up for that?"

Oh, yeah. They were up for that. I had them now. Leaning forward. Wanting to hear.

"Does everybody know the show *The Apprentice*?"

"Yes!" Of course they knew it. In its second season, the show was a sensation.

"Does anybody know who's sponsoring the March 31 episode?"

Somebody yelled out, "Domino's!?"

"That's right," I said. "And do you know what the challenge to the apprentices is going to be?"

Another voice from the back of the room. "To come up with a new pizza style!"

"That's right," I said. "So here's the idea. We create our own TV ad and run it right in the middle of the episode. We put the challenge to Domino's. Tell them the whole idea of amateurs making pizza is absurd. And tell Domino's *they're* fired!"

Howls of excitement. Laughter. Clapping.

"What do you think?" I asked. "Do you think we should do it?"

Franchisees leaping out of their seats. "Yes! Let's go for it!" They were on board.

We gave the go-ahead. Zimmerman zoomed into action. Within two weeks we had shot and cut the ad. We purchased ad time on sixty-four local outlets in our major markets, essentially giving us national coverage.

March 31, the big day came. The ad ran. It featured John sitting in a big leather chair in a boardroom not unlike the one where Trump sat in judgment on his apprentices. John turns to the camera and says, "Why get a pizza made by apprentices when you can order a pizza made by the pros at Papa John's?" Then, in the dramatic final moment, he looks at the camera. "To our competition, I say," John pauses: "*You're fired!*"

The franchisees loved it. The press ate it up. And it had the desired effect. It was an early statement to the Papa John's people that we were not going to accept the status quo and that we were willing to put ourselves forward in an assertive way—but with a touch of humor. The following two years we saw good growth and gained advantage over Domino's.

. . .

Three years later, in January of 2009, I left Papa John's to join Dunkin' Brands. I found myself in a much larger company, with an iconic brand name, international operations, and tremendous potential. However, just like Papa John's, I felt that there was a little something missing from Dunkin' Donuts when I joined: that spark, that sense of willingness to question things and thumb your nose at the status quo. As I would put it now, the company did not have what I would call a robust challenge culture. But I felt that the seeds were there to create one, and I believed that we—corporate staff, franchisees, and the board—could do it together. And I figured we had a couple of advantages on our side, although they might not sound like advantages today. The first was the lousy recession economy. The second was the initial public offering (IPO) planned for Dunkin' Brands within the next few years.

People often ask me what it was like to join a company right smack in the middle of a recession. Well, it was actually a perfect time because the economy, the business environment, and the company itself were under severe pressure and everyone felt a lot of stress. The Dunkin' franchisees were struggling with their economics, as was the world at large. It was the very best time to challenge the status quo because the status quo was so clearly unacceptable.

The second factor was that, when I joined Dunkin', we were privately held, which meant we could take a longer-term view of things and not worry too much about quarterly results. At the same time, we were planning to take the company public within the next few years, so that gave us a kind of deadline and a clear focus. Although Dunkin' was in decent shape, it was not, as I sensed right away, a red-hot, forward-thinking company, the kind that attracts scads of investors to an IPO. That might have been more acceptable in a strong economy, but a public offering during an economic downturn would be riskier because investors would be looking for companies that were ahead of the pack, with lots of potential for growth and improved profitability.

All these factors meant that bold action was needed and could be taken in a considered way.

Challenge cultures are not created overnight or by executive decree. They have to be modeled, shaped, developed, and refined over time. The incoming leader who wants to build a challenge culture begins by asking questions. This does two things: it sets an example that you want others to follow and it generates vital information that will inform your decisions about changes that might need to be made.

I did not waste any time getting started. I came on board as CEO of Dunkin' Brands in January 2009 and immediately plunged into conversations with Dunkin' people. I reached out, in particular, to franchisees, the independent businesspeople who own the Dunkin' shops around the world. Although these people are the heart and soul of the Dunkin' business, they are not corporate employees.

In any franchise business, including Dunkin', the franchisor owns the brand and the franchisees purchase the right to use the brand, typically within a designated territory. The franchisee is responsible for a number of business activities, such as pricing, and each franchisee competes with other franchisees. The franchisor cannot dictate everything the franchisees do but has a number of methods and tools to maintain consistency and vibrancy of the brand—the most important of these is influence.

When you want to effect change in a system like ours, the *only* really effective way to do so is by creating a challenge culture that enables you to build and leverage influence. You need positive questioning and persuasive pushback to develop new ideas and to gain understanding, buy-in, and support for them. Otherwise, no change will occur.

Now, you may wonder, if the franchise system is so distinct, do the principles of the challenge culture also apply to other types of organizations? The answer is: yes, they do apply. The challenge culture looks essentially the same in any company that comprises multiple groups and disciplines, geographies and units, which must be brought together in strategy and action. So while some of the specific mechanisms of culture development in a franchise operation may be a little different than in other types of organizations, the essentials are the same.

. . .

In my conversations with Dunkin' people in those first few weeks of 2009, I was eager to get to know them, hear what was on their minds, and learn as much as I could about the company.

One of my early calls was with a franchisee, I'll call him Russ, who owned a number of stores in the South, including Texas. He did not waste any time telling me that he was thinking about selling out and leaving the Dunkin' system.

This was one of my first opportunities to ask the "why" questions and, by so doing, show him how I intended to manage and also encourage him to participate in improving whatever he thought was lacking at Dunkin'.

"Why would you think about leaving?" I knew that his business was not as profitable as he wanted it to be, but it was hardly on the brink of disaster.

"Many reasons," he said, uncomfortably. He seemed reluctant to sound negative in his comments. That's a barrier to challenge: we equate pushback with pessimism and negativity. Nobody likes that. So, sometimes you have to take the first step. Give permission to people to open up.

"Is it the economy?" I ventured. "Or some of the closings?" Recently, a large Dunkin' franchise operation, with fifty-six stores, had filed for bankruptcy. Others were struggling through the downturn. Maybe Russ was spooked.

"Partly," he said. "But I think *I* could probably get through this OK. If . . . "

"If?" I asked. "If what?"

It was an open question. He could have dodged it, but he didn't.

"Listen," he said, "for the past four or five years or so, it's been all about growth at Dunkin', right? Lots of new units. New geographies. I opened three new restaurants in Texas."

"I know. That's great."

"Yes, it could be great, but even though corporate wanted to expand geographically, seems to me there was no real strategy for expansion. They just wanted to grow fast. To do that, they brought in a bunch of new owners who had the cash to sign these huge development agreements to open a bunch of stores, but a lot of them didn't understand the specific market or even have restaurant experience." In 2009, it was true that Dunkin' was not doing well in some of the newly expanded regions, particularly Texas.

"What didn't they understand?" I asked.

Russ chuckled. "Well, for one thing, the goddamn menu. If you don't have a kolache or an apple fritter on the menu in Texas, forget it."

"Right." Russ was getting warmed up now, so I didn't think he needed any more prompting.

"Plus, cost of goods!" Russ exclaimed. "What about cost of goods? They're way higher in the South than they are in the Northeast. Even with expansion, we don't have enough stores to generate the kind of buying power you have in New England. So our supply chain is shakier, costs are higher, and profits are lower than they should be." This was true. At the time, we operated with a number of regional supply chains, and pricing for supplies and materials varied from region to region. Prices were generally higher for shops in smaller or newer markets. Two years later, we challenged the status quo, nationalized the supply chain, and brought pricing into parity from region to region.

But I'm getting ahead of the story. "OK, Russ, have you discussed these issues?"

Russ paused and cleared his throat. "With management you mean?"

"Yes."

"No. Not exactly," Russ admitted. "I didn't think that would get good results."

"Why not?"

Russ hesitated again. We were getting into complicated territory.

"Things can get contentious, you know? If corporate doesn't think you're on track, they can find all kinds of reasons to penalize or fine you. I mean, the proof is in the fact that there are so many lawsuits pending against Dunkin' right now."

"Russ, listen, I appreciate your discussing this with me," I said. "You should always feel free to ask a question or bring up a concern. If we don't ask questions and if we don't push back on the status quo, we won't have enough knowledge or understanding to make changes we need to make."

"Yep," Russ said, and the conversation continued for another few minutes.

I can tell you one thing for certain: conversations like that one get out. They multiply. The simple fact that it was possible to have a direct conversation with the CEO, to bring up real and fundamental concerns, and to be heard made an impression on

Russ, and he spread the word. He did not, in the end, leave the system.

In many other discussions with people throughout the organization, I heard a lot of similar concerns. The business environment was at the top of almost everyone's list. The world was changing dramatically and not only because of the financial crisis. Tom Friedman in his book *Thank You for Being Late* pinpoints 2007 as the year when the world exploded into warp speed—with the introduction of the iPhone, the rise of social media, and the emergence of cloud computing.

I also heard that Dunkin' was a bit behind the change curve. Customer expectations were changing rapidly. They wanted everything: high quality, greater choice, more speed, operational excellence, and social purpose. Competition was coming at us from new directions, particularly convenience stores and gas stations. Coffee was a huge business and an attractive market, with high margins but lots of competition. Technology was disrupting the entire industry, in product innovation as well as online ordering and delivery systems. No company of any size could get along without an online presence and online ordering.

Another concern was the private equity (PE) ownership structure. At the time, Dunkin' Brands was owned by three private equity firms: Bain Capital, the Carlyle Group, and Thomas H. Lee Partners. The trio bought Dunkin' in early 2006, bringing to an end a period of corporate turmoil that had begun all the way back in 1990. That's the year that Allied Lyons, a British drinks and restaurant group, bought out Dunkin', which had been a publicly traded company since 1968. Four years later, Allied Lyons merged with Pedro Domecq, and then, in 2005, Pernod Ricard, the French conglomerate, purchased the merged entity, Allied Domecq, and decided to sell off some of its brands, including Dunkin'. That's when the three equity firms stepped in.

As everyone at Dunkin' knew, private equity firms purchase undervalued companies, make improvements, and then sell them or take them public. So everybody expected a public offering and knew that I had been brought in to get Dunkin' ready. They assumed that changes would be required if the offering was going to be a success. The previous few years the company had focused on growth, and indeed, Dunkin' had seen significant expansion in the number of restaurant units. But other aspects of the business had not gotten enough attention, including our long-range systems approach, real estate strategy, supply chain management, stakeholder relationships, and technology.

Naturally, everybody, including the franchisees, was jittery. What kind of changes would be made? When would the company go public? What would it mean for their jobs and businesses? And I'm sure they were wondering what this guy Travis could bring to the party.

. . .

In a way, I came to Dunkin' at the right time, not only in terms of the economy but also in my career: I had experienced and helped shape a lot of change, especially at Papa John's, where we became the online pizza leader. Although my ideas about the challenge culture were well formed, I hadn't yet articulated them in a formal way.

I began developing the challenge culture ideas at Grand Metropolitan, the big British conglomerate, which I joined in 1985 in a position in human resources. There, with CEO Allen Sheppard, we articulated the key elements of a successful culture, one of which was the necessity of challenge.

When Grand Met acquired Burger King, I moved to Miami as senior vice president human resources and then was thrust into my first operating role as Burger King's managing director for Europe, the Middle East, and Africa, based in London. Burger King was a pretty traditional organization, and I saw there how hierarchies can actually tamp down challenge and how that can stultify a company. After Grand Met I spent ten years with Blockbuster, the video rental company, where I developed my fascination with technology and where I learned an important lesson in that regard: you have to challenge your own status quo before technology comes along and does it for you.

From 2005 to 2008, I was at Papa John's. I was president and CEO, and John Schnatter, the founder, retained the title of chairman. Although John was always open to new ideas—like our *Apprentice* ad—he was still the ultimate authority, no matter what the organizational hierarchy looked like on paper. He was, and still is, a brilliant entrepreneur who has built an amazing company. But, and I think he would agree, the challenge pretty much goes one way. John challenges everything but does not feel that comfortable with a whole lot of pushback.

Through all these positions, I had gained a great deal of understanding of how challenge works in different kinds of organizations because their structures and industries can be very different.

So how did I see it working at Dunkin'? Well, first you have to understand a bit about the company. People assume that Dunkin' Brands is a huge enterprise, and in some ways, they're right. If we were ranked by total system sales, just over $11 billion in 2017, we'd be a Fortune 250 company. Ranked by total number of system employees, about two hundred thousand people, we'd be on the list of the top fifty private employers in the United States. Measured by number of units, we are a major global entity, with over twenty thousand points of presence in sixty-nine countries worldwide.

Looked at in terms of revenue, however, Dunkin' is relatively small. Corporate revenue is less than a billion dollars. That's because, as a franchise operation, our revenue comes almost entirely from fees paid by the franchisees. However, we realize a very high profit margin, with nearly 55 percent of our revenue going to the bottom line. Lots of companies typically make profit in the single digits. Twenty percent is considered high. Fifty-five percent is astronomical.

Throughout my corporate career, I also developed a reverence for brands, and Dunkin' Donuts is one of the world's greatest. The company was founded in 1950 in Quincy, Massachusetts, by Bill Rosenberg, a wonderfully savvy entrepreneur. Bill expanded the operation throughout New England until Dunkin' shops seemed to be on every city street corner and in every town and village. As the company grew, Dunkin' gradually became the iconic brand it is today. For more than a decade, our advertising line "America Runs on Dunkin'" rang true for tens of millions of customers. (And it still does.) And you know that you're part of the national culture when you get spoofed on *Saturday Night Live,* as we were in 2016. Vanilla Nut Taps— I will say no more.

. . .

The evolution of my thinking about corporate culture actually goes back even further than my Grand Met tenure, to my university days in the 1970s. I was studying what was then known as personnel management, and I was deeply influenced by a paper, written in 1966, called "Industrial Sociology and Industrial Relations," by the sociologist Alan Fox. His theory, which became influential worldwide, is that there are two fundamental perspectives on employment in organizations: the unitary and the pluralistic. The unitary view holds that employers and employees basically share common interests. The pluralistic approach holds that organizations are composed of multiple parties with different interests that must constantly be negotiated.

Today, fifty years after Fox published his paper, there are not many unitary companies around anymore; you'd have to look at smaller, privately held, family-owned, or employee-owned companies—such as Publix Super Markets or Gensler, the architectural firm—to find an organization where employer and employee interests are fundamentally the same. Almost all large companies today are pluralistic. Apple, the world's most valuable company, depends on its developers, manufacturers, partners, and customers to build and manage the brand.

At Dunkin', we think of our constituencies as if they are concentric circles, all configured around the same fundamental goal—success for Dunkin'—but with different perspectives on virtually everything. Although the franchisees depend on the corporation for managing the brand, they don't always align with what corporate thinks is right. Nor does corporate management always agree with the board of directors about how to execute on overall goals. Corporate employees have their point of view, as do suppliers, partners, advisers, and, of course, customers.

Pluralistic organizations are, by their nature, particularly suited to and best managed through the development of a challenge culture. As CEO, I did have some authority to make binding corporate decisions, but without the buy-in of the franchisees, and without the support of employees and partners, any unilateral move can lead to resentment and often produce unintended or unexpected consequences.

I am not talking about achieving alignment, which suggests that there could be consensus or virtually unanimous agreement on a strategy or initiative. Diverse constituencies will never be entirely on the same page, and you shouldn't try to get them there. However, it *is* possible, and necessary, to enable the constituencies to engage with each other on issues that pertain to them and to give them a voice where they should have one. For the very reason that the process does not usually create consensus, some people will walk away from it without prevailing. However, the challenge process crystallizes and defines the issues, so that everybody knows where everybody stands and why decisions have been made as they have.

That's what you want in a challenge culture. But just as you can't mandate change, you can't create a challenge culture with the wave of a wand. You have to model it, build it into the organization, make it explicit, and get everybody up to speed on what it is, how it works, and how to work within it.

It starts, of course, with the leadership team.

CHAPTER TWO

Leaders Must Model

Paul Takes a Stand

The first meeting of my management team, in January 2009, was a total bust.

We assembled in the conference room at corporate headquarters in Canton, Massachusetts, a suburb about fifteen miles south of Boston, not far from Quincy, the town where Dunkin' was founded.

There were ten members of the leadership team in the meeting, most in the room, a few on the phone. All the key disciplines were represented: the heads of U.S., international, marketing, human resources, legal, strategy, finance, and operations and some of their staff people. I didn't know any of them very well; the majority of them were long-term Dunkin' people who had worked together for years and knew the operations of the company far better than I did.

I welcomed everyone to the meeting and set out my agenda for the session: the goal was to explain my values, talk about the culture I wanted us to build at Dunkin', and discuss together any changes we might need or want to make as we prepared for the public offering.

"Anybody want to add anything to that agenda?" I asked. "Any further thoughts? Questions?"

I looked around the room. All I got were little head shakes and murmurs of approval. Nobody had anything to add. No burning questions. No hearty agreement. No dissent.

"OK," I said. "Good." But it wasn't good. I suddenly felt very heavy, as if the atmosphere in the room was thickening and pushing me down. I'm sure you know the feeling.

"Well then, to start off, let me briefly tell you a little about myself," I said. "And where I'm coming from."

Stony faces. They looked as if they were preparing to be shot.

"I actually began my career in HR," I said, as if that might be of some surprise or interest to the people in the room. Not so much. Blank looks.

I briefly skipped through the highlights of my career: my father the entrepreneur, the Brit upbringing, the stints at Grand Met, Burger King, Papa John's, and Blockbuster. No comments. No questions. Just little noncommittal head bobs.

Then I began laying out my vision for Dunkin' Brands: how I wanted to create a culture where all the constituencies could collaborate to improve operations, move forward with technology, innovate in food and beverage offerings, widen our customer base, expand into new geographies in the U.S. and abroad, while leveraging the fabulous Dunkin' and Baskin-Robbins brands. And, of course, achieve a successful public offering within the next two to three years.

As I talked, I could feel the room fill up with fear, anxiety, uncertainty, hesitation, resistance, and doubt.

At the end of the meeting, which lasted about an hour, I felt profoundly frustrated. Clearly the leadership team, as it was then configured, did not have the challenge skills I was expecting and knew we needed. In a challenge culture, the meeting would have gone very differently. People would have felt free to make suggestions, ask questions, push back, and voice concerns and enthusiasms. What I got instead was guardedness and protectionism.

I knew that things would have to change.

The first thing I did was make the leadership team meeting a weekly event, instead of monthly. We needed more time together. And I wanted to know sooner rather than later whether this group could shed the habits they had developed during years in the Dunkin' culture. I realized that they, like the franchisees I spoke with, had been operating in an authoritarian world where there had been little effort to bring the constituencies together. Would they change? Could they change? Did they want to change?

The answer for eight of the ten was no.

There was no wholesale housecleaning, no purge. Rather, one by one, it became clear that the person and the new culture were not compatible. Some left of their own accord. Some I dismissed.

Throughout that period, I followed a few rules: state expectations, change people when needed, recruit people who can help build the culture, surround the team with talent.

You need to state your expectations of people and the culture very clearly, and do it early and often. I had done this in that first meeting and continued to do so. You have to be explicit about what you want and why you want it, and you have to say it over and over, while you're modeling it. There is no shortcut.

If people cannot change, you'll have to change the personnel. I don't believe that it is always necessary for a new management team to oust the old team and bring in a whole new one. When I joined Papa John's, for example, I did not change one member of the team. But when it is necessary, the changes must be made resolutely and, again, with the reasons made explicit.

It's essential to recruit people that you know will help reinforce the culture you want. People with skills in challenge, who aren't afraid to question, who know the value of pushback.

Finally, be sure to surround your leadership team with talented people who have a range of perspectives and can help the leaders look at the business in new ways.

Not long after that first meeting, I began to bring in new leadership team members. The first was Karen Raskopf, who came in to lead corporate communications. Karen had been with me at Blockbuster. We knew each other well, and I knew that Karen was a skilled pushbacker. Not confrontational, not negative. But always ready and able to ask the essential question or bring up the uncomfortable truth, without ever disrespecting or discrediting. Plus, she had done a stint with 7-Eleven, one of Dunkin's archenemies, so she had a broad view of the industry and could challenge the Dunkin' status quo mind-set.

Also in 2009, another key import was Rich Emmett, who came in as senior vice president and general counsel. Rich and I had worked together at Papa John's before he moved on to Quiznos. He had also spent time in private practice, so he knew the law from many angles. Rich has a very different challenge style than I do. I tend to be rather extroverted and can get heated up when the conversation gets passionate. Rich, however, is one of those guys you might read about in Susan Cain's book *Quiet: The Power of Introverts in a World That Can't Stop Talking*. He listens carefully. He considers everything. He speaks up only when he thinks he has something of value to say. The quiet questioner, as I have learned from Rich, can be incredibly effective when everybody else in the room is in a lather.

That year, we also brought in John Costello, who was something of a marketing legend. The list of firms he had worked for, advised, or served as director for is impressive, including Home Depot, Yahoo, Sears, Nielsen, and Procter & Gamble. He had experience with technology, retail, advertising, and research and had served on a number of not-for-profit boards as well. Although he started out in a consulting role for Dunkin', his ability to ask the right questions and challenge us soon proved so valuable we asked him to join the management team full-time.

But not all of the leadership team people came from outside the company; some were Dunkin' staffers who had been eager to see change come along. One of these Dunkin' hands was Scott Murphy, who had been with the company five years.

Although he had not been a member of the leadership team, he clearly had great talent and embraced the tenets of the challenge culture. He earned his MBA at MIT, then spent a number of years with A.T. Kearney, the management consultancy, before joining Dunkin' in 2004. Not only was he a half decade ahead of me in terms of knowledge, but I soon realized that he was an analytic whiz. Scott was a question asker, for sure.

Late in 2009, I brought in another experienced hand who proved to be key to our ability to build a challenge culture. That was Paul Twohig, who came in as president of Dunkin' Donuts U.S., the senior operating executive of the most important unit in the business. Paul was an old hand at the restaurant industry with a lot of experience in the quick service sector, both in corporate and as a franchisee, and I knew him from my Burger King days. Paul, too, is a challenger, but one with a different style from Karen, Rich, Scott, or me. He is quite introverted, reserved, and very soft-spoken, but he has a sharp wit and occasionally a bite to his comments, even a touch of well-targeted cynicism when called for. Of all the team members, Paul was the one who had absolutely no fear or reservations about challenging me. As a result, I came to rely on him for counsel.

It was Paul who really helped change the tenor of the leadership team meetings. I remember very well one of the first meetings he attended, in early 2010, because it was so different from that very dead-silent session I had struggled through the year before.

The main agenda item for that meeting was our general and administrative costs (G&A). In my discussions with the board and key leaders individually, we had begun to identify several overall objectives and areas we needed to focus on before the IPO. One of these was costs. It was an issue that would affect everybody on the team. It would have a big impact on our growth plans and the IPO offering. As everybody knows, it's tough to cut costs and invest in growth at the same time.

I didn't know how the meeting would go. It was an important discussion to have and one that required real consideration. I needed information and clarity, and as a group, we had to reach a decision about any changes we would make.

In addition to the issue itself, I saw the meeting as a test of how the newly configured leadership team would function together. I wanted to make it explicit, once again, that I expected everybody to have a voice in the discussion, whether they were the new guys or experienced Dunkin' hands. I encouraged challenge, questioning, pushback, discussion.

I kicked off the conversation by saying I thought our costs were too high and we needed to find ways to trim them. Everybody made sounds of general agreement. One way to do that, I proposed, was to take a look at corporate hiring. There were a high number of new hires in the budget, which was a positive thing, but I argued that we probably could get along with a few less. The noises changed in character. Not quite so agreeing in tone.

I was deliberately being a bit provocative, I confess, precisely because I wanted to get a dialogue going about how our costs supported our strategy. I could have issued a directive that we had to cut costs by X percent or that we had to chop the number of new hires by X amount. But that would have precluded discussion.

We talked through the budget in detail and reviewed which of the proposed hires could be eliminated. There was some discussion, a bit of pushback, but no substantive debate. I realized that as each new position was discussed, people gradually said less and less about it. The atmosphere got downright uncomfortable. I wasn't getting the kind of dialogue going that I wanted and that we needed. I couldn't tell where people really stood.

Sometimes, I realized, you have to push *forward* to get people to push back. I turned to Paul. He had plenty of authority as president to offer his opinion. He began his career at Burger King, became a regional manager for the chain, and then bought a franchise. After that, he spent several years at Boston Market as a franchisee, followed by ten years in two stints as senior vice president with Starbucks. He had also been COO of Panera Bread. So Paul certainly had the chops to challenge me on the new hire plan because he understood the issue from the point of view of a corporate executive and as a store owner. But I didn't know what he would say. We hadn't talked about it in detail prior to the meeting.

"Paul," I said, "where do you stand on this?"

Paul thought for a moment and looked around the room. People were probably expecting Paul to back me up and perhaps thinking that I had turned to him precisely for that reason. Maybe they were right.

But he didn't.

"Nigel," Paul said, "I think you're going way too far on this."

Everybody got quiet. I looked at Paul. I was a little surprised, actually, because I thought he might argue for even deeper cost cuts.

"OK," I said. "Why is that?"

"Because we've agreed to accelerate growth, especially outside New England," Paul said. "If we're going to do that right, we're going to need a lot of strong talent to help us do it. Cutting costs in hiring is not going to get us there. We need the people. We need to spend the money. We can't cut our way to greatness."

The atmosphere in the room changed dramatically; everybody was paying very close attention. Paul's challenge to me was significant. He didn't agree with me. The issue was substantive. It affected everyone. But he had made his argument calmly. And I had accepted his comment. I looked around the room, but before I could say anything, Paul did something very smart that crystallized the moment by making explicit what he had just done.

"Hey, Nigel," he said with a chuckle, "you told me coming into this job that one of my roles was to speak up when I think you're going too far on something. You've been saying—ad nauseam, I should add—that you want a culture of challenge. Well, you got it."

Blips of laughter. Apparently, it was OK to challenge the boss on policy, and not only that, it was also OK to make a little fun of him, too.

"OK," I said. "Good enough. What does everybody else think?"

From that moment on, the conversation began to flow swift and sure. We got into a lengthy discussion about costs, hiring, and growth. Ultimately, we arrived at a modified plan. It wasn't a compromise or a concession or even a consensus, really. It was a plan made better through testing, questioning, and challenging. And, in the long run, we did achieve the growth targets we had set, in large part because we hired the people we needed.

The central point of the story is the action that Paul took. He didn't just make a challenge; he stated that he was doing so and that it was a role I had encouraged him to fulfill. Everybody on the leadership team witnessed the moment: Paul's challenge and my response to it. They saw that challenge could be made, that it would not be put down, that it could lead to positive results, and they learned eventually that there would be no unpleasant consequences. From that moment, people on the team began to feel more comfortable challenging me and one another about ideas and decisions. That attitude cascaded throughout the organization into their own teams, whose members also became more willing to challenge and more accepting of challenge from others. And so the idea of challenge gradually, bit by bit, infused itself into the Dunkin' culture.

· · ·

To many people, the virtues of this kind of challenge may seem obvious. Doesn't every company value questioning and encourage dialogue? The answer is that most profess to want an open atmosphere and say that questioning is encouraged, but the reality is quite different. The sad truth is that too many organizations in virtually every arena of endeavor operate with authorities that discourage challenge and questioning. Starting in 2016 and into 2017, we began to see tremendous pushback to these cultures of authoritarianism, rigidity, and fear. In the world of media, the challenge resulted in the fall of such prominent figures as Roger Ailes, Harvey Weinstein, and Matt Lauer, variously accused of authoritarianism, abuse of power, sexual harassment, and covering up their misdeeds. Travis Kalanick of Uber resigned, and John Stumpf of Wells Fargo and Jeff Immelt of GE retired, at least in part because they had failed to listen and to accept challenge. And on it went, in politics, sports, hospitality, and the arts (even ballet).

There is a TV ad for cars.com, the online car sales company, that portrays this kind of business environment well. A group of businesspeople are in a meeting. They look like the members of the perfect, diverse management team: multicultural, multigenerational, multigender. The big boss is sitting at the head of the long conference table. Stacks of reports tower before them. Clearly, the group has just finished discussing some kind of important proposal. The camera pushes in on one guy who fiddles with his pencil and looks uncomfortable. We hear the boss proclaiming, "This is a very *smart* plan. So we're all onboard?" Everybody instantly raises their hands. Except for the one guy. He chucks the report aside. "Nah," he says, "this is a stupid plan." Cut to the dissenting guy standing on the sidewalk outside the office building. He's holding a cardboard box containing a sales trophy, a picture frame, and a plant, obviously from his cleaned-out desk. Fired for pushing back.

It's only an ad—and saying that something is "stupid" is not the kind of informed and positive challenge we want—but it portrays an atmosphere prevalent in many workplaces and one we've seen all too often in real workplaces, from Wells Fargo to Samsung.

I call it the you're-fired culture, where people do not challenge each other or question ideas for the simple reason that they're afraid they'll be reprimanded, ostracized, demoted, marginalized, ridiculed, or fired. When people believe their positions are on the line, they are less likely to voice an opinion, question an idea, or push back on a plan. As a result, divergent viewpoints are discouraged, dubious actions continue, decisions get made unilaterally, the loudest voices prevail, initiatives that shouldn't be pursued go forward. There are clear winners and abject losers. Eventually, good people get frustrated, discouraged, and stifled. Many leave.

The you're-fired culture seems particularly prevalent in the United States. Trump and *The Apprentice* epitomized and glamorized it as a competitive workplace that rewarded results and where the leaders were bold, decisive, and even regal. Trump became famous just for delivering his triumphant line, "You're fired!" But Trump hardly invented the concept, although he did try to trademark it. (His bid was rejected.) There are fewer employment protections in the U.S., where employment is generally considered "at will," than there are in Europe, where it is harder to fire people and they have more rights and benefits when they are let go. This sense that one's connection to an organization can be severed at any time, and with almost a sense of glee, is frightening to people and bad for the stability of an organization. No wonder people are reluctant to speak up in a way that could put their job in jeopardy.

Wells Fargo is an extreme example of a you're-fired culture. Over a period of years, the company engaged in a variety of dubious practices designed to bring in more customers, sell more products, charge more fees, and boost revenues and profits. The pressure on employees to meet sales targets, especially at lower levels in the organization, was so great that they began to engage in questionable practices such as signing up customers for services without their approval or knowledge. "The whispers among employees had been around for years," was the lead in a *Wall Street Journal* article on the case. Indeed, an internal investigation had flagged the practices in 2004. But employees said they felt intense pressure to reach sales targets and were reluctant to speak up for fear of losing their jobs.

When the practices finally came to public light, the company responded the same way, not by admitting their mistakes or forbidding the practices but by firing five thousand low-level workers. Rather than send a message that Wells Fargo had turned a page, it sent a chill through the organization and squelched further protest. The culture of fear ran so deep that, just a year later, Wells Fargo was found to be up to the same old tricks and some new ones came to light. In the auto financing business, for example, it was revealed that Wells Fargo salespeople had coerced customers into buying collision coverage they weren't actually required to have.

That does not mean that Wells Fargo completely got away with their bad behavior or that the executives lived to manage another day. John Stumpf, CEO of Wells Fargo, learned this lesson the hard way—on the hot seat at the United States Senate enduring hours of intense interrogation by the members of the Banking Committee. Just a few of the questions they threw at him:

How could this pattern of corrosive misconduct of two million unauthorized new customer accounts have continued over more than five years despite public reports?

Why were 5,300 lower-level employees scapegoated and terminated?

What does this pattern of misconduct say about the firm's cherished culture of integrity?

Elizabeth Warren, a member of the Banking Committee, accused Stumpf of "gutless leadership." That is a nightmare scenario, and Wells Fargo was seriously damaged by the experience. Stumpf took the fall. He retired almost immediately after the hearings.

The lesson: if you don't allow enough challenge within your organization, someone else may very well end up doing the questioning for you, and it won't be anywhere near as much fun. It's not likely you'll end up testifying before a congressional committee, but it is highly probable that you will find yourself dealing with other outsiders—such as activist investors—asking questions. These are individuals or firms that invest in companies and purposely engage with their management, especially when they are dismayed by wayward or dubious practices or by the conduct of the company's leaders. Activist investors have become increasingly aggressive in recent years. According to *The Activist Investing Annual Review 2017*, a report issued by the Harvard Law School Forum on Corporate Governance and Regulation, "the juggernaut of shareholder engagement kept rolling in 2016." The study states that, in 2016, activist investors made public demands of 758 companies worldwide, an increase of 13 percent over the previous year. These demands typically include challenges to strategy or calls for changes in governance. The message from these activists is clear: if you don't challenge yourself internally, outside activist stakeholders probably will.

· · ·

We must always keep in mind that companies are fragile things. They can quickly go from success to trouble, as we've seen so many times in the past decade alone, often precisely because the culture does not allow for challenging the status quo or questioning of practices.

In 2016, Samsung rushed its Galaxy Note 7 out the door in order to beat the new Apple iPhone to market. The Note 7 was launched in August, and soon thereafter, Note 7 phones were bursting into flames in users' hands. In September, Samsung suspended sales and issued a recall of millions of the phones. In early October, the Federal Aviation Administration (FAA) banned the phones from all U.S. flights. Later that month, Samsung announced that the recall had drained 98 percent of the profit from its mobile division, which is Samsung's core business. Overall company profit was down by 30 percent, a massive hit. Share price fell 4 percent. Estimates of the total cost of the debacle ranged from $5 to $17 billion. Samsung was hardly ruined, but the company lost money, time, and share of market, and its reputation suffered. It's difficult to know exactly how the phone was allowed to launch with these flaws, but some speculated that it was partly because of Samsung's culture, which reputedly lacked transparency. According to one report, engineers were reluctant to talk about the situation for fear of being thought of as "troublemakers." Another observer described a culture of "unusual secrecy."

There are endless examples of companies that have suffered because the culture could not manage challenge. Yahoo refused to recognize the Google onslaught, and although it was one of the pioneering Internet companies, the company was sold to Verizon in 2016. At Volkswagen, the upper echelons of leadership enforced a culture of secrecy around a massive emissions cheating scheme. No one, it seems, was powerful enough to push back against the initiative. When that inevitably came to light, Volkswagen found itself dealing with a huge scandal, a crisis of confidence, a massive recall, and the loss of billions of dollars. For years management at Fox News tamped down complaints about sexual harassment until, finally, the dam burst and the questions came pouring out. Roger Ailes and Bill O'Reilly, two powerful men accused of offenses, were ousted. Ailes died soon thereafter. And at Blockbuster, where I was president and COO, we did not challenge ourselves hard enough or listen attentively enough to questions about our strategy. As I'll relate later, the result (although long after I had departed the company) was an existential crisis. In the end, Blockbuster completely collapsed and disappeared.

Lesson: not allowing questioning can have terminal consequences.

. . .

What produces such cultures? There is plenty of research into the matter.

Edgar Schein, professor at MIT Sloan School of Management, has been studying executive behavior for years and is the author of a book called *Humble Inquiry: The Gentle Art of Asking Instead of Telling.* Schein writes about what he calls the "culture of tell." This is one in which people "take it for granted that telling is more valued than asking." Schein says that corporate employees get into the telling mode at a particular point in their careers: when they have been "formally promoted into a position of power."

Schein writes about an amazing session he had with a group of his students. He asked them a simple question: "What does it mean to you to be promoted to manager?"

What do you think they replied? Schein reports that, without the least hesitation, they all said, *It means I can now tell others what to do.*

Another academic, David Maxfield, a social scientist, describes this workplace environment in a slightly different way: he calls it the "culture of silence." It's not always that people are afraid of losing their jobs if they question things, he says. It's that questioning and dialogue are not considered essential management methods. People simply do not debate important issues or address concerns or even engage in much dialogue. They get their assignments, keep their heads down, and do their work. In an article in *Harvard Business Review*, Maxfield describes how this kind of silence "eats away" at a company. He cites an example of a workplace where everybody spent months implementing a project plan, even though the people involved knew—or at least should have known—that it had potentially fatal flaws. It failed.

There is a third cultural model that I call the "culture of confrontation."

It's important to make a distinction between challenge and confrontation. It's easy to assume they are essentially the same, but they're not. The key difference is that, in the challenge culture, the point of questioning is to stimulate conversation and debate and, ultimately, to bring forth new understanding and arrive at good decisions and effective solutions.

In a confrontation culture, people engage in challenge primarily to assert themselves, to gain personal power, to push through their own agendas, to put down others, and, ultimately, to win for themselves and make others lose. People attack, insult, intimidate. Questioning is interrogation. Dialogue is like combat.

Two examples come to mind. Bridgewater is the world's biggest hedge fund manager, making more money for its investors than any other hedge fund ever. Bridgewater is well known for its brutal culture where meetings get extremely contentious and people are encouraged to confront one another. Bridgewater has reportedly gone so far as to show a video to new hires that includes a scene of a female employee bursting into tears at a meeting. Founder Ray Dalio believes in what he calls "total honesty." He stresses the importance of pain to achieve progress and determine truth. He has made his ideas explicit in a set of principles, which he privately published for his company and then expressed in a 2017 book called *Principles.*

The second example is Uber, the ride-sharing company. They endorse a concept they call "principled confrontation." This is very much in the mode of the style of the founder, Travis Kalanick, who began the company in 2009 and grew it into one of the world's most valuable companies in less than a decade. Kalanick was well known for his brash, confrontational, aggressive, in-your-face style, as was his A team of senior executives.

What's intriguing is that both of these companies ran into trouble while I was writing this book and both because of cultural problems. At Bridgewater, performance slumped, and Dalio announced that he would step aside from day-to-day management responsibilities amid turmoil about who would succeed him.

Things were worse at Uber, largely because Kalanick's approach had not been so well-defined or explicit as Dalio's. Amid charges of too much conflict, including sexual harassment, Kalanick was forced to resign, along with many of his A team.

Unlike these cultures of confrontation, companies with a challenge culture see questioning as normal operating procedure, but the questioning is always within the context of a civil dialogue. Conversation among people with different viewpoints is purposeful: to evaluate information and discuss ideas in order to solve a problem or decide on a course of action. It includes questions and answers, pushback and analysis. By civil, I mean that the people involved are respectful of one another, observe the ground rules of discussion, including active listening, and, very important, have the best interests of the company in mind.

A civil dialogue is not a debate to the death. Those involved are not seeking to conquer the others. No one gets trashed.

. . .

In addition to the research done by academics in the field, consultancies, too, have taken the lead in defining and adhering to principles of culture. McKinsey & Company, the legendary management consulting firm, makes challenge a part of its mission and values. The firm states that it seeks to "create an unrivaled environment for exceptional people."

One essential way they do that is to "uphold the obligation to dissent."

That is a powerful idea: the *obligation* to dissent. Not only is questioning and challenge encouraged and accepted, at McKinsey dissent is seen as a kind of duty. Everybody and anybody in the organization can, and is expected to, speak his or her mind about any issue at hand. The assumption is that everybody can contribute and everybody wants to improve the company, including the newest hire, the youngest person, or a manager without direct experience in the discipline or subject area being discussed.

Fred Gluck, managing director at McKinsey from 1988 to 1994, described what it was like to experience this obligation to dissent. In 1967, as a young recent hire, Gluck was working on a strategy study for a client, and he thought the team was "not delivering the right value." One evening he bumped into Marvin Bower, McKinsey's founder, who asked Gluck how things were going. Gluck told him what he thought: things weren't going that well. He explained what was wrong. The following morning Gluck got a note saying he should go see Bower. Gluck feared what might happen. Perhaps he wouldn't get any more assignments? Wrong. Bower had taken his dissent to heart and discussed it with the partner who was leading the study team. The partner and Bower decided to ditch the approach, refund their fee to the client, and take a new tack. Gluck says he "walked out thinking this is a firm I want to be part of."

Not surprisingly, Steve Jobs made the idea of challenge explicit in a different way than McKinsey does. He didn't talk so much about dissent but rather about how everyone's contribution can help to create a better product.

He tells a story that equates collaboration with the polishing of stones. When Jobs was a kid, he lived down the street from a man in his eighties. Although the guy was "a little scary looking," Jobs got to know him a bit. One day the man showed Jobs his passion: a dusty old rock tumbler he had in his garage, just a "motor and a coffee can and a little band between them." The two got some rocks and put them in the can with some liquid and polishing grit. They closed the can. The man turned on the motor and said to Jobs, "Come back tomorrow."

The next day, the two opened the can. The ordinary rocks had been transformed into beautiful polished stones, just through rubbing against each other and "creating a little bit of friction." For Jobs, that became a metaphor for a team "working really hard on something they're passionate about. It's that through the team, through that group of incredibly talented people bumping up against each other, having arguments, having fights sometimes, making some noise, and working together they polish each other and they polish the ideas, and what comes out are these really beautiful stones."

That story resonates with me perhaps because it reminds me of my own early experiences with collaboration, challenge, and questioning.

CHAPTER THREE

Overcoming Challenge Aversion

*The Difference Between Dad, Socrates,
and Blockbuster*

I n my high school days, from the time I was fourteen to about sixteen, I worked for my dad's company when he needed help. He started the business in 1957, after he left a firm called Ascher Cordage, where he had worked for some years. Ascher sold rope and twine and had facilities in Curtain Road in London. Dad had gotten into a dustup with the owner, Old Man Ascher, and decided to go out on his own. He and my mother started a similar company, called R&J Travis, specializing in paper and string. Through the years, they expanded the business to include the sales of wholesale toys, the manufacturing of water inflatables, kids' costumes, and professional uniforms. I am proud that he became a successful serial entrepreneur. (The company, led by my brother, Malcolm Travis, until his recent retirement, is still going strong.)

R&J Travis (later renamed as Travis Designs) was a tiny family operation when I worked there in the 1960s. One of our products was a toy called Jokari, which was basically a ball attached to a wooden block with a long elastic band. My job was to hammer a hook into the block to attach the band. I'd bang hooks into blocks all day long. We also made windbreaks for use on the beach, and my task was to nail the canvas fabric onto the wooden frame.

One day I finished up a pile of windbreaks and was sitting around twiddling my thumbs when Dad came in.

"What are you doing?" Dad asked. His tone sounded ominous and suspicious that I was up to no good.

I told him I had finished the work and was taking a break.

"Well, you could at least *try* to look like you're busy," he barked. Dad was a very energetic guy, always active and not particularly sympathetic to idleness.

"Why?" I asked. I didn't really see why I should pretend to look busy. He was my dad, after all, and I had finished the work he asked me to do.

"Why?" Dad asked. "You're asking why?"

He didn't seem to have an answer to my simple question. Maybe pretending to be busy had been an important part of the job at Ascher Cordage. Maybe Dad was like MIT professor Schein's students: he believed that becoming a manager meant he had the God-given right to tell others what to do.

Finally he said, "Why is just a crooked letter," and pushed off. Say what?

That is a fair example of an unproductive dialogue, from Dad's first confrontational question, "What are you doing?" to my unhelpful response, to his inscrutable statement: "Why is just a crooked letter." That wasn't the first time he had said that. I still think about it. What did it mean? I think it meant he really didn't like being questioned, particularly by his son.

. . .

Asking questions is an essential element of the challenge culture, but organizations of any shape or size—large or small—do not naturally encourage questioning.

I've found the proclivity for questioning extends even beyond the leadership team to the board of directors. I wasn't sure how it would be at Dunkin', but I quickly found out during my employment interviews with the board in late 2008. We covered a range of topics in those exploratory talks. One of the issues I discussed with them was the need for company-owned stores. As I've said, I believed that, in order to be competitive and successful in the eventual IPO, we would have to make changes to operations, the brand, and our management of technology. Since we couldn't mandate change to franchisees, we would have to provide a model for them. One effective way to do that is to use company-owned stores to test and refine new concepts, practices, and products. At the time, however, Dunkin' was 100 percent franchisee owned—all the stores were owned and operated by independent businesspeople.

I wasted no time making my views known to the directors about the value of company-owned restaurants. I pushed hard on the issue and was surprised and delighted that I got a lot of smart pushback from them. They didn't reject my idea because it ran counter to their current policy. Rather, they asked questions. They plunged into the issue.

Why did I feel so strongly about company-owned stores?
How would it affect relationships with current franchisees?
What would it cost?
What would the stores look like?
How many would we need?
Where would they be located?
Who would operate them?
What kind of staffing requirements would there be?
How long would it take to get the program up and running?
What were the benefits?
What were the risks?

I pushed forward so relentlessly and they shot questions back so intensely that I made the incorrect assumption that their questions amounted to disagreement and disapproval and that, as a result, I would not get the job.

Wrong. The board directors had conclusively demonstrated that they not only tolerated questioning, but they also deeply valued it. I took that as a very good sign. Soon after I joined we began converting several franchise stores into company units. And, nine years later, three of those original directors still sit on the Dunkin' board. That is highly unusual. After most public offerings, the equity partners swiftly exit the board. What's more, our directors are as engaged as ever and still asking endless questions. There is no doubt in my mind that the challenging style of our board has been a constant reason for our success over the years.

. . .

I got lucky, I guess. As I've said, vigorous questioning is not always so prevalent in corporate settings. In fact it's more the exception than the rule, as Warren Berger, an expert on innovation, knows very well. He is the author of *A More Beautiful Question: The Power of Inquiry to Spark Breakthrough Ideas,* and he has conducted workshops for members of many management teams. (I met him when he conducted a seminar at my kids' school.) Warren has studied dozens of companies to try to understand why some were more innovative than others and came to the conclusion that asking "beautiful" questions was the way to get to good solutions.

"A beautiful question," Warren writes, "is an ambitious yet actionable question that can begin to shift the way we perceive or think about something—and that might serve as a catalyst to bring about change."

In his research, however, Warren found that very few companies encouraged beautiful questioning or questioning of any kind, for that matter. "I found few companies that actually encouraged questioning in any substantive way. There were no departments or training programs focused on questioning; no policies, guidelines, best practices. On the contrary, many companies—whether consciously or not—have established cultures that tend to discourage inquiry in the form of someone's asking, for example, *Why are we doing this particular thing in this particular way?*

Warren is essentially describing the difference between the cultures of fear and "you're fired" and that of the challenge culture, and he is far from alone in arguing for the value of questioning. Simon Sinek, an author and consultant, focuses on the fundamental "why" question in his book, *Start with Why: How Great Leaders Inspire Everyone to Take Action.* He writes that if we start with the "wrong questions" and don't seek to find the cause of *why* people think what they do, "then even the right answers will always steer us wrong . . . eventually. The truth, you see, is always revealed . . . eventually."

As Sinek and MIT professor Schein and many others argue, our society places a high value on knowing things, delivering answers, being concrete. There is nothing wrong with that. Deep knowledge, being explicit, and possessing facts and data are essential in all aspects of decision making. But we also know that knowledge without purpose, and data without understanding, can be useless. People in large organizations often find themselves asking themselves and each other (usually behind management's backs): *Why are we doing this again?* So it's very important, as Sinek puts it, to start with why and to build a culture that encourages employees to speak up and ask questions of their leadership.

Deep questions often reveal deeper truths. In my dialogue with the board directors, for example, we got down to the fundamental question of why Dunkin' did *not* have company-owned stores. As a result of our discussion, we determined that the previous owners of Dunkin' had deliberately chosen not to get deeply involved in operations and had left innovation up to the individual franchisees. The owners had focused on rapid expansion. But their lack of knowledge of restaurant operations had resulted in some poor sitings, lackluster performance in some areas, and inconsistent practices across the system. In our back-and-forth, I think the board members learned as much about the company as I did.

. . .

We should not be surprised that questioning is risky and, at the same time, so valuable. We need only take a look at the most famous and brilliant questioner of all, the Greek philosopher Socrates (470–399 BC).

Before Socrates's time, philosophers were generally of the "tell" variety. They made grand pronouncements on weighty issues, such as the nature of the universe. "All is water," declared the philosopher Thales.

Socrates, in the search for truth, did not wish to make pronouncements. He wanted his students to "discover within themselves a multitude of beautiful things, which they themselves bring forth into the light."

To do this, Socrates would explore a topic by engaging in conversation with his students. (The most famous of these, Plato, wrote down the dialogues.) Socrates would often start by professing ignorance or confusion about a subject. For example, to begin a conversation about the nature of knowledge, Socrates admits he is uncertain about the issue and cajoles his students into helping him understand. "I can't get a proper grasp of what knowledge is," he says. "Could we manage to put it into words?"

This is obviously a different approach from the environment that Schein describes, where definitively knowing something is seen as the ideal.

Socrates's question entices one of his students to jump in with an answer. The student replies that knowledge means subjects like geometry, astronomy, music, and arithmetic. "They must be knowledge, surely."

Now Socrates starts to refine the question and focus the discussion. To do this, he is careful not to say to his student, "You're wrong." Instead, he thanks him for his "frank and generous answer." But then Socrates says that the student has not really answered the question that was asked. He hadn't asked about "how many branches of knowledge there are." No, Socrates says, "we wanted to know what knowledge itself is."

In the course of the conversation, Socrates continually seeks to gain agreement, point by point. When discussing the nature of justice, for example, he asks, "Is it the role of a just man to harm anyone?"

His student replies: "Certainly, he must harm those who are both bad and his enemies."

Then Socrates takes an unexpected detour to reach a conclusion.

Socrates: Do horses become better or worse when they are harmed?

Student: Worse.

Socrates: Then won't we say the same about human beings, too, that when they are harmed they become worse in human virtue?

Student: Indeed.

Socrates: But isn't justice a human virtue?

Student: Yes, certainly.

Socrates: Then people who are harmed must become more unjust.

The student agrees. Socrates gradually builds every dialogue through a succession of such agreements so that when they come to a conclusion it is difficult to refute. In the conversation about justice, they reach an agreement that the just person is one who never inflicts harm on another.

Along the way, Socrates seeks feedback about his line of questioning, to be sure his students are with him. At one point in the discussion of knowledge, for example, Socrates asks, "Am I talking nonsense?"

This aspect of the Socratic method is essential to the challenge culture. You have to get people agreeing before you get to the disagreeing part. In that early management meeting, for example, my team all agreed that we wanted to accelerate growth. We agreed that we needed to cut costs. We could then identify that our disagreement was over the specific tactics that would enable us to drive growth and cut costs and reached the conclusion that it was not through a wholesale reduction of staffing level. And, indeed, I turned to Paul Twohig to explicitly solicit feedback. I didn't use the words, "Am I talking nonsense?" but the effect was the same: it gave the others an opening to make their opinions known.

This kind of conversation through questioning has an important additional benefit. It shows everybody involved how you have arrived at a conclusion. Today we would call this transparency. I have found that understanding the reasoning behind a conclusion can make a huge difference in business. If people know why you're doing something, they can usually accept it, even if they don't endorse it. That was true of the Dunkin' board of directors and my plan for corporate-owned stores.

Questioning can be a tricky business, however. People, including me (and my dad), do not always like to be questioned. We sometimes get annoyed at the questioner, especially when he or she gets too challenging or too close to an uncomfortable truth.

For Socrates, questioning proved fatal. As it turned out, he did not live in a culture that valued challenge as much as he did. Socrates was so persistent with his questioning that the conversations could get acrimonious, and he became known as a gadfly, an irritating person. Eventually, he provoked so much unrest at every level of Athenian society that he was charged with corrupting his students, brought to trial, and sentenced to death.

So there are worse things than getting fired. Questioning undeniably carries risk. It can be perceived by those in power as a threat to their authority and even to the nature of the organization.

That is why it is so important to build a whole *culture* of challenge, where people understand how and when to question and where questioning is the norm, not an aberration.

· · ·

Challenging the status quo can be risky, then, but it's important to understand that *not* challenging it can be far more dangerous. I learned this the hard way, and it turned out to be disastrous.

I refer to my time at Blockbuster. After twenty-five years of operation, the company filed for bankruptcy in 2010, and today, Blockbuster is no more. (Except for a handful of stores operating independently, several of them in Alaska.)

This makes me sad because in its heyday, which was essentially the decade I was there, Blockbuster was an iconic brand and an important part of the social and family lives of millions of Americans. In cities and towns across the country, people would go to their local Blockbuster store on Friday and Saturday night to pick out a movie on VHS or DVD. Families would search the aisles together. People would bump into friends and compare notes about which movies they loved or hated. (Watch the movie *The Holiday* if you want to revisit those happy times.) Customers often knew the owner of the store. Local high school students worked there after school and on weekends. There was a sense of community and shared interest. At Blockbuster's peak, we operated about nine thousand stores worldwide and employed about sixty thousand people in the United States.

The company had huge potential and could have continued to keep growing, further build its leadership in the industry, and expand worldwide. That is *if* there had been a culture of challenge internally. And *if* the company had responded to the external challenges it faced.

There wasn't. It didn't.

I joined Blockbuster in 1994 after nearly a decade with Grand Met, five of those years with Burger King, at a time when Blockbuster was going gangbusters. Blockbuster was founded in 1985 by the entrepreneur Dave Cook, who opened his first store in Dallas. He sold the company two years later for $18.5 million to Waste Management, Inc., founded by Wayne Huizenga, who later became famous as a serial entrepreneur, sports magnate, and philanthropist.

Under Huizenga's leadership, Blockbuster went into high growth mode. In addition to organic expansion, the company binged on acquisition in the late 1980s and early 1990s. It bought three other video rental chains—Major Video and Erol's in the U.S. and Ritz in the U.K. In 1992, it swallowed up two music retail chains, Sound Warehouse and Music Plus, to create the Blockbuster Music unit. By 1992 Blockbuster was opening a new store every twenty-four hours and had about 2,800 units. In the fall of 1993, a year before I arrived, Blockbuster got into content production by buying a stake in the Spelling Entertainment Group, producers of such mega TV hits as *The Love Boat* and *Dynasty*. In 1993, with revenues in the billions, Blockbuster management approached Viacom, the media giant, with a merger proposition and entered into negotiations that lasted some time.

I came on board as vice president, Europe, based in Uxbridge, a commercial suburb west of London. (And just down the street from my old office at Burger King.) Although the U.S. business was exploding, Blockbuster's European presence then consisted of a straggly collection of stores in Spain and the United Kingdom and a single lonely store in Italy. Blockbuster was obviously not yet a European powerhouse. It was my assignment to make it so.

I soon learned that Blockbuster was in disarray in Europe, with a weak management team, a collection of unrationalized companies and brands, and no coherent strategy beyond the incessant opening of new stores. I suspected the same was true in the U.S., although I was not privy to the profit and loss there.

But it had capital and a sterling brand, and within three months of my arrival, Viacom and Blockbuster completed a complicated stock-swap deal valued at $8.4 billion. Blockbuster contributed $1.5 billion in cash that Viacom needed for its ultimately successful quest to purchase Paramount Communications, Inc., home of Paramount Pictures, the movie studio. Blockbuster got stock and options and a position of power on the Viacom board.

I found myself in a conglomerate once again and one that, like Grand Met, was struggling to establish an effective management team and coherent culture. In early 1996, Blockbuster brought in a new CEO, Bill Fields. He had spent twenty-five years at Wal-Mart, serving ultimately as president and CEO of the Wal-Mart Retail Stores Division. In that job, Bill had responsibility for a huge network of more than two thousand stores and six hundred thousand employees and was involved in all aspects of the business, from strategy to logistics. There is no doubt that Bill knew retail inside and out, and there is no debating that Wal-Mart had developed a management approach that helped make it one of the biggest and most successful companies on earth. It's not surprising, then, that Bill tried to apply the Wal-Mart way to Blockbuster. As a *Fortune* article of the day put it, "You can take the man out of Wal-Mart, but you can't take Wal-Mart out of the man."

Some of Bill's initiatives improved matters at Blockbuster. Bill brought in a number of new systems, including an executive information system (EIS). This was a sales tracking system that collected data from all Blockbuster stores around the world, packaged and presented the information in various ways, and made it available to the management team at 5:30 A.M. each morning. Having access to this vast amount of up-to-the-minute data made a huge difference to our ability to understand what was happening in the field and make better decisions. This action proved to be a life changer for me, and I have never managed to quit the drug of looking at sales results at 5:30 A.M. every morning. Twenty-two years and counting! Bill also brought in a real estate system that was enormously helpful in making choices about the performance differences in locations and identifying the best new store sites. Both systems proved useful to me in my subsequent positions at Papa John's and Dunkin'.

In other ways, Bill's indoctrination in the Wal-Mart philosophy was less effective for us. For example, in every Wal-Mart store you will see a sign above the exit that reads: *Thank you for shopping at Wal-Mart.* Soon enough, every exit at Blockbuster had a sign reading *Thank you for shopping at Blockbuster.* Nothing seriously wrong with that, except our customers didn't really think of their visit as "shopping." But Bill saw retail as retail, and to him, saying "thank you" was an essential part of customer relations. Our major business, however, was not pure retail but rather the renting of entertainment products, as Bill's successor John Antioco demonstrated.

Bill also followed the Wal-Mart way when it came to managing the leadership team and running the corporate operations. Early in his tenure, Bill organized an off-site strategy session and chose a skeet-shooting ranch in South Texas as the location. Sixteen of us arrived at the venue and discovered that we would be sleeping three to a room, in keeping with Wal-Mart's frugal approach to management costs. That was not the most popular decision of Bill's reign. We spent three days together, racing through the South Texas plains and brush country in trucks, shooting skeet. We'd return to the ranch for lunch and sit around a blazing fire. Bill kept a TV tuned to the financial news and kept glancing at it to check the Wal-Mart stock price. I guess he still had a big holding.

We did settle on a strategy during that off-site skeet-strategy session, but not through the kind of rigorous analysis, questioning, and back-and-forth I had anticipated. No, during the key meeting, Bill said, "I brought you all here because we need to agree on a Blockbuster strategy."

We nodded and got ready for discussion.

Bill handed out a single sheet of paper. On it were written five strategy points. Bill gave us a minute to read them, although it only took about ten seconds.

"So," Bill said, "everyone agree?"

Guess what? Everyone agreed. That was the end of our strategy debate, and the five points were the sum total of our strategy going forward.

The rest of the meeting proceeded without major incident. Except for the moment when our CFO accidentally fired his rifle during training and nearly shot himself in the foot.

Perhaps the action that signaled the beginning of the end for Bill came in November 1996. At the time, our headquarters was in Ft. Lauderdale. Wayne Huizenga had maintained a luxurious suite of offices on the top floor of the high-rise. I heard a rumor that Bill wasn't thrilled to be operating in the rather large shadow of the former honcho—who was then the owner of both the Miami Dolphins and the Miami Marlins. Whatever the reason, he proposed to Viacom, our parent company, that we move offices. The Viacom board approved the plan, no doubt thinking that Bill had another Ft. Lauderdale location in mind. Instead, Bill announced that the entire operation would move to Dallas. We began making the move in the spring of 1997 and, in the process, put a severe strain on the management team and the company as a whole, and we lost a large number of employees.

Bill himself never occupied the new offices. In April, he quit after just thirteen months on the job. John Antioco took over the CEO spot. I worked with him for seven years, and he remains a great friend. During that time, I kept climbing the hierarchical ladder. In 1998, I moved from the U.K. to the new Dallas headquarters. (I've lived in the U.S. ever since.) In 1998, I was named executive vice president and president, Worldwide Retail Operations, and president and COO in 2001. I learned a lot about the rental business, development, and back office systems.

In the ten-year period I was at Blockbuster, we enjoyed a lot of success. We increased global sales over 50 percent. I helped build our international business to reach twenty-six countries with revenue of $1.8 billion and established a worldwide franchise network of three hundred franchisees in fifteen countries.

Beneath the good news, however, there were troubles. The story of Blockbuster's demise is typically told as a technological cautionary tale: we didn't see the rise of DVD by mail, video on demand, and online streaming. The reality is that we did see the signs but failed to challenge ourselves and question the status quo so that we would be roused to make a timely response. The Blockbuster assumption was that people would always want to go to a physical store, rent a physical movie, and take it home to watch. Maybe the form would evolve, as it was moving then from cassette to DVD, but the human behavior would never change. Management was hooked on the physical model. Opening stores was what we did and what we were organized around.

Blockbuster was a development company as much as a movie rental company.

But, as early as 1996, there were signals that the business of renting movies was changing in fundamental ways, and they weren't particularly weak signals. Antioco, however, galvanized the team behind our rental heritage and drove the business through innovative approaches such as revenue sharing with the Hollywood studios so that we could guarantee that the hottest movie releases would be in stock on the weekends. We had several years of real success, but eventually the impact of technology began to catch up with us. The most obvious sign was the emergence of Netflix, which was founded in 1997 by Reed Hastings, to offer a subscription DVD-by-mail service, with no late fees. Hastings tells the story that the concept was inspired by his frustration with Blockbuster. He had rented *Apollo 13* and didn't get it back to the store for six weeks, by which time he owed forty dollars. (Late fees accounted for as much as 16 percent of Blockbuster's revenue in some years.) Hastings saw his health club membership as a better business model. There you paid a monthly fee and could work out as much or as little as you wanted. (Hastings later said he had made up the whole story for effect, but it's still credible.)

At first, Blockbuster did essentially nothing to respond to the Netflix challenge, seeing it as likely to be successful only in areas with high-speed Internet access, such as San Francisco and Austin. Our assumption, which proved wrong, was that Netflix would be a niche player, its service too dependent on high technology.

The great irony is that, in 2002, we had the chance to purchase Netflix, our greatest nemesis and eventual obliterator, for the pocket-change price of $100 million. We passed. Even in 2002, as Netflix went public and headed toward profitability, Blockbuster still focused on growth through geographic expansion and store proliferation. We acted as if our main rivals were other physical retailers including Wal-Mart and Best Buy. I share the blame for this miss.

That year, in a presentation to the board of directors, management argued that the way to achieve budget goals was to re-energize U.S. sales growth. That could be done by maintaining tight store controls, managing costs, building new stores in key markets, improving brand image, and investing in infrastructure.

The very last bullet on the list should have been the very first: *Test concept renewal ideas that can create platforms for growth.*

In fairness to us, we did make several attempts to create new growth platforms, many of which I championed or supported. The most intriguing of these was our foray into video on demand. In 2000, we decided we would do a limited test of the service in a handful of cities, and to ensure a response, we would offer the service free. To help fund the initiative, we sought a partner and found one in Enron, the company that later became infamous for its financial transgressions. But at the time, Enron was seen as one of the smartest, most successful companies in the world. They had an investment in optical fiber and saw video on demand as a promising market for it. The partnership progressed fine, but the test proved disappointing, and we didn't roll out the service. Although Blockbuster reported a loss on the venture, Enron somehow reported it as a profit, an example of its expertise in the manipulation of financial data to their benefit. (The chicanery eventually brought Enron to grief and dissolution, and for some executives, it resulted in prison, disgrace, and death.)

At Blockbuster, we made other attempts to build new platforms, including ventures in games and vending. In 2002, in response to the growing market for games and, particularly, game trading, Blockbuster purchased the Dallas-based Movie Trading Company and GameStation. That year, 2004, Redbox was founded, and it began to demonstrate there was huge potential in the DVD vending machine business. In 2001, we explored that category with a pilot vending program, but concluded it would not work in the United States. Redbox proved that our conclusion was wrong. It was a painful lesson and one I have never forgotten. Part of the challenge culture is to learn your lessons and apply the knowledge studiously. As I write this book, we are testing vending in many countries around the world for both Dunkin' brands.

Despite the fizzles at Blockbuster, the company skyrocketed to the very top of its game in 2004. Stores bustled with business. We developed an online service that proved very attractive to customers. They could order a movie online, get it by mail, and then return the DVD to the store. Netflix could not match this offer, and our online service attracted a lot of subscribers, even more new ones than were joining Netflix. To further differentiate this service, we included coupons for free rentals that could be redeemed in stores. This, too, met with great success and increased store revenue because these customers ended up spending more in store than did the store-only customer.

In 2004, despite the fast-changing environment, we achieved record profits.

In August of that year, amid all this success, the Blockbuster board signed a new five-year contract with CEO John Antioco. I was fifty-four years old. I had anticipated getting a shot at the CEO position. Now I'd have to wait five years, maybe longer, to take it. I began to look beyond Blockbuster and became CEO at Papa John's.

Not long after I left Blockbuster in October 2004, things started to fall apart. (Not just because I left!) In 2005, Viacom took advantage of Blockbuster's success to split the company off, probably a year too soon. Viacom released 80 percent of the stock into the market, which proved too much for it to absorb. A lot of the shares ended up in the hands of hedge funds, which eventually opened the door for the entrance of the famed corporate raider Carl Icahn.

When, at the end of 2004, Blockbuster began an initiative to buy Hollywood Video, Icahn bought positions in both companies. The Federal Trade Commission (FTC) did not approve the sale. Icahn raised a stink and then launched a proxy fight in 2005, which gave him a controlling interest.

Icahn feuded with Antioco over compensation, and in July 2007, Antioco left and was replaced by James W. Keyes, who had been president and CEO of 7-Eleven. The new strategy was to continue the store-based model, dump the DVD by mail service, and get into streaming video. But Blockbuster did not invest heavily enough in the online service and continued to overinvest in physical expansion and acquisition. They tried to purchase Circuit City in 2008. They reinstated late fees to increase revenue. Circuit City went bankrupt.

In 2010, things unraveled at a sickening rate. In July, Blockbuster was kicked off the New York Stock Exchange (stock symbol BBI). In August, it failed to meet an interest payment. In September, Blockbuster filed for bankruptcy protection. In 2011, Dish network purchased Blockbuster, with the intention of transforming it into a Netflix competitor. But that plan fizzled. Stores were closed, and by 2014, only a tiny fraction of the thousands of Blockbuster stores continued operations.

During the same period, Netflix went from strength to strength. In 2013, the company successfully ventured into content creation with *House of Cards* and today claims to produce more series and films than any other television entity. In 2016, Netflix reported nearly $9 billion in revenue with some ninety-eight million subscribers in 190 countries. It was at 314 on the *Fortune* 500 list of the largest companies in the United States, number 20 on the magazine's list of Fastest-Growing Companies, and number 14 on its list of World's Most Admired Companies.

You could argue that Blockbuster went down because of a failure to adopt new technology and a new business model, and that would be true. But the more fundamental issue was, in my opinion, the lack of a challenge culture. We didn't have the values or the habits that encouraged vigorous examination, questioning of the status quo, and challenge to our assumptions about the future. Part of the reason for that was management turmoil. There had been many changes at the top over the years. (Bill Fields lasted just thirteen months, short even by today's standards.) The parent company invested in other parts of the enterprise, rather than building and improving the Blockbuster business. One proposed purchase, of the games retailer Electronics Boutique, was rejected. That was probably a mistake. A similar business, GameStop, is still in business today. If Blockbuster had moved decisively into games, the company might still be around.

Reflecting on my time there, I do not feel that senior management—me included—worked well enough together to develop a coherent and competitive strategy to analyze trends, set long-range objectives, and monitor performance. As a result, we didn't articulate a vision for the industry and our place in it. We didn't have a clear strategic process, and so our attempts at building new growth platforms were all done in an ad hoc manner.

By way of explanation if not excuse, I will say that it's extremely difficult to imagine one's demise when you're enjoying the success we were having in 2004, with subscriptions on the rise and record profits.

It was textbook, really. When you look at companies that get in trouble, you usually find that the risk factors and problems were well known internally. That is what we saw at Wells Fargo and Samsung. But the right questions were not asked or answered. Programs that should have been killed were allowed to continue. Challenge was discouraged and external threats ignored. Management was too focused on profit and market goals. Employees were more concerned about holding on to their jobs than keeping the company moving.

So when I joined Dunkin' in 2009, after five years at Papa John's, I was determined to develop a culture different from any I had experienced thus far. I certainly did not want to repeat the mistakes we had made at Blockbuster. I definitely *did* want to adopt the best elements of the challenging collaborative environment I had first experienced at Grand Met.

And maybe, without really thinking about it, much as I admired my father and his entrepreneurial spirit, I was trying to show Dad that "why" is not just a crooked letter. The ability to ask why and to question leadership is essential to enterprise success.

CHAPTER FOUR

Developing People for Challenge

Why Allen Sheppard
Kept a "Light Grip on the Throat"

There is another element that played an important role in my development of the challenge culture ideas: my background in human resources.

I never intended to be a CEO or, for that matter, any operational executive. I spent the first twenty years of my career in human resources, and that's where I expected to spend my entire working life, but it didn't work out that way. I became an operating executive in 1991 at the age of thirty-nine.

But, looking back, I see it was this indirect path to senior operational management that enabled me to realize the importance of the challenge culture and learn how one can be created: usually it requires disrupting a long-standing status quo, reshaping an organization, rewriting the rules, and reconfiguring the management team. Just as we would do at Dunkin'.

My fascination with human resources began in high school, as I started thinking about university and my career beyond. I took a vocational aptitude test, and the consultant who administered it advised that I was a natural for social work. I told her I didn't want to do social work, I wanted to go into business, perhaps it was in the blood. She said, "Well then, why don't you do social work in business? It's called personnel management." As I soon learned, that was not a particularly good description of what the human resource manager actually did then or does now. In those days, HR was responsible for the nitty-gritty details of employment policy and execution: hiring, compensation, benefits, work scheduling, and all of that. It didn't really involve what I thought of as social work. Today, however, human resources people are at the very center of corporate activity, responsible for management development. That means bringing the right people into the company and helping them contribute and succeed. HR is also deeply involved in organizational structure, culture, and learning.

Anyway, I took the counselor's advice and looked for a university program in personnel management. I decided that the University of Essex was the best place for me, but my dad wasn't keen on the place. It was far enough away that I'd have to live on campus, which would add expense. Actually, that was a bit of a ruse; Dad wasn't particularly keen on university at all. He grumbled that it would be "too academic" and "not practical enough" and that it would probably turn me into a "raging lefty." It was 1968, an incredibly tumultuous political year, especially in the United States, with the assassination of Martin Luther King, Richard Nixon's election, and protests against the Vietnam War. Essex, like many American universities, was a hotbed of political activity and protest.

In the end, Dad put his foot down on Essex but didn't say no to higher education altogether. I ended up at Middlesex University in London (my campus was then known as Enfield College of Technology), commuted from home by car, and did business studies with a focus on personnel management. I still regret that decision because I think it impeded my maturing process.

But maybe there were benefits to it, as well, because I was driven to make the most of the college experience. Not only did I immerse myself in business theory, such as Fox's ideas on pluralism, but I got my first taste of entrepreneurialism and what it meant to run one's own enterprise. I had always wanted to be a

DJ and landed a gig on a lunchtime radio show in my first year at school. It went so well that I teamed up with an engineer friend, Dave Bradbrook, and we took the show out of the studio and into the dance hall. People liked us and word got around. Pretty soon we were getting gigs off campus, doing weddings, parties, and club dates. I used to joke that we played everything but funerals, and maybe we would have done those, too, if anybody had asked. We got so much work that we gave ourselves a proper name, Corporate Sound, which made us seem much bigger and more impressive than we were. People would call up and ask, "Can I hire one of your units?" Of course, we only had one "unit," but I'd act as if we had a bunch of them. "Hang on," I'd say, "let me check our booking schedule."

I kept the business going right through university. I probably did thirty weddings a year and some Saturdays in June I did two. I worked most weekends, Friday, Saturday, and Sunday nights. Christmas was the busiest period. I'd work every night from December 8 through the 24 and be exhausted come Christmas Day. I loved it, and I made pretty good money, around £100 per gig (around £1,300 or $1,744 today).

Maybe Dad was right about university not being practical enough, because in 1970 I felt the need to get in some real-life business experience. I took a year away from college to work at Esso, the U.K. unit of Exxon, in labor relations and continued to DJ, as well. In the Esso job I got a good sense of what it was like to work in a big company and caught a glimpse of what pluralism looked like in real life and found it could be contentious, especially between management and labor.

I went back to school after that work experience and in my senior year, 1972, interviewed for a full-time job. I talked with a number of companies and felt very fortunate that I got multiple offers—from four companies with HR positions, an insurance company in general management, and even one job as a soccer coach in a school. In the end, I chose Kraft Foods, because it was the most interesting of the corporate openings. It also paid the most, at £2,000 per annum (about £26,000 or $35,000 today).

In those days, the standard procedure was that the college graduate would commit to a job in the spring of senior year, take the summer off, and start work in September. My plan was to go to the United States for the summer, and I was really looking forward to it. I had always been fascinated by the States and, as a DJ, loved American music. But Kraft was having none of it. They said, oh no, we need you to start right away. My first day on the job I had to catch a 12:50 A.M. train from Paddington Station in West London to Haverfordwest, Wales, so I could report to the plant there first thing in the morning. It would be another eight years before I finally got to America.

I spent the next thirteen years in a series of very intriguing corporate jobs, each of which gave me new perspectives on management and contributed to my views on the importance of challenge.

At Kraft, I learned a great deal about the traditional practice of personnel management, which, as I said, was largely concerned with compensation, benefits, and employee relations with the white-collar office staff. I sensed that these practices, while necessary, were hardly sufficient to the full development of people in their positions.

Then I joined Rolls-Royce, where I did similar work in labor relations but mostly involving daily negotiations with shop floor employees. It also got very intense and personal. For example, I visited countless employees who were on sick leave. Sometimes I could wish them well and a speedy recovery. Sometimes the situation was grave and the purpose of my visit was to talk about benefits for the soon-to-be widow. At Rolls-Royce, an employee got a better pension deal if they took early retirement rather than waited for a death benefit. But when I explained this, the sick employee would become anxious that, if they took retirement, they would not be able to return to work, if and when they recovered. Sometimes they did come back to work; sometimes they didn't. I attended my share of funerals. These were hardly "soft" functions, as people sometimes characterize the responsibilities of the HR manager. In fact, I look back at my career and see that some of the skills that a general manager needs—a combination of toughness, compassion, and empathy—came from my work in human resources.

In January 1977, I was recruited by Massey Ferguson, makers of farm equipment, and there I was exposed for the first time to international business and began to see the effect of national culture on business culture. As a young HR officer, the experience was a huge eye-opener. For example, I was responsible for supporting agricultural engineers and other professional staffers in many European countries, including Switzerland and Poland, as well as countries in Africa and the Middle East, including Kenya, Libya, and Iran. I had to quickly learn the intricacies and formalities of the Swiss cantonal system of government. I supported managers in Iran and visited Benghazi, Libya, and both experiences helped me understand the pressures of doing business in countries with authoritarian regimes, where questioning and pushback are discouraged, sometimes by force. Seeing what an authoritarian culture really looks like throws the challenge culture into high relief.

In 1982, after I'd spent a decade in business, personnel management was starting to change. In addition to the compensation issues, HR was getting more and more involved in leadership development and organizational change. During that period, I moved on from Massey Ferguson to Parker Hannifin, makers of precision industrial products. There I was amazed and excited to find that HR was involved in the fundamental forces that shape a culture. One of the key issues we addressed was how to create a safe environment where employees would feel empowered and encouraged to ask questions, make challenges, and take individual initiative. We wanted to make it possible for people to be proactive, screw up sometimes, learn from their mistakes, help and support one another even when things went wrong, and not fear they would be punished or lose their jobs.

Very clearly, a big part of the answer was, and still is, training and communication. At Parker Hannifin, I was responsible for a training course called Management for Action, which I led many times. One of the main discussion points was this issue of the safe employee environment, and I can tell you that it was all new stuff for most of the plant managers. They had spent their careers thinking about efficiency, productivity, and yield. The idea of questioning, challenge, and discourse was completely foreign to them.

Even the basic concept of people management was new for many of them. They thought about managing machines and the production process. As for people? Well, some were better workers than others. Training was necessary, yes, but it took time out of the day and could have a negative effect on short-term productivity. Development and continuous improvement of the human "asset"? They just didn't think that way.

I will never forget one session when this point of view was made blindingly clear to me. After the session, a plant manager came up to me. I'll call him Rex. He was in his midforties and probably had five hundred people reporting to him. He seemed genuinely curious about what we had discussed in the session.

"You know, Nigel," Rex said, "this management thing . . . " He paused. I thought maybe he was going to say it was all rubbish.

"This management thing, well, it's really *quite interesting.*"

I had to agree with him. And I felt quite pleased ("chuffed," as we say in England) that I had been able to open Rex's eyes to the human side of the production process. Up until then, to Rex, managing people had meant filling open slots, assigning tasks, scheduling work, approving raises and promotions, handling wage disputes, and the like.

· · ·

I would consider all of these work experiences to be part of my formative years, a period of higher education in the challenge culture, but it was not until I joined Grand Metropolitan, in March of 1985, that the concepts really began to crystallize.

My new position had a very different title than I was used to: director of manpower resourcing for the Express Foods Group unit of Grand Metropolitan or Grand Met, as it was usually called. Not "personnel officer" or "HR manager" or the like. I was in charge of manpower resourcing. If you forgive for a moment the gender-specific manpower, the title signified a very different view of people development than I was accustomed to. People were a source of power and an important resource; they were not just interchangeable workers who had to be hired, fired, paid, and shuffled about.

Grand Met, too, was a very different kind of business than any I had worked in previously: a large, global conglomerate. It had been in the making for several decades. In 1969, Grand Met acquired Express Dairy, a family-owned company that had been making daily milk deliveries to English doorsteps since 1864. Over the years, the company had gotten involved in a variety of nondairy food ventures and was renamed Express Foods. As the company grew and became more complex, the lack of professional management began to show. By the early eighties, the unit was struggling: they had not rationalized and modernized their systems or updated their products. Profits were plummeting, and employees were demotivated and discouraged.

Allen Sheppard changed all that. In 1984, Allen was named head of U.K. operations for all Grand Met units, and he soon turned his attention to Express Foods. He was not about to settle for the poor status quo in that company, and he made the first step in challenging it by installing a new management team under CEO Clive Strowger. After Clive and his team did their due diligence, they set about cutting costs, rationalizing operations, improving quality, developing new products, and building the brand. They stuck their noses into everything and asked questions of everybody.

Which factory operations could be consolidated into fewer facilities?
Could a yogurt production line be adapted to handle the making of other types of products?
Could the delivery fleet be improved?
Did we have the workforce right in each location?

Express Foods was my first experience of a company that had been allowed to run itself into the ground by accepting things as they had always been done. By the time I joined the company in 1985, however, profits were beginning to recover and morale was improving. It was a dramatic turnaround situation, and I saw how essential it was that management had questioned everything.

I also saw that the senior managers could be pretty aggressive and even abrasive if they found things not to their liking. That was the 1980s style. They demanded a lot from their people and put each individual through a rigorous performance evaluation process on a regular basis, including biannual management development reviews at board level. There was little tolerance for inadequate performance, and new people had to show their stuff right away. My boss, David Tagg, talked energetically about how Grand Met people had to demonstrate what they could do in their first hundred days on the job. Three months to learn, engage, contribute, and begin to make a difference. The value of hitting the ground running is a lesson that I have applied throughout my career.

In early 1986, having brought Express Foods back from the brink, Allen was named CEO of Grand Met, and he turned his attention to other units. He brought me into the corporate center to become group management development director for all of Grand Met. As such, I had responsibility for senior recruitment and management development for all the units in this massive, incredibly diversified global conglomerate—with multiple operating units and 130,000 employees. This was human resources in its most expansive and progressive form: a big, central operation, where we were involved in developing strategy, building management capability, improving education and training, facilitating organizational development, and fostering cultural change.

Of course, it was the eighties, and the business environment was very different then. And Grand Met was very much a creature of the acquisitive, aggressive, expansionist, swashbuckling times. What's more, it had its roots in much earlier days, when business was even less concerned about a people-centric culture. Grand Met was originally the brainchild of a colorful British entrepreneur, Max Joseph, born in 1910, who started out in real estate and was wealthy by age thirty, with a Rolls-Royce and a home in Hampstead, one of London's toniest neighborhoods. Joseph began buying up hotels in 1947, amassed extensive properties and assets, and went public in 1961 as Grand Metropolitan. He kept on buying and diversifying, driven by the theory that a huge portfolio of physical assets could generate enough profits to support the debt required to acquire even more physical assets. It was all about finance and assets, buying and selling, profit and more profit.

By 1985, when I joined, Grand Met had become a huge sprawling mass of businesses, which included breweries, restaurants, betting and gaming operations, food companies, pet food makers, hotels, branded wines and spirits, and a number of U.S. consumer businesses, including Pepsi-bottling operations and Alpo pet food. Allen Sheppard had joined Grand Met in 1975 as managing director of its brewing unit, Watney Mann & Truman.

Grand Met had acquired the jewel for its crown in 1981, with the purchase of InterContinental Hotels, for $500 million. But the crown soon proved rather unwieldy, and that acquisition actually marked the beginning of the end of the strategy of achieving growth through asset accumulation. In 1983, when Grand Met got into health care with the purchase of Pearle Vision, the financial managers and analysts in the City (London's equivalent of Wall Street) began to have their doubts about Grand Met's prospects, and the company lost the premium status it had enjoyed.

Clearly, the status quo could no longer be tolerated; Grand Met needed a complete strategic, organizational, and cultural overhaul, which is why the board had given the nod to Allen to take over as chair. He had won the vote over the other finalist, the aristocratic Anthony Tennant, a figure that Americans would likely think of as a classic British businessperson—rather formal and patrician. The board sensed it needed a questioner and a shaker-upper. Allen, the brilliant son of the working class, was seen as the scrappy challenger who would be more than willing to engage in discourse with anyone at any time. He was also, by that time, one of Great Britain's most illustrious business figures. Within a week or two of his ascendancy in 1986, Allen had begun assembling a new senior management team, and that's when he brought me into the center.

Allen's strategy was simple in concept. We would transform Grand Met from a lumpy conglomerate into the world's leading food and drinks company. Execution of the strategy was, however, not so simple. To achieve our strategic goals, we absolutely had to challenge the corporate status quo, which had been in place for some thirty years, and that proved to be quite an exercise. We embarked on an initiative Allen called Operation Declutter, which was essentially a massive program of review, rationalization, reconfiguration, deacquisition, and new acquisition.

Another way to describe Operation Declutter is as a meta example of Sinek's concept of "starting with why." Allen questioned the purpose of every Grand Met unit, and over a two-year period, from 1986 to 1988, we divested a number of businesses that did not fit the food and drinks focus, including the unit that had been considered at the core of Grand Met just a few years earlier, InterContinental Hotels. Its sale for $2.27 billion to a Japanese consortium helped support a number of other businesses that sharpened our focus. These included the biggest one, the $5.7 billion 1988 hostile takeover of the U.S. food giant Pillsbury, whose stable of brands included Häagen-Dazs, Green Giant, and—as it turned out, important for me—Burger King.

This was corporate action of a whole new scale and scope for me. I doubt that we could have accomplished what we did without an appetite and an aptitude for challenge. There is no question that Allen, in both his personality and style of management, along with my boss David Tagg, the group services director, had a tremendous influence on our thinking. David in particular was very powerful, and much of what I am today I put down to his tutelage.

Grand Met, as I think about it now, was an intriguing combination of a culture of challenge and a culture of fear, and this seeming duality sprang largely from the character of our fearless leader. Allen was a no-nonsense guy who had a natural taste for egalitarian collaboration *and* authoritarian confrontation. He famously referred to his management approach as "controlled conflict," which sounds quite a lot like Uber's idea of "principled confrontation."

By controlled conflict, Allen meant that the job of management was to encourage the expression of disparate views, put disagreements on the table, and create an environment where decisions could be thrashed out. This was, in essence, a challenge culture. When it worked, I could see how healthy and productive the approach could be.

However, Allen also embraced the brutal, primal, win-lose attitude that has been a part of Western business practice for centuries. This part of his management philosophy he liked to call the "light grip on the throat." That meant he always wanted his people to know that he was the ultimate authority; he had his hand on the throat and could clamp down at any time. That was more like the you're-fired culture, where the threat of dismissal or marginalization was always present.

So, at Grand Met, we had a hybrid culture: plenty of productive and positive challenge but always set against a backdrop of lingering anxiety and tension. "I'll go to meetings and take a very strong line," Allen said. "I expect people to counterpunch, and I get quite irritated when they don't." Allen deeply believed in change and constant motion. He said he would rather launch ten new products and have six fail than launch nothing new at all. He also had another characteristic that made the challenge fun and the tension bearable: a wry sense of humor. Allen's approach worked for the time and the place and the organization. Those were the days of rapid acquisition, and Grand Met was essentially an assemblage of very disparate operating units. Talk about pluralistic. Beyond the need to be profitable and achieve growth, there was very little that a dog-food maker and a five-star hotel chain had in common. To keep Grand Met moving forward, Allen felt he needed to retain some control, allow some independence, encourage some challenge, and enforce some authority.

It was a complicated and sometimes confusing environment and, eventually, could not sustain itself. Allen finally decided the conglomerate had to be disassembled and a new approach taken, much more like a true challenge culture. He was not one for long-winded mission and values statements, but he did want to capture our organizational philosophy in writing so that our foundational tenets would be explicit. We distilled it into eleven bullet points that barely fill a page:

- Decentralized authority
- Open communications
- Challenge culture
- Small corporate center adding value
- Avoidance of bureaucracy
- Strong performance orientation
- No compromise on high management standards
- Development of people
- Tolerance of different personalities and styles
- Action orientation
- Major role in trade and industry affairs

That list is as relevant today as it was in 1988, although now I would put "challenge culture" at the top because, in a way, all the others are contained within that idea.

. . .

The acquisition of Burger King gave me a chance to finally make the trip to America. On January 16, 1989, almost immediately after the Pillsbury acquisition was completed, I flew to Miami, Florida, to become senior vice president, human resources, for the new Grand Met unit. My immediate boss was Barry

Gibbons, Burger King's newly appointed chairman and CEO, a fellow British transplant who Allen had plucked from the Berni and Host Group Limited, the restaurant unit of Grand Met. Neither of us had much experience in the U.S. We were soon to find that it was incredibly different from working in London, and both of us were shell-shocked at first. I was awed by the sheer size of the company and the power of the brand and by the scope of the fast-food industry, in which so many Americans at that time had started their working careers.

Barry, by his own admission, had very little clue about any of that, but he rightly sensed that culture would be a major issue in his new assignment. "The culture of an organization—whether business or otherwise—is an odd phenomenon," Barry wrote in his insightful and very amusing book, *Pushing Doors Marked Pull*. Although he dismissed most analyses of corporate culture as "bollocks," Barry realized that he was "heading for a seismic culture clash" at Burger King. He knew that he, himself, an ex-rocker and noncorporate type, would be part of that clash.

One incident that demonstrated our innocent ignorance of all things American came soon after our arrival. Barry and I flew to Orlando to meet with a new marketing executive. At the airport, Burger King had arranged for a stretch limo to pick us up.

"Where to?" asked the driver.

Barry gave him the name of the hotel.

The driver looked surprised. "Say that again?"

Barry repeated our destination.

The driver shook his head, said "OK," and moved off.

We creeped forward about four hundred yards and came to a stop.

"Here you go," said the driver.

Barry looked at me. "What the hell . . . ?"

I laughed. "Ask him to wait and give us a ride back."

Welcome to the U.S.A.!

At the time we joined, Burger King was in the doldrums and needed a reset. Another company in need of a spark. Founded in 1953, it was America's No. 2 burger chain, after McDonald's, with annual sales of some $6 billion, but it had become sluggish and bloated. The company employed over 41,000 people, about 1,500 of them in corporate positions. About 100 of those worked in splendor at the headquarters in Miami. Barry was shocked to discover that each of the top managers there had a budget of $50,000 to decorate their offices.

Clearly, the Burger King operation did not adhere to Grand Met's organizational philosophy, especially the concepts of a small corporate center that added value and the avoidance of bureaucracy. Barry charged me with devising a plan for reducing head count and reorganizing the corporate center. With that in mind, I went to see Ron Petty, then global president and an industry icon, on my first day on the job that January. I asked him how many people he thought could be taken out of his headquarters organization.

"Not one," he said.

Hmm.

One of the benefits of being an outsider to an organization, as I was, is that it is easy to ask basic questions, and that is what I did for the next several weeks. I had come to Miami without my family, I was living in a hotel, and I knew nobody outside the company, so I had no obligations other than to learn everything I could about our new acquisition. Every evening, I went out to dinner with an executive or manager. Every morning, I had breakfast with another one. All day long, I talked with people, asked questions, and learned about the company, how people worked, and why things were the way they were. In this effort, I collaborated closely with one of my direct reports, Bob Morrison, and we called our initiative Project Aries.

Just as I did years later with the franchisees when I first joined Dunkin', I drilled down, trying to get at the root causes of Burger King's inefficiency and lackadaisical performance. I learned there were many contributing factors. Some were large, such as the dense bureaucracy; some were seemingly minor. For example, at that time, Burger King restaurants were known for being poorly maintained and sloppily run. I had many conversations with district managers, who had responsibility for ensuring company standards of operation at the store level. Theoretically, they spent their days visiting stores, making inspections, and working with store operators. But that, I learned, was not what was actually happening. The district managers traveled long distances by car and had to connect with many people each day. When they got to a store they made a beeline for the telephone so they could check in with corporate, call their office to pick up messages, and try to reach other managers throughout the system, often with the same message or piece of information. After finishing their phone calls, they barely had time to look at store operations before getting in the car to drive to the next location.

This was 1989 and cell phones were expensive and not in wide use, so we couldn't give everyone a mobile to increase their productivity, but we could install a technology that was then coming into general application: voice mail. This would enable the district managers to leave messages with multiple people at one time, and pick up a load of messages left for them all at once, without having to make multiple calls and repeated attempts to reach their bosses, colleagues, or direct reports. With the freed-up time they could do what they were supposed to be doing: helping store managers improve their operations. (Yes, this was 1989 and voice mail was revolutionary!)

By the end of March, I had talked to enough people and asked enough questions that I had a good understanding of how the corporate organization worked and didn't work. Bob Morrison and I developed a new organizational plan, and I went to discuss it with Barry.

"How many people do you think we can take out of corporate?" he asked.

"Probably 30 percent," I said.

Barry almost fell off his chair. "That's three times more than I expected," he said.

In April, we let go 550 people from the corporate organization, including 100 from Ron Petty's group at headquarters. In addition, the roles and responsibilities of almost every position were changed and refined. This may sound antithetical to the challenge culture, which I have defined as being the opposite of the you're-fired approach. But this was foundational. We had to remove the bloat, cut the excess, focus the activity, and instill the Grand Met organizational philosophy.

I must quickly add that we took great care in the process. I insisted that the managers had to meet personally with each person who was being let go, and that's exactly what happened. There was no general announcement or mass pink slipping. We talked to each person individually, and the exit packages were generous. Years later, one of the people I let go even said to me, "Nigel, that was the best thing that ever happened to me." He now owns a big network of Applebee's restaurants.

I am not suggesting that all the people we let go were happy about it. Nor do I believe that firing should be a preferred management tool. I tell this story to make the point that sometimes drastic measures must be taken to clear the ground and get the organization and staffing right before you start building a challenge culture.

And, in the end, Project Aries brought results. We trimmed thirteen layers of management. Gone were the fancy office budgets and stretch limos. We improved the supply chain and revitalized marketing. We expanded internationally by purchasing the U.K. Wimpy burger chain and remaking their restaurants as Burger King units. (Barry Gibbons became famous as "the man who brought the Whopper to Great Britain.") In 1990, Burger King's profits began to rise.

. . .

From my experience at Grand Met, including my time at Burger King, I came to believe that human resources has to be a forward-looking function in any business. It must play a central role in ensuring that management development and organizational structure support corporate philosophy. An aggressive HR function pushes everything to do with culture, people, and organizational change.

This was true with all the acquisitions Grand Met made. When they brought a new company into the group, we looked carefully at three positions: the CEO, the finance director, and the human resources director. When we purchased Burger King, we brought in new people in all three positions: Barry Gibbons as CEO; Bob Stetson, who had been with Pearle Vision, as finance leader; and me in HR. The idea was to build a team of people who understood the Grand Met organizational philosophy and everything worked from there.

When I first came to America in 1988, this is not what I saw in most companies. I was surprised and frankly appalled by the standard of the human resources function in this country compared with the United Kingdom and other countries in Europe. Many were still operating as administrators. I believe that the true value of HR comes in recruiting the right people, creating the right organization structure, developing the right talent, and constantly training people—particularly with changing technological needs—and this is becoming more and more the standard in the United States. It is certainly how we think about HR at Dunkin'.

But what is the "right" talent for the challenge culture? What are the right skills? This is an intriguing and fundamental question. Allen Sheppard's brand of "controlled conflict" and my style of incessant questioning do not always come naturally to everybody. Indeed, many businesspeople can be reluctant to challenge other people, ideas, and the status quo. It's not that they don't want to make a challenge (although some don't), it's that they simply don't know how to go about it in a way that will gain a result and not be unpleasant or dangerous for them. Living in a challenge culture requires a set of skills that many people don't have or haven't developed or that haven't been required of them. The skills are sometimes referred to as "soft" or "qualitative" skills, and they include collaboration, communication, problem solving, and critical thinking.

Collaboration is the ability to work productively with other people. This skill is fundamental to the challenge culture. It is the ability to listen to different viewpoints and to work in group settings for the benefit of the goal of the group, even if you have some reservations about the agreed plan of action. In some companies, sole contributors can be successful without having to collaborate, but most organizations face complex problems that require multifunctional operations. Collaboration is a skill that can be taught at any age but, ideally, is learned young. I have been very impressed with the emphasis put on collaboration at the Charles River School in Dover, Massachusetts, where both of my young kids go. They start collaborating at the age of four, working together to create presentations, sing songs, choreograph dances, and do other group projects.

Communication is the ability to articulate ideas, express emotions, engage in dialogue, question, listen, and respond. I talk about communication in more depth later in the book, but it's important to understand it as a key soft skill that makes organizations run well. At Dunkin', we constantly increase the amount of communication to employees so they can be fully engaged in the business and know what is going on. In a challenge culture, information is not seen as a weapon or tool of authority but as an important resource to be shared. When I come across a relevant article or receive a useful report, I always think about who might benefit from the information and pass it along to them.

Problem solving involves being able to define problems and devise and execute solutions. In the 1980s and 1990s, problem solving typically involved problem identification, solution development, and evaluation of results. Today, we must add another skill to those activities: the ability to search for, organize, and evaluate information that pertains to the problems. That's because there is such a huge amount of knowledge available on any and every subject from a huge range of sources, most of them online. Knowledge management has become a key aspect of problem solving.

Critical thinking comprises the skills involved in evaluating concepts, synthesizing information, applying judgment, and

forming an opinion. A perfect illustration of this skill is the identification and selection of candidates for senior positions. In 2016,
we needed to fill the position of president of Dunkin' U.S.A. and
had several good candidates. It was an important role, given that
it was our biggest unit and being president in the U.S. was a perfect way to be groomed for the CEO role. So we underwent a
rigorous process of evaluation, information gathering, analysis,
and judgment. All of the candidates went through a variety of
testing procedures, administered by external consultants, to identify their personality traits. I spent a good deal of time soliciting
and reviewing references for each candidate. I interviewed each
candidate at least four times, each conversation in a different situation, so I could see how they responded to different environments: formal and informal settings; office and restaurant; group
and one-on-one engagements. Throughout the process, I com-
piled a written assessment of each candidate, in the same form
for each, so I captured every aspect of their career, personality,
family life, and work history. That enabled me to evaluate each
candidate and compare each one to every other in a rigorous
way and consistent format. That is the kind of critical-thinking
process that needs to be applied to any key decision.

Qualitative skills, as essential as they are, seem to be in surprisingly short supply in today's workforce, largely because there
is so much focus placed on the quantitative or technical skills—
finance, software development, coding, engineering—that are
valued in the technology and financial services industries and
because of our almost religious belief in data, especially big data.

The *Wall Street Journal* cites some revealing statistics about the
importance of qualitative skills today. They report that companies say that qualitative skills "can make the difference between
a stand-out employee and one who just gets by," especially today when routine tasks have been automated and so many jobs
demand "empathy, or other abilities that computers can't easily
simulate." In the *Journal*'s survey of nine hundred executives, 92
percent of them said that "soft skills were equally important or

more important than technical skills." Just as striking, 89 percent of the executives polled said they were having difficulty finding people with those skills.

It is certainly my bias, since I came up through HR, that the human resources function is where the needed skills of the challenge culture can best be fostered and encouraged and hired in, but that is also my conviction and experience as a chief executive officer. At Dunkin', our human resources people are key players in developing talent, building teams, training, managing a culture, and ensuring that soft skills and hard skills come together, especially in management and leadership positions—because these are the people who must model the challenge culture day in and day out.

And it is essential to keep reviewing and reassessing your people as business conditions change, new initiatives are pursued, and time goes by. Do we have the right people in the right places? Do they have the skills necessary for the tasks and projects they are responsible for? Are we developing our people appropriately? Do we need to reconsider staffing levels and assignments? The best mix of people today may not be the ideal one for tomorrow.

. . .

In 1991, after two years with Burger King in Miami, my career in human resources came to an end. One day Barry Gibbons took me aside.

"Nigel, listen," he said. "You're so involved in the business and so interested in it, you really ought to be running something."

"Barry," I replied, "all I've ever wanted to do is be the best HR person I could be."

"No, no, no mate," he said. "You've got to go run something."

The next thing I knew I was on my way back to London with a new title: managing director, Europe, Middle East, and Africa. My management team there was very skeptical of this HR guy who had just had operational greatness thrust upon him. I decided to put my faith in one of the key elements of the Grand Met philosophy: open communications.

"Look," I said to my new colleagues, "I don't know much about any of your disciplines. I know a few things about HR. I know a bit about management and leadership. But I don't know a hell of a lot about finance. I'm reasonably familiar with that thing you call the P&L. But the balance sheet is pretty much beyond me."

They could only laugh. "You're just going to have to help me learn all this stuff," I said.

And guess what, that is just what they did.

In my new role as an operational leader, I began to learn what was necessary to make the concept of the challenge culture really work in practice.

CHAPTER FIVE

Setting the Rules of Engagement

How We Launched K-Cups

Not everybody is an Allen Sheppard, who relished asking questions and challenging the status quo. In fact, I have found that many people are naturally averse to challenging one another or to asking what they see as too many questions. That's probably because they have never learned the skills or been exposed to such an environment. As I've said previously, there are plenty of families and companies where challenge is not encouraged and where questioning is considered rude. As a result, people simply don't know how to go about questioning in a way that will get a result and not be unpleasant or too risky for them.

One of my nonbusiness activities has shown me the truth of this over and over again: soccer coaching. When I was a kid I dreamed of being a professional coach. I got my preliminary soccer coaching badge in the U.K. at age eighteen. Over the years, I have coached at a senior amateur level in the U.K. and youth soccer on and off for forty-odd years. At the moment, I coach two youth soccer teams, one of eleven-year-old girls and the other of thirteen-year-old boys. In 2017, I put together and led a consortium to purchase and reinvigorate the Leyton Orient Football Club, the professional London soccer organization that has been my home team since I can remember. (More on that story in chapter nine.)

In both my amateur coaching and my work with the professional team, I have learned an incredible amount about the development, management, and implementation of the challenge culture: sport involves a special kind of challenge, but its skills are relevant to business.

One of the most important roles of the soccer coach, or any kind of sports coach, is that of teacher. This is especially true when it comes to young players, who do not start out with the capabilities they need to play soccer effectively, although some have greater natural talent than others.

One of the key behaviors that does not come quickly or easily to a lot of kids is the simple act of challenging another player. Kids are great at asking questions and challenging their parents, but they tend to avoid challenging one another. When an opposing team player comes at them, they are more likely to get out of the way than they are to step forward and try to block a shot, force the player to pass, or take the ball away. But those are the things they must learn to do if they want to get and keep the ball and, ultimately, win the game. Similarly, the businessperson who is not adept at challenge may try to avoid or deflect questions and is more likely to step back than to "lean in" to the discourse, to borrow Sheryl Sandberg's term for being actively engaged.

Some soccer coaches seem to assume that the way to get kids to make a challenge is to yell at them. "Come on! You gotta step up to it! Go for it!" Of course, this does not work. Coaches have to help kids understand that challenge actually involves a set of specific skills, each of which can be defined and practiced. Nor does such sloganeering work in the corporate setting. Too often, companies make grand statements about the importance of debate but, in practice, do not really encourage it.

On the soccer field, one of the skills required in challenge is the physical maneuvering and footwork needed to take the ball away from another player. But a lot of kids can't focus on that skill because of their natural tendency to shy away from the player barreling toward them. So, in practice sessions, we do a simple exercise that removes the incoming threat so the kids can focus on the task of using their feet to get the ball.

I have the kids on my team number off as ones or twos. The number ones take the ball and run away from the twos. The twos have to run after them, try to catch up and take the ball. It is a very different thing to run after another player than it is to run at them head on, but it still requires the same kind of footwork and ball handling to take the ball away. The players then switch roles and the ones try to get the ball from the twos. When they feel they have gained skill in footwork and ball handling, they have more confidence on the field and are less likely to shy away from a scramble for the ball. In other words, the development of specific, component skills contributes to the ability to challenge.

So, just as challenge can be broken down into core skills in soccer, challenge skills can be defined in the business environment, including purposeful questioning, civil discourse, and productive, explicit disagreement.

. . .

People do not naturally love to be questioned. They may see it as an affront to their authority or an attack on their beliefs. (I have often seen this when board members challenge management.) One-on-one questioning can seem personal, raw, and confrontational, with potential for embarrassment.

In the presidential campaign of 2016, we saw just how uncomfortable questioning can be, as we watched Hillary Clinton and Donald Trump hurl questions (and accusations) directly at each other. In postdebate analyses, both candidates were widely criticized for the nature of the questioning being too personal, too aggressive, too nasty, and too focused on exposing, trapping, or making the other candidate look foolish, badly informed, or insensitive. As a *Wall Street Journal* reporter described the second debate, "This was raw and angry politics as blood sport and served perhaps only to underscore even more how unappetizing political debate has become."

Another observation about the 2016 presidential debates was that they simply reflected the tenor of the times. Questioning has never been easy and has always had the potential to go astray, but that's a far greater hazard today when there are so many channels of expression available, including TV, online, and social media. The likelihood that challenge can turn into attack is most prevalent in social media, where it's easy to post confrontational comments without having to actually engage in dialogue with anyone. What's more, many sites allow people to post comments under an online moniker or anonymously. This emboldens many people and seems to increase the intensity of comment. In these venues, questioning often escalates into confrontation and, indeed, can become a blood sport. Many participants focus on scoring points and winning for their own glory.

With Dunkin', people comment about us on social media constantly and about everything, from store operations to menu offerings to specific instances of customer service, good or bad. Some of it can get very personal and indeed abusive on occasion. These comments can really take a toll on company leaders, store managers, and line workers. They feel attacked, with no way to express their own view of the issue or side of the story. The immediate impulse is to respond, but we know that this can often lead to escalation and more attacks. So, we have had to think hard about how we should monitor social media and when and how we should respond. At Dunkin' we devote a good deal of resources to monitoring what customers say about our products, brands, and service and in distributing those comments to those who might benefit from the views. This alone takes a lot of work and judgment: to identify the real issues and separate them from the nonsense that pervades social media channels. Sometimes we find valuable questions and worthwhile challenges posed by commenters. But clearly social media trolls don't follow the same rules of engagement we espouse, so we have to diligently apply our soft skills of critical thinking and analysis.

When the national culture at large seems to thrive on the kind of conflict and attack we see in social media, it's all the more difficult—and all the more important—for companies to model, teach, and manage the challenge process.

. . .

How do we keep questioning on track in the business environment? First, by defining its *purpose*. If people understand the purpose of intense questioning and believe that the purpose is worthy and valuable, and not personally threatening to them, the questioning will be more readily accepted and the answers come more freely and truthfully, willingly, and completely.

Again, we can look to Socrates for the model. In its highest form, as Socrates defined it, the purpose of questioning is to discover the truth. We in business may not spend much time trying to figure out the nature of the universe, as Socrates and his students did, but we should always try to get to the truth of any situation. If we're looking to make a new hire, analyze a problem, set a strategy, or take any kind of important decision, we want to get at the truth.

Theoretically, anyway, getting at the truth of a situation is good for everybody involved in a business enterprise and is thus a shared purpose, bigger and more important than the goals of any individual participant.

Defining and stating purpose is one of the important aspects of the extensive interviewing I do with candidates for a new position. When conducting an interview, it's important to make it clear that the purpose of the questioning is to gather information and build understanding, not to make on-the-spot judgments. When interviewing candidates for a job, I know that, eventually, their skills and characteristics will become evident and will have an effect on our culture and performance, so the more we know the earlier, the better. I really want to know how they would like to improve and whether the company could benefit from their efforts to do so. So the goal of intense questioning is not to find reasons to reject a candidate. It often enables us to help them, once hired, to build on their strengths and achieve greater success more quickly in their new positions than if we had to learn about their traits on the job.

Interviews are truly fascinating situations, and I always try to allow the interviewee to engage however he or she wants to in the interview because the person's actions and behaviors will give a sense of his or her priorities and behaviors.

Sometimes these actions will be quite minor but hugely revealing. For example, I was interviewing a candidate for an important position on the management team. I'll call him Leo. We did one of the several interviews at a restaurant. I booked a private room so we would not be distracted and so Leo could feel freer to be himself.

It was summer and the dining room was warm. Within a few minutes of sitting down, Leo took off his coat and tossed it on a side chair. OK, fair enough. But he was still warm. Suddenly, in the middle of a sentence, Leo got up and went to the air conditioner controls and started tinkering with them, as we continued to talk. He hadn't asked what I thought of the temperature. He didn't suggest that he might adjust the controls. Leo sat down again but still didn't seem to be satisfied. He jumped up again and this time yanked open a window, again without discussing his actions with me.

This bit of Leo's behavior was just one piece of data, but it indicated to me that he was quite focused on his own issues, was not particularly attuned to others, and liked control.

One of the reasons I conduct more than one interview is so I can ask questions of people in different environments. A person can be skilled at interviewing across the table in an office but will come across very differently elsewhere. I always take candidates for a visit to one or two of our Dunkin' locations, and I usually learn much more about them as we walk and talk than I would in a conference room. Action reveals purpose.

My favorite interview environment is anywhere outside the office—a golf course, a restaurant, on a boat, at competitors' locations, or in our own shops. Sometimes I will take a candidate to visit several Dunkin' or Baskin-Robbins shops and talk about how they compare and contrast. This gives us the chance to talk about a wide range of operational issues and for me to observe the candidate interacting with staff and customers.

I also like to personally conduct interviews with the candidates' references, rather than relying on a headhunter, recruitment agency, or our own HR staff to do them. This is an unusual practice for a CEO, I know, but it is a valuable and effective one. A recruiter is a less reliable source of information because he or she has a vested interest in the candidate. A recruiter is not looking to explore the candidate's shortcomings or failures or self-doubts, all of which can be highly relevant, but rather to present the candidate in the best possible light. It is only by listening to and observing very carefully the reference's in-person comments that a deeper understanding of the candidate will come out—in the awkward pauses, the facial expressions, the genuine enthusiasm, the hedged statements, or the overselling.

The reference interview gives me an opportunity to really dig into the candidate's depth of skill and knowledge.

Does the candidate understand the complexities of working in a franchise operation?

Is the candidate aware of the vital importance of technology in retail ordering?

Does the candidate get the cadence of a retail business, with its focus on managing comp sales, stock-outs, and inventory?

Only through questioning can you understand the candidate's expertise, capabilities, and suitability for a position.

Because people are so wary of questioning—and because it can go so wrong—we have to make it explicit that the purpose of questioning is the search for truth and the ultimate goal is to arrive at decisions and actions that benefit the enterprise as a whole. The goal is *not* to win the debate for yourself or put the other person down.

. . .

Questioning, then, is one of the key skills involved in challenge. It can have many purposes beyond information gathering—and one of the most essential of these is to open a dialogue. In a dialogue, people engage more as they do in a soccer game or tennis match than they do in a job interview. They question one another, offer answers, pose more questions based on those answers, analyze, and synthesize. One question leads to another. The questioner becomes the questioned. An answer provokes a whole new set of questions. The goal is to get at a deeper, more complete, and often more complex truth than you can through questioning alone.

In such dialogic exchanges, the material that emerges ranges from hard facts and quantifiable information to ideas and opinions, attitudes and biases, and the entire range of emotions, from fear to delight.

When emotions get involved in questioning, the dialogue can get heated, contentious, and even nasty. When that happens, the purpose of the dialogue can get lost. The dialogue can become divisive among groups and disruptive to our ability to perform together. So we need to keep the discourse civil, which means that it stays within the bounds and norms of the organization and, above all, that it stays focused on issues, not on individual personalities or specific groups.

You may have come across the term *ad hominem*, which is Latin, meaning "related to a particular person." An ad hominem comment is one that is personal and related to the person's character or motives. President Trump became known for his ad hominem comments. When North Korean leader Kim

Jong-un described Trump as "old" in a tweet, Trump responded by tweeting back that he would never call Kim "short and fat," which in fact was exactly what he was doing.

The ad hominem, or personal comment, is in contrast to the *ad rem* argument, which is also Latin, meaning "to the matter or subject at hand" or "relevant." An ad hominem comment, then, is directed at the person and an ad rem comment is focused on an issue or idea. If Trump had taken the ad rem approach, he would have tweeted something about Kim's nuclear policy, not his physique.

The most troubling ad hominem statements are negative ones, and they can get in the way of creating a challenge culture and ruin civil discourse because they undercut the idea of shared purpose. The Trump administration offers many more examples of the ad hominem approach. Trump, when presented with an issue he wants to avoid or an argument he wants to rebut, will often convert the dialogue into an attack on the person bringing up the issue. This became ritualized through his use of epithets, most of them negative. There were nicknames for individuals, such as Crooked Hillary, Lyin' Ted Cruz, and Beleaguered Jeff Sessions. And there were slights for entities and groups such as the "failing *New York Times*" or the "bad hombres" from Mexico.

Throughout the first year of Trump's term, the results of this ad hominem approach had a clear and nonpositive effect on the White House as a workplace: people within his organization attacked each other, leaked information, and sought to protect themselves and their positions, and there was a high turnover rate. It was an extreme example of how an organization that discourages questioning and focuses on personalities rather than issues can create a culture of fear and dysfunction. Trump, like some business leaders, seemed to value this environment, believing that uncertainty and discomfort could produce fresh ideas and positive disruption. My view, however, is that questions should be asked in a manner that the recipient deems to be constructive. This is especially important when acting in a board position.

People in any organization quickly learn the cultural rules, including those that govern civil discourse, and generally are careful to follow them and know when a violation occurs. The Trump administration offers an example of how different these rules can be in different organizational cultures. Not long after Anthony Scaramucci joined the White House staff as communications director, he engaged in a phone dialogue with *New Yorker* reporter Ryan Lizza. Scaramucci clearly did not understand, or respect, the bounds of civil discourse as most reporters, Washington politicos, and White House staffers understand it. Not only did he violate norms regarding the use of profanity (he used a lot), he ignored the well-known but largely unspoken rules of engagement between reporters and interviewees. Specifically, Scaramucci seemed unaware of the on-the-record and off-the-record protocols. Above all, Scaramucci engaged in vicious ad hominem attacks, calling Reince Priebus, then the chief of staff, a "paranoid schizophrenic," among other names I don't need to mention.

Scaramucci's comments, once published, caused such a firestorm of backlash that he doubled down on the personal attacks, saying that he had made a mistake in trusting a reporter and would never do so again. This, too, is a typical Trump administration tactic—although it has been practiced by others for centuries—which is to discredit the challenger's group or class, not just the individual. The implication is that no charge made by a reporter can be trusted because reporters are an unworthy class of citizens.

Trump's spokesperson, Sarah Sanders, initially defended Scaramucci and his remarks, saying the president liked the "kind of competition" that Scaramucci brought to the White House because it gets the "best results." Scaramucci himself said that, while he sometimes used "colorful language," his deeper goal was to "serve the country" and not himself. But Scaramucci had challenged the status quo too far, going beyond civil discourse. He was removed from his position a few days later.

In the business environment, I believe, the purpose of questioning must always be understood as a shared search for the truth, and the practice of civil discourse must always be focused on issues, rather than personalities.

One practical way to ensure that questioning and dialogue remain civil is to make the rules of engagement explicit. You may want to put them in writing. Distribute them. Refer to them. State them aloud. Every company will express them differently and in its own terms.

The goal of questioning: to get at the truth.
Shared purpose underlies civil discourse.
Challenge ideas, not people.

Just as important as explicitly expressing the rules is to model them and also to enforce them, publicly and consistently, whenever there is an infraction. This means that your actions must be consistent with what you say. And you must constantly point out, through all your communications channels, that your actions and words are in line. If and when they aren't, you need to explain why.

Another way to keep things civil is to keep notes and create a record of meetings or engagements. This is a simple way to demonstrate genuine interest in the dialogue and to suggest that you want to have the information needed to follow up on what has been discussed. It is also an excellent way to keep people honest about how they represent a discussion to others. (Ryan Lizza took notes *and* recorded his phone call with Scaramucci.)

I learned the importance of keeping a record soon after I joined Dunkin'. I met with a group of franchisees in New York and engaged in a long back-and-forth about a number of issues. The meeting was critical because New York is our biggest market (not Boston, as people think), and the franchisees there were in the middle of a significant growth phase. As the new guy on the block, I needed to make an impression on them, but I also wanted to model my approach: listening, learning, and keeping track. What's more, I could use the notes to refer back to the meeting and keep everybody honest about what had been said and agreed upon.

After the meeting, one of the participants was debriefing our regional director. "We couldn't believe Nigel took so many notes!" he said. The point they were making was that I had listened, taken detailed notes, and stated my understanding of their concerns: that we had to be more aggressive on driving sales and also focus on their store profitability more than in the past.

Keeping minutes is, of course, standard procedure in high-level gatherings such as board meetings, but I strongly recommend it for other engagements where you have significant back-and-forth on important issues.

. . .

The process of questioning and civil discourse runs the risk of turning into confrontation, but the great benefit is well worth the risk: you will get to the very bottom of any disagreement and be able to make it explicit, so it can be thoroughly discussed and dealt with.

It is when a disagreement is developing that tensions will run high, but the disagreement need not devolve into hand-to-hand combat if the participants know how to question purposefully, carry on a civil discourse, and share a greater goal: the good of the enterprise. When two parties share a higher objective but disagree on how best to attain it, what unites them is stronger than what divides them. The eighteenth-century political theorist Jean-Jacques Rousseau called this the "social contract," by which citizens maintained a civil society.

It is by deeply exploring these disagreements—rather than avoiding them—that we most often come up with new ideas, better solutions, and stronger commitments.

This was the case with our introduction of Dunkin' Donuts K-Cup pods, those single-serve portions for use in Keurig brewing machines. The story begins in 2010, the year after I joined the company, when we entered into negotiations with the owners of Keurig to manufacture and distribute Dunkin' Donuts single-serve K-Cup portion packs.

There was not much disagreement about this initiative, at least on the Dunkin' side of the partnership. We had done a fair amount of questioning and had engaged in a lot of discussion at the board level, among corporate staff, and with franchisees. Everybody agreed that the initiative would serve the higher purpose: it would benefit Dunkin' Brands as a whole, with no obvious negative impact on any constituent. This lack of friction was largely because our intention was that Dunkin' K-Cups would be sold exclusively in Dunkin' Donuts restaurants, would not require a large upfront capital investment, and had great potential for us to expand into a new category.

Success came almost immediately. We announced the partnership in February 2011, and by summer, we were selling Dunkin' K-Cup pods in five flavors: Original Blend, Dunkin' Decaf, French Vanilla, Hazelnut, and Dunkin' Dark. The Dunkin' K-Cups flew out of the stores. Everybody was happy: customers, corporate, and franchisees. Why not? The K-Cups provided a profitable revenue stream. By association with two growing and respected brands, Green Mountain and Keurig, we strengthened our own brand. And by making Dunkin' available at home in a new format, we extended our customer base to people who did not visit the shops.

With the encouraging performance of the Dunkin' K-Cup pods in Dunkin' restaurants, corporate management and the board now set their sights on the obvious next step: selling the hot new product in grocery stores and other retail outlets. The board wanted to make the move as quickly as possible and urged management to bring in a distribution partner, J.M. Smucker, and get going. But I knew the concept would be controversial and there would be disagreement and pushback because the franchisees would almost certainly see the sale of K-Cups in grocery stores as a cannibalization of their businesses.

I knew we would have to do a lot of questioning, offer a lot of answers, and engage in as civil a discourse as we possibly could in order to gain support for the move.

By asking a string of whys with a wide range of participants, I came to a deeper understanding of the fundamental reason for the franchisees' reluctance. Yes, there was the issue of lost income, but at the very heart of the matter, the root cause was the lack of shared purpose. Because of the way the company had been managed for several years before going into private ownership, the franchisees had lost trust and no longer believed that brand management had the best interests of the franchisees at heart. There was not a sense of shared goals. Corporate questioning was often seen as malicious by the franchisees—a way to uncover rule infractions so management could impose fines or defranchise owners they didn't like. No wonder Dunkin' had stalled in terms of innovation and improvement.

I saw the process of discussing the move into grocery stores with K-Cups as a way to change all that, to demonstrate that we could share a common purpose, disagree on strategies, and still work out a solution that benefitted the whole. And that is exactly what happened.

The process took about two years. Yes, corporate had the authority to move quickly and autonomously. But that would have done nothing to build trust or demonstrate our commitment to a shared goal. It would have been an authoritarian, confrontational approach.

I continued the questioning and discourse process, and the issues became clearer and clearer.

First, the franchisees believed that the sale of a Dunkin' K-Cup at a grocery store was equivalent to the *loss* of a K-Cup sale at a Dunkin' store. So we conducted a good deal of research and engaged consultants to help us better understand the reality of the market. Our research showed that, to the consumer, a retail store purchase is a very different occasion from a Dunkin' store purchase. The consumer has a world of shopping choices when it comes to K-Cup pods. They can buy them at hardware stores and big box stores, such as Best Buy, Target, or Bed Bath & Beyond. The consumer who has K-Cups on the shopping list is going to buy the brand that is available at any of those outlets. If they can't buy Dunkin', they'll buy Green Mountain or some other brand. They will not likely make a special trip to a Dunkin' shop just to buy pods.

This discussion brought out a lot of the "soft" stuff. In particular, it surfaced an underlying emotional issue for the franchisees. They saw the Dunkin' Brands as special, distinct, and better than other coffee brands. They wanted to believe that a consumer was so loyal to Dunkin' that they would go out of their way to buy K-Cups at the Dunkin' shop if they weren't available elsewhere.

But the research showed that the sales of K-Cups were skyrocketing and also that competitive brands, including Starbucks, were *not* losing revenue as the result of their branded K-Cups sales through nonbranded outlets. In fact, they had opened a whole new revenue stream.

At last, the franchisees acknowledged the reality that, while customers love Dunkin', their love has some limits. Better to sell K-Cups in retail stores and keep the brand relevant than to offer them exclusively in the Dunkin' shops and miss out on increased volume and lots of exposure.

Second was the matter of profit. Selling Dunkin' K-Cups in retail outlets did not involve the franchisees in any way. They would not have to invest in product development or promotion, but the K-Cups would essentially sell on the strength of the brand and the reputation of the store network. If, in fact, all the constituencies were acting for the good of the entire system, how would the franchisees benefit?

To reach an agreement on this issue some process innovation—involving corporate, J.M. Smucker, and the franchisees— was required. Smucker, in addition to manufacturing famous jams and other packaged goods, offers distribution and store category management services. We contracted with them to place the Dunkin' K-Cup pods in non-Dunkin' locations. They would send Dunkin' corporate a check for sales, after deducting their fees. We would then split the profits, fifty-fifty, with the franchisees. Their share would be placed in a pool and distributed twice a year, with each franchisee receiving a check proportional to their relative sales volume.

The board got a little impatient with the process, but I knew that if we steamrolled the franchisees on this issue, we would have a very hard time getting support for other initiatives that did require their involvement. So I was transparent with the board about the discussion, and I held firm that we had to see the process through.

Yes, it took longer than we expected or would have liked. In fact, I often ask people how many breakfasts with franchisee leaders it took to get the deal done. Answer: seventeen. I was fortunate that Clayton Turnbull, my cochair on the Brand Advisory Council (BAC), attended most of them. (Both Dunkin' corporate and the franchisees are represented by a chair on the BAC. More on the Advisory Council system later.) We found that once the franchisees set aside their emotional attachment to an unfounded belief in the extent of brand loyalty and once we negotiated terms that essentially gave them a royalty on sales in a whole new market, they agreed. That is not to say that every one of them was totally satisfied with the deal, but they understood the issues, they knew that we had negotiated in good faith, and they realized that they had gotten a better deal than corporate was legally bound to offer.

As I've said, I don't expect to reach complete agreement or unwavering alignment in a pluralistic organization, but I do believe you can achieve a "directed consensus," which is what we did with K-Cups. It is a blend of managerial direction, transparent debate, explicit articulation of disagreements, and core (if not unanimous) support for a well-considered solution. In a you're-fired hierarchical culture, this approach might be considered too conciliatory, not tough enough. Not so. It produced a win-win for us. Franchisee margins increased, and Dunkin' gained market share.

We launched the Dunkin' Donuts K-Cup pods in July 2015 in grocery stores and thousands of other retailers. Just as the product had been a success in Dunkin' shops, it enjoyed almost immediate success in retail markets. We sold about three hundred million units in the first year, and the product was named one of the top new consumer packaged goods products for 2016 by IRI, an industry research group, in their annual Pacesetters report.

Not only was the product a hit, but I credit that initiative with beginning to change the culture at Dunkin' from one of mistrustful confrontation to one of productive challenge. That was perhaps even more important than the launch of the successful new product.

. . .

It's true that Dunkin' had gone through a period when challenge mostly meant confrontation (before my time), but there is another thread to Dunkin' history that shows the company also has a tradition of purposeful questioning, and it stems from Dunkin's founder, entrepreneur Bill Rosenberg. After he had built Dunkin' into an international brand, Bill stepped back from day-to-day operations and devoted himself to a very different passion: breeding racehorses. In his autobiography, *Time to Make the Donuts,* Bill talks about the time that one of his winningest colts developed a limp and couldn't race.

Bill went to the vet in search of answers, but the doctor said he didn't know what the problem was. Bill looked to his trainer, who was known as an expert in the profession, but he confessed he didn't know either. "Well, why don't you ask around then?" Bill asked the trainer. Bill thought that other owners or vets might have encountered the same problem. But the trainer didn't want to ask anybody else. "He didn't want to be embarrassed and appear as if he didn't know what to do," Bill wrote.

Bill did not mind looking like he didn't know what to do because he didn't. He just wanted to solve the problem. He embarked on a questioning campaign, talking over the issues with eight or nine people with experience in the racing world. As a result of his questioning and his discourse with them, Bill came up with a solution that got the colt back on the track. "In the end," Bill wrote, "because I knew nothing, I ended up learning more and gathering more useful information than the 'expert'."

You don't have to be a Socrates or even a Bill Rosenberg to learn how to ask good questions, manage productive disagreement, and come up with effective solutions. But, in addition to attaining the skills, you have to give people opportunities and the forums to exercise them. That can be formal or informal; in groups or one-on-ones.

At Dunkin', one of our favorite forums for questioning and discourse is, appropriately enough, the coffee chat.

CHAPTER SIX

Ask Me Anything

Sixty Coffee Chats and Counting

T he coffee chat is just what it sounds like. It's just me in a room with a bunch of Dunkin' people. They are invited from across disciplines, so they don't normally work together and may not even know each other. They can bring up any topic. They can make statements. Engage in dialogue with each other. Ignore me completely, if they want. (There is plenty of coffee available.)

People can ask any question, within the bounds of civility:

Do you think Dunkin' is moving in the right strategic direction?

What are we going to do about the sales dip in the PM day-part?

I heard a rumor that Dunkin' is going to be acquired. Is that true?

How are we using the data we collect from On-the-Go mobile ordering?

Why do franchisees sometimes get information before corporate employees do?

What are we doing to increase the number of women in IT senior management?

Do we have a problem with sexual harassment?

How can we improve our meetings?

There's a lot of innovation going on in international markets; how can we apply it back home?

How did sales of Fruited Iced Teas go?

Is Amazon really pursuing coffee delivery by drone?

I first started holding coffee chats when I was at Papa John's, where we called them "Tea Times with Nigel." People didn't think that name would fly so well at Dunkin' since our brand is practically synonymous with coffee.

We have held dozens of coffee chats since I came on board in 2009. I have done them with groups of as few as ten or twelve employees at corporate headquarters in Canton. I've led them with as many as three hundred franchisees in hotel ballrooms around the United States.

The purpose of the coffee chat is to provide an open and safe forum for people to ask questions, share information, articulate ideas, express feelings, and surface disagreements. For the corporate sessions, we invite only people who do *not* have direct engagement with the senior level of management, those who hold positions below the vice president level: directors, managers, planners, coordinators, analysts, specialists, technologists, and interns. Ideally, they represent a range of departments and disciplines: marketing, operations, customer relations, R&D, technology, learning design, IT, finance, development—a diagonal slice of the organization. I'm the only senior executive in the room. I may know some of the participants, but none of them report directly to me.

By this time, the basics of the coffee chat are well understood by Dunkin' people. It is not a gripe session or an opportunity to complain, diss your boss (he or she won't be in the room), snipe at your coworkers, or moan about the company or the world in general. Perhaps surprisingly, this has never been an issue. I am constantly delighted at how positive and engaged people generally are in these events. They value the opportunity to express themselves, ask questions, be heard, and learn. They don't want to blow it by whining.

I learned this in a session I did some years ago at Burger King, when I was senior vice president for human resources. Unlike the chats we do at Dunkin', that BK meeting brought together a single group—truck drivers, the guys who deliver supplies to the restaurants. I felt sure they would want to grill me about compensation or overtime policies. They didn't. They immediately focused on the intricacies of route design: how the process of laying out driving routes could be improved to increase efficiency, reduce costs, and boost on-time delivery percentage. I barely said a word for about forty minutes as they discussed that topic before I could wedge in a question about overtime policy. They looked at me blankly until one of them made a remark about some minor adjustment we might consider. That non-debate lasted about three minutes before they went back to the issue that most concerned them: how to redesign their routes to better serve customers.

This experience reinforced a simple fact: most employees want to do the best job they can. Some may say that I am naïve in this assumption, but I would argue that this positive approach has served me well. In this regard, I like to think of Barry Gibbons, my boss at Burger King, whose motto was: "Trust people until they let you down."

A coffee chat is an open-ended, two-way conversation. We set no agenda. I make no formal presentation. We don't use slides, a whiteboard, or video. I facilitate the discussion, but I don't dominate it. In fact, I always start by saying that this is not a Q&A with Nigel! The right scene setting is critical, and if you start well, you find that people will ask questions of each other and engage in discussion across the room.

Everything is on the table. No issue should be off limits, so long as we stay within the bounds of civil discourse, as we define it at Dunkin'. We operate on the assumption that everybody in the room has the best interests of the company at heart (as well as their own interests, of course), that they will show respect for one another, and that they will not engage in personal, ad hominem comments or make attacks on individuals.

It's important to understand that coffee chats are not de-signed as decision-making events. Nor do we think of them as a mechanism for quantifying opinion. We don't take any polls. The whole point of these meetings is that they are *chats*. We don't have the pressure to come to a conclusion, reach a consen-sus, achieve alignment, resolve an issue, make a decision, or agree on an action to be taken. By removing those expectations, peo-ple feel freer to bring up thorny issues and to speak their minds. They know they will not be evaluated by their boss. They won't be held responsible for the performance of their ideas. There will be no unpleasant consequences for speaking up. If you bring up a controversial topic at a chat, or express disagreement with me or others, you're not going to suffer negative consequences. It is my belief that people do not have enough face-to-face time to just talk about the business and the company and to be heard by senior management in an informal setting.

Of course, there is no guarantee that action will be taken on your issue, but there is an assurance that your participation will be respected, you will know what I and others think about it, and you won't be penalized for asking tough questions or ex-pressing your views.

Is this just a feel-good exercise?

Well, first of all, what's wrong with feeling good?

Second, just because the coffee chat is not a decision-making exercise does not mean it doesn't *influence* decisions and af-fect actions. We take notes during every chat, and I report back to my management team on the content. We keep people in-formed, through a variety of communications channels, about the coffee chats that have been held and what was discussed. I try to give public credit to coffee chats that have raised issues of importance, especially when they have contributed to some kind of change—in awareness, understanding, process, or policy.

During the rash of sexual harassment allegations in the fall of 2017 (starting with those against Harvey Weinstein), that topic was a coffee chat issue. The general feeling expressed was that the environment at Dunkin' headquarters was collegial and respectful. No one had witnessed any instances of sexual harassment or misconduct; they felt confident that, if they did, we had the resources in place to deal with it. However, the conversation compelled us to review our harassment training to ensure it was up to date and being conducted competently.

In that case, the discussion provided the opportunity for people to speak up about an issue that was on the nation's mind and had unsettled people in organizations of all kinds.

Sometimes, a coffee chat discussion surfaces a tension or reveals a problem that has not been on management's radar screen, has not been adequately addressed, or needs further attention.

These issues are rarely as complex or as fundamental as sexual harassment, but they are typically ones that have an important impact on our people's daily lives and their ability to perform at their best. That was the case with a corporate chat that got us into the issue of work scheduling.

My executive assistant, Ruth O'Quin, organized the event as she always does. She made up a list of about twenty people who had not participated in a coffee chat already and sent them an invitation to participate. About fifteen of them were able to attend (participation is voluntary), and they showed up at the second-floor conference room ready to go at eleven o'clock. We had a good representation of disciplines and departments there. The age skewed young, with more women than men. Naturally, we all had a cup of coffee or tea at hand.

I greeted everybody and thanked them for coming. To get things rolling, I tossed out a few subjects we might talk about—food safety, new product performance, a new executive hire, comp sales, franchisee relations, share price, competitors—but said we didn't have to address any of those things. We could discuss anything related to the business. Amazingly enough, in the sixty-odd coffee chats I've held in the past few years, we have rarely discussed the same issue twice.

In this chat, it didn't take long for us to hit on an issue that resonated with most people in the room: managing work schedules to accommodate family responsibilities. This is an essential matter for many of our corporate staff of about 1,200 people, including me. I have two young kids—a thirteen-year-old boy and an eleven-year-old girl—so I understand the complexities of managing work and family scheduling. That is, I thought I understood, until the group challenged me about company policy.

One young woman, I'll call her Jane, a customer relations coordinator, had two kids in day care, one of them with special needs. Her husband's work schedule shifted unpredictably from week to week. "Nigel," she said (everybody calls me Nigel), "I don't have enough flexibility in the number of hours I work here at Dunkin' and when I work them. My husband doesn't have much control over his schedule. I may have to leave unexpectedly in the middle of the day to take care of my special needs child. I know I'm not the only person dealing with this." Her comment prompted several others to speak up with similar concerns.

At the time, I believed that Dunkin' had a pretty progressive approach to work schedules, but the discussion made it abundantly clear that we had to go further. And, as often happens, the challenge to scheduling policy opened up the discussion to a whole range of issues related to work scheduling. Partly as a result of that conversation, we eventually revised corporate policy to allow for much more flexibility in scheduling. We also changed our policy on paid parental leave, adding four more weeks of paid time off—beyond the standard six weeks already provided—for both mother and father.

Many coffee chats lead to policy changes, but even if they don't, they produce rich conversations, and I always learn a lot that influences how I think. If you wait to have a dialogue until an issue turns urgent, you've waited too long. One of the recurring issues, for example, is technology change. In one chat, people asked me about my experience at Blockbuster and what I had learned. They really took to heart the lesson of staying ahead of the technology change curve. Specifically, that discussion strengthened internal support for our On-the-Go Mobile Ordering app that had recently been introduced.

Even the least engaging coffee chat serves a useful purpose: it reinforces the culture we want at Dunkin'.

. . .

In a coffee chat, or anywhere else for that matter, people who ask a question love to be praised with the comment, *That's a great question!* The more coffee chats I do, and the more I observe situations in which people ask questions of one another—interviews, meetings, conferences, presentations, you name it—the more I think about what that means. What makes for a "great" question?

In general, a good question is one that has a contributory effect on a conversation: it brings forth information, clarifies ideas, acknowledges emotions, and generates more questions. A really good or great question is one that generates something that did not exist before: it opens up new avenues of inquiry, produces new insights, leads to new actions, produces change of some kind.

So question formulation is an important skill in the challenge culture, but most people are not educated in the formulation of questions, with the exception, perhaps, of a few specialized professions—such as lawyers, journalists, scientists. The rest of us learn by doing. Over the years I have been exposed to so much questioning—from potential employers, the kids on my soccer teams, industry analysts, the press, directors, consultants, employees, fellow executives, not to mention every member of my family, including my dad—that I have come to really value useful and probing questions because they force you to think.

There is a lot of literature on what questioning is and why it's important—I've already mentioned the work of both Simon Sinek and Warren Berger—so let me touch on some of the basics that I think are most essential to master in the challenge culture.

First, is the designation "open" or "closed." A closed question is generally a sharply focused question and can typically be answered with a brief, relatively unambiguous response: a yes, a no, a number, a quantitative piece of information.

For example: Have you ever played professional football?
Either you have or you haven't. Yes or no.

Or:

Which team has won the most World Cup tournaments?
Answer: Brazil. There is only one correct response.

Closed questions are relatively easy to formulate and straight-forward to answer. They can help engagement, and people are often more willing to answer them, at least at first, than open questions. At a coffee chat with franchisees, for example, we got onto the topic of the Dunkin' mobile app and future opportunities for it. At some point, I asked a simple closed question: "How many people in this room do *not* have a cell phone?" Two people rather sheepishly raised their hands. Everybody laughed, a sure sign of good energy and engagement.

Closed questions are effective for gathering information and getting the facts straight. In our coffee chat discussion about work scheduling, for example, I asked closed questions of Jane and the others:

"How many hours do you work per week?"

"What time do you normally get to the office? When do you need to leave?"

"What time do you pick up your kids at day care?"

"What are your spouse's work hours?"

Closed questions are useful in creating a groundwork of information that everybody can refer to. This is akin to the activity known as discovery in a legal proceeding. Socrates did the same thing, by asking a series of yes/no questions with the purpose of getting agreement on quantitative information before moving on to areas that would require discussion.

Simon Sinek, author of *Start with Why*, calls these "what" questions because they deal in facts and tangibles. The great fictional detectives, from Sherlock Holmes to Nancy Drew, Fox Mulder to Jane Rizzoli, are adept at asking "what" questions. As Holmes put it to one of his new clients, "Pray give us the essential facts, Sir, and afterwards I can question you as to those details which seem to me most important."

Closed questions are typically neutral in nature. People don't usually feel threatened by answering them. On the contrary, people like closed questions. There is a feeling of satisfaction that comes from laying out the facts. In our discussion of work schedules, for example, people learned a lot just by understanding the essential facts of the situations of the others in the room. It's one thing to say that you need more flexibility in scheduling and quite another for people to understand that you have a sixty-minute commute each way, that your spouse travels out of state three days per week, and that your child's counselor can only meet every other Tuesday at 10:00 A.M.

People also respond well to closed questions because there is generally a "right" answer and a "wrong" answer, which is satisfying. We all like to know something for sure, to be right.

Open questions, by contrast, are a whole different kettle of fish. They require *qualitative* answers. They cannot always or easily be answered with a yes, a no, or a quantitative fact. They are the how and the why questions that demand more from the dialogue participants. They may involve opinion, interpretation, point of view, speculation, analysis, and emotion.

For example: "How does the issue of work scheduling affect your department?"

People in different departments will likely have a range of views on the impact of work scheduling. It may be a factor in productivity, hiring, morale, availability for travel, profitability. These are matters that are not satisfactorily answered with a yes or no. The answer, "Yes, work scheduling affects us," doesn't add much to the conversation. It is not what I would call a good answer. We need to know more. It may well be that people have not really thought through the effects; questioning will compel them to do so.

Open questions can sometimes enter into personal territory.

For example: "How do the problems you face in managing work and home schedules affect you and your family?"

This is a good question because it can provoke many responses, from an unrevealing "it makes life more complicated" to a much more nuanced explanation, such as:

"Well, we decided that we had to buy a second car, which we hadn't planned on and hadn't budgeted for. So we had to work more hours to generate a little more income, which just made the problems worse. We also had to deal with parking, which took time and added stress. We began to debate whether one of us should change jobs or quit or try to work at home."

Now the issues of finance, health, relationships, and career had been put on the table. That's what open questions can do.

Open questions are tricky to formulate. They can very easily express a point of view, contain a bias, or suggest an answer. When that happens, the respondent may feel pressured to reply in a certain way. This reduces the freedom and range of the conversation, rather than expanding it.

In the coffee chat discussion, for example, I could have asked Jane a question that expressed my point of view on Dunkin' work policy.

"So, Jane, why do you think Dunkin' doesn't care about families?"

The question makes an assumption vis-à-vis Jane's feelings about Dunkin' policy and puts words in her mouth. She never said that Dunkin' "didn't care" about families, but that's what the question presumes. Now she has to figure out how to deal with the misrepresentation. It forces her to take sides: either she is for Dunkin' or against it and, by extension, for or against me. The question puts everyone on guard, erodes trust, and polarizes the group. That is not what we want in a civil dialogue.

A neutral, open question regarding work scheduling might be: "What changes could be made at Dunkin' to help you better manage your work and home schedules?"

This question does not imply a point of view. It does not suggest that Dunkin's policies are fine or that they could use improvement. It asks the speaker, and the group, to collaborate in thinking about possible changes.

. . .

Good questions, whether open or closed, encourage dialogue. They are not statements that produce no response, nor are they instruments of interrogation. A dialogue is like a soccer game. I pass the ball to you and you may pass it back to me or send it to someone else. I can never be sure when the ball will come to me again. When it does, my teammates and opponents will be in different positions from where we started so I will have to make my next move based on new information.

In a dialogue, there is no set list of questions, just as there is no set agenda in a coffee chat, which is why listening becomes so important. A question may point the conversation in a certain direction, but the answer may open up an unexpected path. You have to listen carefully for new content and be willing to follow promising leads, rather than just ticking off a list of questions formulated before the meeting starts.

In the coffee chat conversation, for example, I asked the group what I thought was a simple, closed question: "How long does it usually take you to get from home to work?"

"On a good day? About forty minutes," said one of the participants.

On a good day? The comment suggested a point of view and that there was more to the story. I could have left it there, but I probed a bit more.

"What do you mean by 'on a good day'? What determines whether it's a good day or not? Is it a question of traffic?"

This opened up a lively conversation about the daily challenges people had with commuting and its impact on their family and work lives. Dunkin' was originally established in the city of Quincy, on Boston's South Shore, and moved headquarters to Canton, a Boston exurb, in 2004. About 10 percent of our employees live in Canton; a few more live in neighboring towns, and for them, the car is the primary method of transport. Some share a vehicle with a spouse and some carpool, which means they don't have autonomy in scheduling their commute. Some take a taxi or car hailing service, which adds expense and uncertainty. Some employees, especially younger ones, live in Boston proper or the metro area, or want to, and many don't own a car. They can catch a commuter rail train, which means they are at the mercy of the schedule. And they still have to get from the train station to the office, which is about five miles away. Dunkin' operates a shuttle bus service, but it too runs on a schedule, which may not fit with theirs.

When the coffee chat started, I did not expect we would get into a discussion of commuting. But by listening and responding, that conversation led us into deeper issues. We made the connection between commuting and hiring, and how we were possibly limiting our candidate pool to people who lived nearby, who owned cars, or who were flexible on working hours and could travel at off-peak hours. It opened up the issue of the effect of commuting on health and wellness: commuting reduces the time people have to devote to physical activity and adds to the stress of their lives. Finally, we discussed the overall effect of these issues on our ability to grow and sustain our business: Should we consider moving our headquarters into the city or to a location with more access to public transportation?

Later, when it came to a discussion of whether to renew our lease on our corporate offices, these views came into consideration. In the end, we decided to stay put but to pursue more ways to reduce the burden of commuting on our employees.

. . .

Another factor that comes into play in any setting that involves questioning and dialogue, such as the coffee chat, is the range of thinking styles and cognitive biases that people have. To participate most effectively in a dialogue, it's helpful to understand these elements so you can recognize them in yourself and others.

One of the fundamentals of discussion in our society, especially among people in the business environment, is a preference for a hardheaded, quantitative approach to discussion and decision making. We trust in data. We see evidence of success primarily in the bottom line. We prefer fact-based arguments. We believe in measurement, the more the better. We love surveys and polls. We want research findings. A satisfying discussion is one that contains lots of facts and data, numbers and tangible evidence, logic and analysis.

This predilection for the hard approach has deep roots. Socrates sought truth through philosophical dialogue that was largely composed of open questions and rarely contained much data. The seventeenth-century French philosopher René Descartes added a new, very large element to the truth-hunting process. Descartes believed that the only information that could be considered indisputable truth was the kind the mind could "clearly and distinctly" grasp—that is, the quantitative. For him, that meant examining the scientific, definable, and measurable properties of any phenomenon. Descartes's thinking emerged at roughly the same time as that of two other scientists, Galileo and Newton, who also had a major effect on how the quest for knowledge should be conducted.

The approach of these philosophers and scientists (the two professions were not so distinct in those days) is essentially what we now call the scientific method. It is largely quantitative in nature. You form a hypothesis. Test it through observation and experiment. Gather data. Make measurements. Confirm, reject, or modify your hypothesis based on the findings.

This approach is well described in the tome *Conjectures and Refutations* by Karl Popper, a work that I studied in college and has had a profound impact on my thinking. I adapt some of Popper's ideas for use in our coffee chats, although I don't directly reference them. When someone proposes an idea, we kick it around and test its potential with people in the room. I have found this approach works particularly well with franchisees, which is one of the reasons I like dealing with them. Franchisees are bright, entrepreneurial, and opinionated and typically speak out boldly in group sessions. To manage such groups, you need the ability to challenge hard, you need a sense of humor, and you sometimes need to employ a bit of strategy.

For example, I held a coffee chat with a group of about one hundred fifty franchisees. In this case, there were a number of items on the agenda that I wanted to discuss, so it was more like a combination of presentation and conversation, question asking and answer seeking.

One of the issues we needed to address was guest satisfaction. I wanted to explore what the franchisees knew about the service our guests were receiving in restaurants and how they felt about their performance in that regard, particularly as it related to our menu offerings.

To get the discussion going, I started with a video of customer comments. It had been shot in a number of restaurants and featured snippets of interviews with a range of people. All the comments were positive, even glowing:

> *I can get in and out of Dunkin' in three minutes.*
> *They get my order right every time. Just the right amount of cream and sugar.*
> *They're very friendly. I had a kid at the drive-through who was just so courteous and friendly.*
> *It's the friendliness that creates loyalty for me.*
> *It's like family, really.*

The video ran for a few minutes. The franchisees felt pretty good at the end of it (although they probably suspected there was more to come). "So, what are the takeaways from this?" I asked.

That was an easy one. Everybody called out the positive messages: *Fast. Friendly. Accurate. Customer service.*

"But," I asked, "how many people feel they are doing really well with customer service in their stores?"

Most said they could do better, which led into a discussion of the issues involved, particularly handling full-service orders, a self-service line, and new menu offerings.

"OK, that was Dunkin' good," I said. Then we rolled a second video. It contained nothing but complaints, problems, and disappointments.

Would it kill them to say "good morning"?
I feel unimportant.
I think the employee morale is better at Starbucks.
They're good at fast, not so good at accurate.
They don't always know the menu.
The order taker didn't speak English very well.
It's so frustrating, I sometimes just walk out.

After watching that, all I had to do was ask the opennest of open-ended questions: "What do you think of that? Is it true?"

Nobody protested. Heads nodded.

"Why?"

The simple why question produced a mixture of factual and quantitative responses, as well as analytical, qualitative thoughts on the issues that affect customer service.

For example, Dunkin' operates in a series of nine "windows." Each is a roughly equal period of time, about six weeks, during which new menu offerings, including limited time offers (LTOs), are available. The number of windows differs from company to company and industry to industry. At Blockbuster, for example, we operated with fifty-two windows, basically a new window each week. Many retailers commonly run four windows, coinciding with the change of seasons. At Dunkin', our cadence of the windows is designed to keep the brand fresh by offering seasonal specialties, new flavors, and product innovations. Even a minor change in the menu—such as a different sauce on the same sandwich—can boost consumer interest and generate additional sales. But there are risks and complications associated with frequent window changes. There are costs involved in promoting the new offerings. The restaurant staff has to learn what the offerings are and how to prepare and serve them. At Dunkin', we already have more than a thousand possible sandwich variations, which means that each new offering adds to the complexity of taking and filling orders. So there is a tension between keeping operations simple and generating consumer interest.

The challenge of learning the new window is made even tougher during certain windows, particularly the late summer and early fall when the college students depart and high school students take their place. The turnover is higher, the education level is lower, and there may be more than the usual number of new items in the window.

We talked about a variety of ways to manage these issues: More training. Menu simplification. Store redesign, with more items available for self-serve. And I carried many of these suggestions back to the management team for further discussion and eventual action. (Menu simplification, for example, became a major initiative.)

. . .

Putting yourself into situations like the coffee chat, where the conversation can't be completely controlled or where outcomes are uncertain, may make you feel vulnerable and unsettled. So it's not surprising thay many leaders prefer to hear presentations and do the questioning themselves. But there are benefits to the coffee chat approach that you don't get in the conference room. Especially in pluralistic organizations, if you run enough of these forums, so that you include people from a range of regions and situations and viewpoints, you can achieve much better buy-in to plans, approaches, and new ideas than you would if you simply announced your plans.

In these meetings, and any situation involving dialogue, it quickly becomes clear that the discussion will include many types of statements and responses. I tend to put them into three boxes or categories: data-based, emotional, and intuitive. The data-based response is quantitative in nature, relying on facts and figures, references, and specific cases to make a point. The emotional contribution comes from the heart and the soul; these are expressions of how one feels about an issue or situation. The intuitive input is really a synthesis of the quantitative and qualitative, a sort of informed instinct. Malcolm Gladwell in his book *Blink* calls it "thinking without thinking."

All these responses are valid and valuable, although the second two are harder to manage than the fact-based inputs. That's because they involve human behaviors and emotions that are difficult to measure, quantify, and, often, to explain. They bring us into the realm of the social sciences, including psychology, sociology, economics, history, political science, and the law. In the past two decades or so, these disciplines have gained momentum in the business world and given us a deep understanding of a range of business issues, including corporate culture, organizational design, leadership, risk, entrepreneurship, teamwork, and customer behavior.

Today, we know that human factors have tremendous bearing even on the disciplines that have been considered the "hardest" ones, such as operations, finance, systems, and information technology.

The appreciation of the social sciences has fueled what might be called the emotional intelligence movement, largely driven by the work of Daniel Goleman and articulated in his first book, *Emotional Intelligence: Why It Can Matter More than IQ*, published in 1995, as well as several subsequent works. Goleman's purpose, he wrote, was to improve our "scientific understanding of the realm of the irrational." The idea struck a chord, and today the study and promotion of emotional intelligence is widespread.

Many other social scientists have contributed to our understanding of how people think and engage in dialogue. In his book *Thinking Fast and Slow*, published in 2011, psychologist Daniel Kahneman explores our thinking process in decision making, with an emphasis on what are often called cognitive biases. Scientists and researchers have identified and named dozens of these biases, and a few of them are extremely relevant to the challenge culture. They show up all the time in business conversations, whether in open forums like the coffee chats or in more focused and structured discussions such as a department meeting or management team retreat, as well as in every water cooler and airplane cabin conversation.

One fundamental cognitive bias is, ironically, the bias blind spot. This is the belief that an individual has that he or she is less biased than other people are. Confirmation bias is another cognitive style that affects most of us, at least some of the time. This is our tendency to look for information and data that confirms what we already believe to be true and to ignore data that contradicts that belief. "If one were to attempt to identify a single problematic aspect of human reasoning that deserves attention above all others," wrote Tufts psychologist Raymond Nickerson, "the confirmation bias would have to be among the candidates for consideration." A third important method of our thinking mechanism is stereotyping, the tendency for people to make certain assumptions about other people, based on their membership in a group or discipline or cultural cohort, without having specific knowledge of that individual.

Stereotyping was one obstacle to change when I arrived at Dunkin'. In particular, some franchisees thought of people working in corporate headquarters in a certain way (as bureaucrats or paper pushers). And some corporate staffers thought of franchisees in a stereotyped way, too (as cowboys or small-town shopkeepers). A major goal for me was to get beyond the stereotypes so we could understand one another and find ways to search for the truth together.

One way to improve our ability to engage in civil dialogue is to understand the context within which each person is working. What do they know about a certain topic? Are they aware of what they know and don't know? How willing are they to be open about their knowledge or lack thereof?

I have a favorite tool that can really help answer these questions called the Johari window. I first became aware of it early in my career, and it has since become a widely used model for understanding and improving self-awareness, achieving personal development, improving communications and interpersonal relationships, enabling group dynamics, and furthering team development and intergroup relationships.

In the Johari window process, a wide range of information is organized into four quadrants:

1. *Open arena.* This defines what a person knows about him- or herself and what others know, too.

2. *Blind spot.* This describes what the person does not know about him- or herself but that others do know.

3. *Hidden area.* This indicates what the person does know about him- or herself but that other people don't know.

4. *Unknown self.* This encompasses the information the person does not know about him- or herself and that other people don't know, either.

You may remember that former Secretary of Defense Donald Rumsfeld had his own version of the Johari window; he talked of the known knowns, the known unknowns, and the unknown unknowns. But he was only one in a long line of national security and other professionals to use the Johari window, first developed in 1955.

This tool can help you better understand your own quadrant, those of others, and the relationship of the perspectives in a group setting. I've found that the understanding can enhance clarity and transparency and facilitate productive dialogue.

You'll find that some people have a very large open arena. They are willing to receive feedback and accept others' views. They are skilled at helping others by expressing their views of them with detail and insight. Such people are often the greatest proponents of the challenge culture. They have a natural predisposition to transparency because they feel they have nothing to hide and are willing to broaden their open area still further. I am, as you might have guessed, one of those people.

. . .

Sometimes there are more obvious, and more basic, issues that affect a dialogue than thinking styles, cognitive biases, and self-awareness—such as the age of the participants in the room, the size of the group, the types of personalities involved in a discussion, the time of day, and the location.

Age is a particularly important factor. Steve Davis, the former head coach of the Leyton Orient Football Club (the sec-ond- oldest London-based football club of which I am now chairman) made me more aware of how big a factor the age of the participants can be. Steve has a wonderful ability to listen, read a group, and adapt his style to the needs of his players. One of his key coaching tools is analysis of game day video. Steve has found that many younger team members will not speak up and give their opinions in a large group, especially when a number of older players are there. (The age of players on a European football team can range from sixteen to thirty-six.) To work around that reluctance, Steve breaks his postgame video analysis sessions into smaller groups and sometimes will do them individually. He goes as small as necessary to get true engage-ment, which means that he and the player are able to openly discuss problems and solutions.

I have also found, as I'm sure you have, that some people nat-urally engage differently in groups. Some talk more than others, no matter who is in the room or how many people there are, while others talk less. There are introverts and extroverts, people who delight in declaring their opinions in a group and others who prefer to listen, process the conversation, and express their ideas and opinions privately or in writing. This is not so much a matter of age but of personality.

Susan Cain in her best-selling book *Quiet* contends that, in our society, the loud voices tend to get more attention than softer ones. People who speak up the most forcefully may be seen as right, even if their comments are not necessarily the most useful or productive, and as I've said, we like rightness and definitive-ness. Some people will rarely, if ever, speak up in a group, even when they have something valuable to say. It may be necessary, therefore, to draw out the introvert.

I will sometimes call on people who have not spoken to solicit a comment. How you do this is key. An open question—"Ralph, what do you think?"—may just put Ralph on the spot and make him want to disappear under the table. A more specific question often works better, at least to get the conversation started: "Jane, I know that you've tried more flexible working schedules in your department. What effect do you think they have had?" You may also have to carefully restate what the introvert has said to be sure it has been heard properly. There are some introverts who just don't want to participate in public discussions, period. If they have something to say that you feel should be heard by the group, you might suggest they find a friend or ally who will act as their mouthpiece and bring forth their point of view. The surrogate might attribute the comment to the introvert or not, whatever they both agree to.

The dynamics of a dialogue can change in the course of the conversation, often rapidly, and so another thing a leader can do to keep everybody on track is to make important moments explicit. Try to read the room, articulate what is happening in the conversation, and act as a spokesperson for the unspoken. As much as possible, the shifting currents should be brought to the surface.

To do this, you can restate an important comment or question to be sure everybody has taken it in and to clarify it, as necessary. ("Sandy, if I heard you right, you're saying that you believe too much flexibility in working hours can cause a drop in productivity?")

You can synthesize viewpoints in a discussion or disagreement. ("So, let me try to summarize what we've heard so far . . . ")

You can make a mood explicit. ("OK, there are obviously very strong feelings about this issue.")

One final point: the leader doesn't have to keep the dialogue moving and enforce the rules of civil discourse singlehandedly.

Ideally, everybody participates in the conversation, not only by making comments but by de facto facilitating as well. As organizational psychologist Roger Schwartz writes in *Harvard Business Review*, "That means if you're a team member and you see that there isn't a clear meeting purpose and process, you don't know your role in the meeting, or people seem to be getting off track, you say something rather than silently criticizing the leader for poor meeting management."

As much as I love engaging in dialogue and leading coffee chats, and as useful as I know they are, I have also come to recognize that people inside a company have difficulty seeing beyond the boundaries of the organization. If we have a shared purpose and a shared way of operating—and especially if we have been with the company for some time—it can get difficult to see the status quo and figure out what needs to be examined. When you're standing among the trees, it's very hard to see the entire forest.

That is why you have to also seek out questions and accept challenge from outsiders.

CHAPTER SEVEN

Outsider Input

Bankers, Media, Students,
and the Tom Hagen Model

I f you really want to open yourself up to intense and purposeful questioning and the incredible learning that can result, I can recommend one surefire method: take your company public.

There are many mechanisms and opportunities to create external challenge to an organization, but in my experience at Dunkin', the most challenging of all is the initial public offering, or IPO. Everything about the process puts the company into challenge mode. You will be asked questions by the bankers who will represent you in the process; by the institutional investors who may buy your stock; by the press and analysts; by your own board; and, finally, the general public will be asking questions about the company to determine if they want to buy in. There is really no other learning experience quite so intense as an IPO.

But I'm getting ahead of myself.

Back to 2009. As I've said, one of the reasons I was brought in as CEO was to get Dunkin' ready for the IPO and to lead the company through the process. Only three years earlier, in December 2005, Dunkin' had gone through a change of ownership when its parent company, Allied Domecq—recently purchased by Pernod Ricard—put Dunkin' up for sale. There was intense interest from private equity groups. They saw Dunkin' as a fantastic brand and a company with a great deal of potential for growth, expansion, and a high return on investment. The offering resulted in an intense, hotly contested auction, and three highly regarded private equity firms emerged as the owners: Bain Capital, the Carlyle Group, and Thomas H. Lee Partners.

In the ensuing three years, Dunkin' realized some of its hoped-for potential. In 2006, the famous "America Runs on Dunkin'" marketing campaign was launched, and in 2007, Dunkin' Donuts coffee was introduced for sale in supermarkets and other retail outlets for the first time. In 2008, the menu was expanded to include all-day oven-toasted sandwiches and flatbreads. We established new partnerships and opened stores in new geographies for Dunkin', including China and the Caribbean.

Yet, there were concerns. The company carried a high debt load. Comparable store sales in Dunkin' U.S. restaurants and in Baskin-Robbins shops declined in 2007 and dipped into the negative in 2008. Systemwide sales growth declined from 2006 to 2008. The stockholders' equity was very much under pressure. In 2009, the economy went to hell.

With these troubling financials in a faltering economy, the owners became concerned that the company would not be ready for an IPO by 2012. They decided that Dunkin' would need to raise its game, and to do so, a management stimulus was in order.

In late 2008, a headhunter contacted me about the CEO position, and I was intrigued, for many reasons. I was eager to be involved again with a big brand and global enterprise. I wanted to lead a company where the CEO would not be constrained by the influence of the founder. And I was especially attracted to the prospect of the IPO because I knew these events could be intense, exciting, enlightening, and huge with opportunity.

The board took the interview process extremely seriously because they saw their next CEO as the person who would be largely responsible for how successful their return on investment would be. Private equity firms typically want to make the move to public ownership within five years of purchase and usually liquidate their holdings within a year after the IPO.

The interview process for the CEO job was intense. There were several candidates in the running. I went through eighteen separate interviews, some with the full board, some with small groups of directors, and some one-on-ones. The process lasted six weeks and was a marathon of questioning unlike any other I have been through. It was a fantastic preview for me of how the board operated and the value they could bring to probing issues.

I believe that it was partially my willingness to engage in this deep questioning and to push back on certain issues, such as company-owned stores, that brought me successfully through the process. I was hired, and with the board, we set a target of 2012 for the IPO, three years hence. As we've seen, I set about reconfiguring the leadership team, improving relations with franchisees, improving systems and technologies, setting the stage for geographic growth, and building the challenge culture.

By 2011, we had made sufficient progress and the economy had recovered enough that we decided we could go public a little ahead of schedule. The huge success of the Dunkin' Donuts K-Cup pods in our restaurants was an important factor in the decision. It had been a very public initiative—signaling a new direction for the company and demonstrating that we could take on big challenges—and had been an inarguable win.

We—me, the board, and the management team—decided to seize the day. I had never taken a company public before (although I had been involved in the Blockbuster IPO process), but I knew that the management team would be tested in the process. I was confident that the group had really jelled, that we had the right set of skills, and that we could successfully take on the rigors of going public. In the estimation of Goldman Sachs, Dunkin' had an "all-star bench" of senior managers. The investment bank calculated that the fifteen most senior Dunkin' Brands executives had an average of nineteen years of experience in the restaurant industry, with a total of 285 "experience years."

It was more than just the skills and the number of years in the business that distinguished the leadership group; it was also that we functioned well together as a team. In addition to the specific hard disciplinary expertise of our leadership group members (law, finance, marketing, etc.), they also had mastery of the soft skills—collaboration, communication, problem solving, and critical thinking—that are so critical to the challenge culture.

I'm not particularly big on titles in corporate organizations. That's largely because the formal title rarely describes the complete role the person plays and the many kinds of value they bring. During the IPO, I came to understand more clearly that team members take on certain responsibilities that do not appear on any organizational chart and make contributions that have little to do with their functional expertise. Two of these roles, for me anyway, are the emotional consigliere and the sparring partner.

Dave Ulrich, a professor at the University of Michigan's Ross School of Management, coined the term *emotional consigliere*. You may remember that Vito Corleone, the mafia don in *The Godfather*, relied on his trusted lawyer, Tom Hagen, as consigliere, but one who delivered much more than legal advice. *Consigliere* is Italian for "counselor" or "adviser," and Hagen's counsel went well beyond how to deal with the law. Hagen is the one who informed the don that Sonny, his oldest boy, had been gunned down on the causeway.

The emotional consigliere is a person who has a close advisory role to a leader (or anyone, for that matter). Typically, the emotional consigliere has a special combination of hard and soft skills—just as Tom Hagen was an expert lawyer and also a skilled and empathic communicator.

I wouldn't compare Paul Twohig to Tom Hagen, or me to the godfather (or business to organized crime), but Paul—the guy who told me I had gone too far in that early leadership team meeting—came to play the role of emotional consigliere to me, especially during the IPO. Paul had vast on-the-ground, operational experience that I did not. He began his career at Burger King, became a regional manager for the chain, and then became a franchisee—so he knew operations from the perspective of both a corporate executive and an owner. He then spent a few years at Boston Market as a franchisee, followed by ten years as senior vice president with Starbucks and a stint as COO of Panera Bread, before I asked him to join Dunkin'. Paul may not have been getting up at 4:30 A.M. to make the donuts, as some of our franchisees did early in their careers, but his knowledge of restaurant operations was so formidable he had the chops to challenge me.

But Paul was far more than a knowledgeable, experienced operations guy. He had the soft skills, as he so clearly demonstrated from that early meeting: he knew how to question, when to question, how to engage in dialogue. He had a keen sense of the moment and an ability to debate without getting involved in personalities.

Paul and I developed good chemistry, possibly because of our complementary differences. He is an introvert who rarely raises his voice and sometimes takes a half-glass-empty view. I am more of an extrovert and sometimes overly optimistic. Although Paul challenged me constantly on operational issues, he also listened and counseled me with insight and great deliberation. During the IPO, we communicated several times a day.

There are risks in relying too much on the counsel of any one person, even a skilled emotional consigliere. Even if the counselor maintains good relationships with others on the leadership team, there is always the chance that this key counselor will be seen as manipulative or trading on his or her position to gain personal benefit. It can also happen that the emotional consigliere may become *too* sympathetic, too in sync with the advisee, and thus unable to provide enough challenge. (That was not the case, I would argue, with either Paul Twohig or Tom Hagen.)

So it's important to recognize that there are limits to what any adviser can provide and to establish other types of relationships within the team—and one of the key ones is the sparring partner. This is a person with different views, approaches, and mindset than yours but who you respect and trust and are willing and able to engage with.

At Dunkin', I had just such a relationship, a superb sparring partner: Paul Carbone, who began as vice president of strategy and finance and later moved into the chief financial officer position. Paul and I argued regularly and disagreed on many issues. We often openly discussed our differences with the board, which helped us make better decisions as a company. Although our disagreements might have looked contentious, our encounters were never personal, and we actually saw them as an invigorating part of our working life. As we prepared for the IPO, I relied on Paul to push back on key deliberations: when to go public, what the valuation should be, what partners to work with.

The other members of the leadership team brought their own set of hard and soft skills to the IPO process. John Costello possessed marketing and brand-building skills honed during his management experience at Procter & Gamble, Nielsen, Yahoo, and a number of tech start-ups. He had a tremendous grasp of data management and technology, as well as brand marketing and product innovation, and had so much varied experience he was always willing to poke his finger into the soft spots of the status quo. Christine Deputy had spent time at Starbucks and, after her tenure with Dunkin', eventually became head of HR at Nordstrom. She led our human resources effort with vigor and was willing to challenge just about anything. Neil Moses came in as CFO and became my indefatigable and unflappable traveling companion during the run-up to the IPO. Two others whom I've already introduced and who had strong challenge skills were Karen Raskopf, senior vice president of corporate communications, and Rich Emmett, general counsel.

The first task in an IPO is to select the investment bank partners who will manage the offering. These banks, known as underwriters, take on responsibility for valuing the company, setting share price, creating the written prospectus, managing the selling process to institutional investors, and handling the actual launch of the company on the stock market.

There is significant risk involved in an IPO, so the offering company typically works with more than one investment bank. We ended up working with a group of fourteen underwriters. The group was led by three firms—J.P. Morgan Securities LLC, Barclays Capital Inc., and Morgan Stanley & Co. LLC—who took on the lead role known as active bookrunner, the principal managers of the process. They were supported by three "passive" bookrunners, who made an investment in the offering but didn't directly participate in the organization and management: Bank of America, Merrill Lynch, and Goldman Sachs & Co. LLC. Nine other underwriting firms participated as co-managers, which meant they were involved in representing the prospectus and selling shares to institutional investors but had no direct management responsibilities. In addition to our fourteen underwriting partners, we engaged a consulting firm, Solebury Capital Group LLC, to advise us on the entire process. Although we relied on the underwriters to put together and manage the IPO, they were essentially independent entities acting largely in their own interests. We needed a consultant, acting exclusively on our behalf, who would know what questions to ask and help us position ourselves for best results. They were, in effect, in the best position to challenge the investment bankers.

The IPO is presented in a written prospectus, prepared by the bookrunners, which lays out the deal in great detail. It is rather sobering to see one's company described, by outsiders, in such straightforward and evaluative terms. There, without benefit of marketing language, is the bare-bones story of the company: strengths, strategy, risks, management, organization.

According to the prospectus our strengths were: strong and established brand, leading market position, high earnings margin, experienced management team, extensive white space opportunity—that is, lots of room to grow.

The stated risks? High indebtedness. Failure to achieve goals if execution of strategy were inadequate. Consumer preferences might change unexpectedly. New and incursive competition could emerge. We might suddenly run out of people interested in opening new restaurants. (That has not been a problem.)

Once the prospectus was ready, the bookrunners organized a roadshow in which I, Neil Moses, other Dunkin' leaders, and representatives of the underwriters embarked on a cross-country tour to make presentations and take questions from the institutional investors. These were the big brokerage houses—such as Fidelity, Janus, Vanguard, and many others—that wanted to make a commitment to buy a certain number of shares, which they would then sell on to their investors, both institutional and individual, on launch day and thereafter.

Beginning in early July, we hit the road. In a period of three weeks, we did about fifty one-on-one meetings and ten group meetings, some in major cities and some online. The live events were typically held at lunchtime in a hotel conference room with as many as seventy brokers in the audience. They came from the big institutional buyers, such as TIAA, who would offer our shares—with the stock symbol DNKN—to a wide range of institutional investors as well as individuals.

The brokerage people probed us on everything:

How are you going to expand on the West Coast when you've already failed twice?

You say that Dunkin' has great potential to expand internationally, but you've struggled badly in China. Why? How will you fix that?

What do you see happening in the coffee sector? The space is getting crowded.

Are you too highly leveraged at five times EBIDTA?

Isn't your growth limited right now because franchisees may have trouble getting financing from traditional lenders, such as banks?

How are you going to compete against the convenience stores who are now offering pretty good coffee?

You have such high margins; how can you possibly sustain them?

You're a small company; how can you retain top talent who want to play in a bigger arena?

Relations with the franchisees have gotten a lot of bad press in the past. What are you going to do to improve relations and clean up some of these issues?

The roadshow experience, in addition to being arduous, was enlightening and valuable. We were obligated to take any and all questions and to provide credible answers. Unlike internal groups, these audiences were not constrained or influenced by their relationship with the company. We had no power over them. And if they chose not to participate in the IPO, there was no real risk to them. In the end, however, our DNKN offering was many times oversubscribed, which means that there was far greater demand for shares than there were shares available to buy.

It all culminated in launch day, July 27, 2011. We opened at $19 a share and closed at $27.85, for a gain of $8.85 or 46.6 percent. More than forty-four million DNKN shares changed hands that day and reached a high of $29.62. We raised about $442 million, which made us one of the largest restaurant IPOs at that time. And the stock continued to rise. As of this writing, shares are trading at close to $60.

I felt many things after the IPO was completed. First, I felt excited and honored. We now had an incredible responsibility to manage the company for the benefit of our millions of shareholders, many thousands of whom were Dunkin' franchisees and employees. That's very different from managing to achieve a return on investment for three private equity firms. As part of the prospectus, we had essentially laid out a road map for growth and success for the coming five years. Now we had to execute and fulfill the promise we had made to our shareholders.

Second, I believed the process of going public had given me a much deeper understanding and detailed knowledge of our company and its place in the industry and, indeed, the society. I wanted to keep that process of discovery going; I saw again just how essential deep inquiry is to the challenge culture.

Third, I felt a weird sense of deflation. What could we do that would top this? How would we keep momentum going? I saw more powerfully than ever that we would have to keep finding new, significant challenges to keep from stagnating. All at once, the dream had become the status quo. It would eventually have to be challenged again. That is true of any significant achievement—earning an academic degree, completing a performance, finishing a work project. Along with the sense of satisfaction goes a feeling of loss, restlessness, boredom. The sooner you can challenge yourself again, the better.

. . .

The IPO deepened my appreciation of the benefits of outside questioning and even gave me an appetite for it.

Perhaps that's why I continue to value the formal outsider questioning event that comes with being a public company: the quarterly earnings announcement, typically known throughout corporate America as earnings day. It's an entire day of communication about corporate performance and related issues, presented primarily for the benefit of multiple external audiences, including financial analysts and the media. The earnings presentation includes a wealth of financial data, such as revenue, net income, and earnings per share, along with management's discussion of the results, as well as news and information about relevant company activities, such as, for us, restaurant openings, organization or staff changes, new products, strategies, and plans.

Some approach earnings day with dread. They think of it as an imposition, even an inquisition. Who are these outsiders to interrogate us about internal matters? What right do they have to pass judgment on our company?

I, on the other hand, rather enjoy it. How often do you get a chance to take questions from, and engage in dialogue with, thirty or forty people who pay close attention to your company and are more than willing—and often more than well prepared—to challenge you at every turn with (mostly) intelligent and well-informed questions? I think of these sessions, therefore, as an opportunity to gain perspective, knowledge, insight, pushback, and challenge from a group of unpaid, relatively unbiased advisors.

If you go into the earnings day with the attitude of the student, not just the lecturer, you may well learn something useful. Sometimes an important issue will surface during the course of the earnings day that compels you to think about it more deeply or in new ways, and that was the case, for example, with the first quarter earnings day sessions we held in May 2017.

The day began at 8:00 A.M. in the second-floor conference room at our Canton headquarters with a conference call between seven Dunkin' senior managers and fourteen financial analysts who represented many of the major financial services firms in the United States, including Morgan Stanley, Goldman Sachs, Bank of America, UBS, J.P. Morgan, Piper Jaffray, Credit Suisse, Barclays, and several others. That amounts to a great deal of influence, buying clout, and brain power.

We presented our results for the quarter, which were characterized by good earnings but slightly disappointing sales comps, largely due to horrendous weather in the Northeast, and discussed a few of the factors that had affected the business. One of these was employment, that is, the high employment rate in the United States at the time. High turnover, as I've discussed, has long been an issue for the quick service industry, and the scarcity of workers was affecting all restaurants in the category. In our presentations, we talked about actions we were taking to improve our retention rate, including simplifications to the menu, automating the ordering process, and working to create an appealing and consistent culture throughout the system.

After our presentations, we took questions. The first came from John Ivankoe, a well-known analyst at J.P. Morgan Securities. John has a keen eye for development and typically asks about our plans for opening new restaurants. Sure enough, John wondered if, given the increased competitive pricing in the market and the pressure on employment, we foresaw a slowdown in franchisee investment in new restaurants. I answered that the rate of franchisee investment showed no signs of slowing and that we felt our development schedule was prudent.

John pushed back: "Let me ask it another way. Should you be growing as quickly as you are, given some of the external and internal challenges that your business is facing?"

I sometimes think of John as an external sparring partner, a member of the extended challenge culture team. Take them where you can find them! "John," I said, "I always love your challenges because they always lead to great animated debates, but we feel that we've got the right plan to deliver our goals . . . We've got to stretch all the development we can get."

Another analyst, Nicole Miller Regan, followed up on the employment issue. She is a managing director and senior research analyst at Piper Jaffray, a leading investment bank and asset management firm. In my prepared remarks, I had mentioned our recent People Summit in Orlando, a three-day event focused on issues of human resources and culture. "Looking back at the meeting . . . with eight hundred franchise and staff members, what did you hear from them?" Nicole asked. "What did they like or not like? What suggestions did they make?"

Culture is not always a top-of-mind issue for financial analysts who are more naturally inclined toward quantifiable information. But Nicole's question led to further discussion of the matter of employment, what role culture plays in attracting and retaining workers, especially on the front lines in our restaurants, and what we were doing in that regard.

The analysts' questions struck me. It was clear that our investors were focused on employment and its related issues: training, retention, and culture. Perhaps even bankers were beginning to value more explicitly the critical role of culture to company health and sustainability?

After the analysts' session, we did interviews with the media, including print and television journalists, most of whom specialized in business and finance, for such outlets as the *Wall Street Journal* and the Associated Press, as well as financial journalists such as Jim Cramer's online newsletter TheStreet. These media questioners, too, had employment on their minds. We talked with them about the role of the quick service restaurant industry as the de facto training ground for America's workforce. Many workers in America get their start in the quick service restaurant industry. The restaurant and food industry is the second-largest employer in the nation. The actions we take in training people, inculcating good habits and values, has a long-term effect on the careers of millions of people and the productivity of the economy as a whole.

The day continued with further interviews and wrapped up with a live webcast to all employees, in which we recapped the messages, interpreted them in the light of employee concerns, and took live questions.

Earnings day is a formalized, even ritualized, exercise in questioning and discourse. During the course of the various sessions, your messages and ideas get tested, transformed, refined, enriched, built out, and stripped down. Sometimes the questions force you to rethink an issue. Sometimes they reassure you that you have considered it well. If we get even one question or response that leads to a new idea or a valuable change of approach, it's worth it.

Sometimes the value of an earnings day engagement is that it brings you up short. It shocks. After a session a few years ago, an analyst from Goldman Sachs put a sell rating on Dunkin' stock. This came as a complete surprise, and we thought it was unwarranted. Some of my colleagues were outraged, and my wife, Joanna, got quite agitated. But I saw no point in getting upset about it. Goldman had an opinion. It's their job to express it. As a result, we plunged into the earnings report more deeply to see what had caused that reaction and if we could, or needed to, do anything about it. (We couldn't find anything specific.)

To shove aside such comments would be to fall into confirmation bias thinking: to reject all information that does not confirm what we want to believe—which was, in this case, that we were doing fine and everything was OK. If assertive questioners can shake up our biases and get us into dialogue, that's a good thing. An even more intense forum is the biennial Investor Day, in which management engages with analysts and major investors. It requires extensive preparation and the process of explaining, and justifying the company's actions over the previous two years is a great example of how challenge can encourage valuable discourse.

. . .

I have another favorite and valued external source of challenge: students. I love talking with student audiences because they always have questions and attitudes that I would not get from the board, management team, institutional investors, or other internal or external audiences, including the media.

On one recent day, I gave two student talks. In the morning, I spoke with kids at the Wellesley High School, the public school in the town of Wellesley, Massachusetts, where we live. In that session, through questions and answers, I learned a number of things. First, I learned that every kid there had purchased something on Amazon recently. That reinforced for me the power and extent of online retailing, even for this young demographic. Second, every kid in the group I spoke with, all of whom were fifteen or sixteen years old, remembered Blockbuster. The last Wellesley store had closed only about three years earlier, and they remembered the place and the experience with fondness. By contrast, neither of my kids, eleven and thirteen years old, have any memory of Blockbuster. That reminded me again of the fragility of market leadership and the importance of staying ahead of technological change. Third, a number of kids in the group had worked in the quick service restaurant industry; some had been employed at both Dunkin' and McDonald's. They told me that the job at Dunkin' was much more complicated than at McDonald's because of the number of menu offerings. I hope that the kids learned a little something from our session; I know that I did.

In the evening, I gave a talk to students at the MIT Sloan School of Management in Cambridge. There were perhaps a hundred MBA students in the big, modern, sloped lecture room. They hailed from countries all over the world, including Germany, Gambia, and the U.K. These were smart, competitive, ambitious people. But that doesn't mean they knew everything about the quick service industry, as I soon found out.

For example, I asked them what they thought the store employee turnover rate was for the quick service industry as a whole.

> *Student 1:* Twenty percent?
> *Me:* OK, anybody else?
> *Student 2:* Forty percent!
> *Me:* OK. Forty percent. Other opinions?
> *Student 3:* Sixty percent!!
> Everybody started laughing. It sounded like an auction.
> *Me:* Any higher bids?
> No further responses.
> *Me:* One hundred fifty percent.
> *Audience:* What? Whoa! No! Really? Wow.
> *Me:* So what are the implications of that turnover rate?
> *Student 4:* High training costs?
> *Me:* Training, yes. Also recruiting and consistency of service. We recently did a survey of franchisees, and they said their biggest issue is finding people to hire.

I then asked the students to think about solutions to the problem of turnover and hiring.

> *Me:* OK, you're all consultants now. I'm your client. I say, look, at Dunkin' Brands, we have this problem. We have high turnover. We can't find people to hire. What's your solution, Mr. or Ms. Consultant?
> *Student 1:* Automation.
> *Student 2:* Job redesign.
> *Student 3:* Algorithms to better define the employees who are likely to stay longer.
> *Student 4:* Schedule flexibility.

Me: OK, those are interesting solutions. There's one other big factor you haven't mentioned.

Student 5: Compensation!

Me: Right. I'm thinking of another one, still. Also begins with a *c.*

Silence. Pause. Finally a student calls out tentatively.

Student 6: Culture?

Me: Culture! All those systems and mechanisms are useful. But yes, I'm thinking of culture. Now, let's say you're a crew person in a Dunkin' store. What kind of culture would you want?

The students said they would want a fun culture. A no-pressure culture. A place where you would get support from your teammates. Where you have the tools, knowledge, and training to do your job.

It was also in this discussion that I became the student and the student became the teacher. A student raised her hand urgently.

Student 7: Nigel, at Starbucks, the training focuses on what they call keystone habits.

Me: Keystone habits? What are those?

Student 7: A keystone habit is a practice or behavior the employee can employ in known, recurring situations. For example, a rushed and irritated customer puts an employee under pressure, who, under stress, delivers an order that isn't right. That's a common situation and one that can get out of hand. The keystone habit defines how to recognize and handle the situation.

Me: Have you worked at Starbucks?

Student 7: No, but I've studied them.

Well, as it turns out, keystone habits are not a Starbucks invention. It's an approach highlighted and named by Charles Duhigg in his insightful book *The Power of Habit: Why We Do What We Do in Life and Business.* In the book he cites the example of

Alcoa, which identified safety habits as key to the turnaround of the company in the 1980s.

The point is that, in this conversation with MBA students, where I was supposedly the expert, I learned something of value. The process of questioning the audience had produced new knowledge for all of us.

Later, I opened the floor to questions. Again, the very nature of the questions themselves gave me information about the next generation of Dunkin' customers and, no doubt, leaders.

They asked:

How do you see Dunkin's long-term sustainability?

How will population shifts, particularly as people move into cities and drive less, affect your business?

What plans do you have to expand Dunkin' internationally and how are they different for Dunkin' and Baskin-Robbins, considering that Baskin is so much bigger in some geographies than Dunkin' is?

How long can you stick with a growth target of 6 percent when the economy is growing at 2 percent or less?

The United States is experiencing a diabetes epidemic, and you're in an industry that could be seen as contributing to that problem. How do you see your company's responsibility to promoting health and wellness?

Would you ever sell one of your brands?

Would you ever make a big acquisition, and if so, what would it be?

It is not so much that I had not thought about these questions, because I had, but the session forced me to articulate my thoughts to an audience who were not in any way beholden to me or the company. Every manager in the quick service industry is asked about health and wellness and nutrition. Honestly, it is a difficult challenge for us and one we wrestle with every day. We have moved with our customers toward a greater awareness and attention to health issues. We list nutrition information about all our products. We have adopted good practices in food sourcing, such as cage-free eggs. We also do our best to respond to the demands of our customers. We constantly try new menu items, and many of them are meant to provide choices with reduced fat, salt, sugar, and artificial ingredients. But if an item doesn't sell, it doesn't sell, and we can't continue to offer it forever.

There is so much to learn from these sessions with outsiders, just from the tenor of the questions, the thinking styles, and attitudes you sense. At the MIT session, for example, I was struck by an issue that I discussed earlier: the sharp focus on the quantitative. Perhaps it was not surprising at MIT, a bastion of science and technology, but it still struck me how sharp the focus was on numbers, data, and financial results and less on taste, attitudes, and emotions.

By the end of the evening, I was pretty exhausted but also exhilarated. I always leave these events feeling passionately committed to further improving the business, taking on new challenges, pushing harder than ever.

CHAPTER EIGHT

The Personal Nudge

*Jumping Off Cliffs When
You're Not Really in the Mood*

I was exhausted, jet-lagged, not in the greatest of moods.
I had just finished an interview with Fox News and was in
a taxi on my way to the hotel when my mobile rang. I had
flown in to New York from the West Coast earlier that day and
was flying out to London the next morning to do more interviews. Karen Raskopf, our head of corporate communications,
was calling. She often gets in touch after an important interview,
to discuss how things went. I could tell, just by the way Karen
drew breath, that she wasn't entirely thrilled.

"Nigel," she said, "we need to talk about the comments you
made on Fox." I didn't even get a "Hi, how are you?"

The interview had been tricky, and I didn't feel particularly pleased with how it had gone. The subject had been immigration. The segment opened with comments by Paul Ryan,
Speaker of the House of Representatives. He took a surprisingly
moderate line, saying that he was open to immigration reform.
When my turn came, I expressed my concern about the lack of
people available to fill jobs in the restaurant industry. I explained
that Dunkin', of course, enforces the law, with a strict policy

that prohibits the employment of undocumented immigrants. I said, however, that I, as a private citizen, believed there should be a path to citizenship for undocumented workers already in the country. With such low unemployment, we could use more people in the pool.

"That's not the way it sounded," Karen told me. "It came across as if you were taking a political stand. It seemed that you were saying that Dunkin's corporate policy is to support the employment of undocumented workers."

"Well, that's not exactly what I said, Karen. I can't help how they chopped it up. Anyway, I don't know what I can do about it now."

"OK," Karen replied. "Well, what we can do is talk about how to handle the U.K. media tomorrow when they ask about immigration."

"Karen, really, the U.K. media doesn't care about U.S. immigration policy," I barked. "They won't even ask me about it."

"Yes, they will, Nigel," she said. "They absolutely will. Doubly so, after your comments on Fox today. So we need to talk it through. Your answers were misinterpreted because they weren't crisp. They weren't what we had discussed. We're going to get a lot of blowback on this."

I did not want to discuss immigration or interviews or my crispness at that moment. I wanted to get to the hotel and sleep.

"I'm very angry at you right now, Karen," I snapped.

"You're angry at me or angry at the media?"

"I'm angry at you!" I bellowed. Of course I wasn't. I was angry at the interview and at myself.

"OK, Nigel," she said calmly. "I'm just doing my job. Remember, we have a challenge culture. Right?"

I grumbled. We pulled up at the hotel. I told Karen I'd call her back after I checked in. Twenty minutes later we talked again. "OK, OK," I said. We talked over the issue, and in five minutes we had it sorted. I flew to the U.K. the next day, and sure enough, the press asked about my comments in the Fox interview.

I called Karen again later. "You were right to push me. Thanks."

She made a noise, a combination of a chuckle and a sigh.

Even with my clarifications to the U.K. media, my comments on Fox did provoke a lot of response. This is true any time you put forward a view in the media on a polarizing issue: you're going to get comments both in support and opposition. They can be intense and troubling. In this case, many people wrote to say they were planning to boycott Dunkin' because of our stated policy on immigration.

Point of the story: living in a challenge culture can be trying. Sometimes you just don't want to formulate purposeful questions or listen carefully to answers or engage in civil dialogue or filter out all those personal ad hominem thoughts that are running through your head. You just want to make a declarative statement, issue a decree, say yes or no, and be done with it. The authoritarian impulse can rise up at any time, and it's hard to push it back down again.

But you have to. The challenge culture succeeds or fails on the commitment and model of the leaders, supporters, and true advocates. The CEO, leadership team, senior managers, and, in the end, everybody in the company needs to do their utmost to adhere to its tenets. Including when they are jet-lagged, stressed, busy, not in the mood, and pressed for time.

Fortunately, challenge is not a 24/7 proposition; you don't need to be in challenge mode 100 percent of your waking hours. The 80/20 rule applies, or perhaps it's more like 90/10: 90 percent business as usual, 10 percent debate and dialogue. You are like an airline pilot. The bulk of the job consists of known tasks and predictable management issues, and only now and again does a real challenge arise from weather, passengers, scheduling, equipment, whatever.

It's in those moments, however, that all your preparations, habits of mind, and good practices kick in. To operate successfully in a challenge culture, you need to be physically fit, focused, and highly productive. Like a professional athlete, you need to maintain your "match-day fitness," as they say in soccer, so you are as well prepared as possible to both deliver challenges and respond to them. You never know from where, or from whom, the challenge is going to come.

So I would like to offer a few of my own personal practices that I believe help keep me as fit and as prepared as possible to function successfully in the challenge culture. These include identifying models for admiration and emulation, keeping physically and emotionally fit, constant learning, and taking on responsibilities very different from the ones I shoulder at work.

. . .

I find that one of the most effective ways to stay motivated for challenge is to look to models I admire, people who are farther out on the edge than I will ever be. I have been fortunate to find sources of inspiration that I value tremendously, particularly people who do things I cannot imagine doing and who encourage me to keep questioning.

One such person is Ellen Brennan. She is the world's women's champion of the extreme sport known as wingsuit flying or wingsuiting. The wingsuit pilot flies through the air like a bat or a flying squirrel, kept aloft by a fabric suit that becomes a wing-like surface as the pilot leaps into the air, stretching arms and legs wide, and the suit automatically inflates into rigidity. The wing creates enough lift to enable the wingsuiter to soar forward as he or she falls. By adjusting the position of the arms, legs, and head, the wingsuiter can control his or her flight with surprising precision—turning, diving, even doing midair somersaults. As the wingsuit pilot approaches the ground, the pilot deploys a built-in parachute for a reasonably gentle touchdown.

There are two categories of wingsuiting: aircraft flying and BASE jumping. Aircraft wingsuiters jump from an airplane, soar through open air, and steer themselves toward an agreeable landing site. BASE jumping is a very different kettle of fish. The wingsuiter takes off from a fixed position, such as a high building, a mountaintop, or a cliff. (BASE stands for buildings, antennas, spans, and earth.) The objective of the BASE jumper is to soar near, past, or through landscape features to increase the sensation of speed that is not so obvious in falling from an airplane. BASE jumpers often choose gorgeous mountain settings with craggy cliffs, spires, even narrow canyons to fly through. An experienced wingsuiter can reach speeds of well over a hundred miles per hour, travel two or three miles in distance, and drop several thousand vertical feet. By all accounts, the flight is exhilarating, gorgeous, and addictive.

Yes, wingsuiting is dangerous, and the sport is dominated by young, single men, which makes Ellen, then age twenty-nine, even more of a standout. She is incredibly dedicated to her sport and is considered to be one of the top female athletes in the field. She has participated in many competitions and is known as the Fastest Flying Woman in the World. She says she got into wingsuiting because she wanted to "explore the boundaries of what we think is possible."

Ellen and Dunkin' have had a relationship since 2016. We approached her about appearing in a television commercial to help launch our On-the-Go Mobile Ordering app. The app enables customers to place their order so that it's ready for them when they arrive at the restaurant. Wait time is cut to zero.

The concept for the TV spot was simple, if a little crazy. (Even more so than The Apprentice spot we did for Papa John's.) Ellen would leap from a clifftop, wearing a wingsuit and helmet emblazoned with the unmistakable Dunkin' logo colors, soar toward a mountainside Dunkin' shop, zoom past a "flyby" pickup station, and grab a suspended Dunkin' bag containing her on-the-go order as she flew past. We'd call it the World's Fastest Dunkin' Run.

Ellen enthusiastically agreed to work with our team in making the spot, despite the incredible challenges involved. "It was a completely crazy idea," she said. "It had never been done. Which is why I wanted to do it." Ellen would be descending more than eight thousand feet, had to maneuver herself into exactly the right position, and would be going about 125 mph at the point of pickup. And, oh yes, no wingsuiter had ever before grabbed an object in full flight. This would be a first.

Ellen threw herself into the preparation, planning, and practice for shooting the spot. She had to break in a new wingsuit, created especially for this spot, which required test flights from an airplane. She had to learn how to pick up a small object at speed, which she did on the ski slope, zooming past a pickup spot on skis. Surprisingly, Ellen was not particularly comfortable with this part of the process. "I don't like going that fast on skis," said the Fastest Flying Woman on earth. She was glad when that part of the training was over.

Ellen and the film crew traveled to the resort area of Chamonix, in the French Alps. They selected a jump site atop a rocky crag, 8,346 feet above sea level. She would soar along a ridge toward the specially constructed Dunkin' hut where the Dunkin' bag was suspended, on breakaway strings, well away from the structure. She would then swoop over the edge of another cliff and set herself down in the valley below.

When it came to the shoot, the start was delayed for several days by bad weather. When the sky finally cleared and the sun came out, it took dozens of flights for Ellen to get her range, determine her best glide path, and figure out how to maneuver herself so her left hand could come into perfect contact with the Dunkin' bag. (Velcro on the bag and her arm helped.) Finally, on the thirtieth flyby, Ellen cleanly snatched her order and let out an enormous whoop. "To accomplish something that's never been done before," she said, "it was unreal."

I met Ellen in April 2017, a year after that amazing spot aired. We had been invited to speak together at the opening session of an industry conference, the Women's Foodservice Forum (WFF) in Orlando. Our topic was the need for women to take risks in developing their careers and the issues they face in managing both their work and home lives.

The appearance posed challenges for both Ellen and me. We had never met and only had about an hour to talk before we went onstage. We would be appearing before an audience of more than three thousand women. That was a challenge for me, as one of the few guys in the house, as well as for Ellen, because it was the largest audience she had ever addressed. Ellen also had to contend with the generational gap of being a twenty-nine-year-old extreme sport athlete dealing with me, a sixty-seven-year-old CEO and amateur soccer coach.

As it happened, Ellen and I hit it off extremely well. After talking about our views on risk and careers, we ditched our prepared script and completely rewrote our remarks. Once we got onstage, Ellen rose to the occasion and was a big hit with the audience. It turned out that she made a significant career change early on. She started out as an intensive care nurse in Salt Lake City but, in 2008, decided to move to France and dedicate herself to flying. Ellen talked about the risks and the rewards of her new extreme lifestyle. "I really feel like I understand life a lot better when I'm flying through the air and seeing everything from a different perspective," she said.

I talked about the risks, less extreme but still significant, that I had taken in my career. The first was when I leaped from the relatively comfortable area of human resources into general management. The second was the move from the country where I was born and raised, the U.K., to the U.S. As I said, both risks paid off brilliantly for me. I have never regretted getting into the operational side of business. Nor would I choose to live anywhere but the United States.

What struck Ellen most about the conference was the response she got from audience members after our talk. Typically, when people meet her for the first time, their first question is, "Isn't it dangerous?" At the WFF event, however, she got a very different question from the women attendees. "How do you get started?" they wanted to know.

"When most people think about taking on a new challenge," Ellen said, "their initial response is fear. They don't want to push their limits. Then there are people who are driven by curiosity, and while they may be apprehensive, they want to push themselves to achievements and experiences that stretch and improve them."

I think of this kind of personal growth challenge as analogous to a rubber band. It seems to have almost unlimited capacity to stretch. I firmly believe too many people, and not just women by any means, think they will break if they try to stretch too far.

. . .

I do not intend to jump off a cliff anytime soon, despite Ellen's encouragement. But her example, and those of others, inspires me. She is able to do what she does as the result of a hundred discrete habits and practices, from the way she trains to the way she packs her gear. It is instructive to examine the habits of superachievers to better understand the specific things they do that contribute to their accomplishments. Tom Brady, for example, the extraordinary quarterback for the New England Patriots, lays out his entire program in his book *TB12*, from the recipe for his green breakfast smoothies to his exercise bands to his sleep habits.

I do not put myself in the Ellen Brennan or Tom Brady category, but I have tried to incorporate a number of lessons and techniques from a variety of sources into my everyday routines. All of them, I believe, contribute to the ability to ask questions and engage in discourse and keep up the challenge way.

First, keeping physically fit.

Life in corporate America can be life in the fast lane. In one recent year, I flew a total of 183,000 air miles on 136 flights, participated in 1,400 meetings, and made hundreds of phone calls. Then there were all the in-between and routine things: getting from place to place, preparing for meetings and events, handling e-mail and paperwork, thinking and planning. That pace of activity puts a strain on the body. So, with some notable exceptions, most successful professionals I know make a point of keeping themselves fit.

With that kind of work and travel schedule, it's difficult to maintain a regular schedule of fitness activity, so I have to build it in where and how I can. Last year, I spent 156 hours working out at the gym, which is pretty good, but that's only an average of three hours per week. I probably get another two hours of intermittent running on the soccer field as I coach my kids' teams.

Then I just look for any and every opportunity to exercise in my everyday activities. The simplest and most convenient method is to walk whenever you can and, when you walk, walk with some energy. At the airport, walk between terminals and try to beat the folks standing on the travelator. You will probably get to the gate or customs line faster than they do. Walk to the restaurant from the hotel. Walk around the office. Get up during the meeting and walk around the room. Take the stairs. If you can add a bit of weight to the walk, so much the better. Carry your own bags. Carry somebody else's bags. Don't worry about having a specific goal of, say, ten thousand steps per day or feel guilty if you don't make the goal. Just walk whenever you can. This is not the American way, as Barry Gibbons and I found out in our four-hundred-yard ride from the Orlando airport to our hotel. But it should be.

Not only does walking benefit your health, it promotes self-reflection. Walking time can be thinking and inspiration time. As Ernest Hemingway said, it's easier to think when you're walking. If you walk while you talk on the phone, you'll be amazed how your thoughts flow and how many miles you'll put in. If you get up in a meeting and take a few steps around the room, the energy level rises and ideas fly faster. Some companies encourage their people to hold meetings while walking, to increase creativity.

"All truly great thoughts are conceived while walking," said philosopher Friedrich Nietzsche. Researchers agree that walking stimulates creative thought, although the exact causes are not certain. Some of them recommend that, for best results, you should walk at a normal pace and avoid places with too many distractions. I find that when walking and running, which I also do as often as I can, questions pop into my mind endlessly. Things that seemed unclear or that I had not been able to challenge suddenly present themselves. That is a gift.

The flipside of vigorous activity is regular rest. Productivity benefits from downtime, taking breaks, and getting sleep. I am a huge advocate of napping. I take naps at the office, at home, on the plane, and I encourage others to do the same. Research supports my belief in the benefits of napping. An expert on the subject, Dr. Sara C. Mednick, lays out twenty benefits of napping on the job in her book, *Take a Nap! Change Your Life*. Here are the five that most resonated with me:

1. *Napping increases your alertness.* Mednick writes that studies by NASA show that napping increases your alertness level by as much as 100 percent, even if you were pretty well rested before the nap.

2. *Napping improves your accuracy.* After a nap, you will work faster and with fewer mistakes, no matter what your job is, whether it's on a manufacturing line, in an office, or on the playing field.

3. *Napping helps you make better decisions.* Large or small decisions can be made with better judgment when you're rested. Studies of pilots, for example, show that pilots who nap are less likely to make an error in judgment at the most critical times of a flight—takeoff and landing—than those who have not napped.

4. *Napping fattens your bottom line.* Mednick reports that "fatigue-related accidents" in U.S. industries result in costs of over $150 million annually. Workers' comp costs go up in workplaces where people are subject to fatigue and aren't allowed to nap.

5. *Napping boosts your creativity.* Mednick writes: "Napping allows your brain to create the loose associations necessary for creative insight and opens the way for a fresh burst of new ideas."

Dr. Mednick enumerates a number of additional health benefits of napping, including keeping your youthful good looks, reducing the risk of heart attack, losing weight, and improving your sex life. If you can accomplish all of that with napping, I have no doubt that your personal productivity and job performance will improve dramatically.

Many of our greatest artists, thinkers, and inventors have been big nappers. Albert Einstein advocated micronapping, short stretches of sleep that do not take you into the deep sleep zone but refresh you and stimulate your thinking. The artist Salvador Dali believed that napping was essential to working long and well. He took a radical approach to the afternoon siesta, believing it should not last a half hour, ten minutes, or even a minute—it should last less than a quarter of a second. To accomplish this, Dali developed a technique he called "slumber with a key." When he felt tired in the afternoon, after many hours of work, he would sit in a hard chair and place a plate on the floor beside him. He would hold a heavy key between his thumb and forefinger, lean back in the chair, stretch out his arms, and close his eyes. As soon as he fell into sleep, his fingers would loosen their grip, and the key would drop on the plate with a clang and wake him up. That much sleep was enough, Dali claimed, for his whole "physical and psychic being to be revivified."

I prefer slightly longer naps, a few minutes, even a half hour, but I agree with Dali's basic idea that you don't want to sleep too deeply. This kind of mini-sleep is known as a hypnagogic nap, the scientific term that refers to the phase of sleep in which the mind is fluid and able to make associations easily. When you wake, you are more able to connect concepts, synthesize, and come up with new approaches to tough issues. You do not wake up feeling groggy and out of it.

I like to think I am the world's best sleeper. I have no evidence to support that claim, but I know that I value sleep, can fall asleep quickly, and feel better, more productive, and more creative when I sleep well and often. I also know that things come into my mind while asleep and that I often wake up with a new question about or, better yet, a new answer to issues that I have been obsessing about.

Traditional corporate culture frowns on daytime, on-the-job napping. But I'm with Winston Churchill on this. "Don't think you will be doing less work because you sleep during the day," he wrote. "That's a foolish notion held by people who have no imaginations."

. . .

Right up there with physical fitness comes learning: mental strength and flexibility. Your ability to formulate good questions, to listen well, to understand the habits of civility, to avoid stereotyping, and to engage with different thinking styles (and avoid biases) is greatly enhanced by your awareness of the world around you, your openness to a range of ideas and people. In short, your embrace of learning.

I advocate two practices for learning: travel and reading.

Every year we travel as a family and visit a different place each trip. One thing I like about traveling is the opportunity to meet people unlike me and go where the experience will shake me up in some way, provide new insight on the status quo I am used to. Not long ago, we visited Dubrovnik, Croatia. It was beautiful and it was also fascinating and I learned a lot. The people of Croatia lived through a brutal war, which influences how they think and behave. They have an edge to them that is distinct and striking. They're not overly charming and don't care to be, but their directness is compelling. I met a young man there, and we talked about what it was like living under the cloud of war. "It was great!" he said. "I didn't have to go to school!" You will not likely get that kind of exchange lying on the beach reading a paperback.

Such journeys make me think about the kinds of experiences my colleagues and employees have lived through and how that affects their views and behaviors. It also further sensitized me to cultural and social conditions in countries outside the United States. So travel when you can. And when you travel, seek out differences, not just the expected. If you travel for work, next time you have a meeting in some unfamiliar place, don't schedule your flights for the greatest efficiency of time. Don't fly out three seconds after the meeting is over. Add on a day, or even a few hours, to get out of the hotel and look around. I don't always follow my own advice, but when I do, I vow to keep pushing myself to do so. It was on business trips that I explored Rio de Janeiro, saw Tabletop Mountain in South Africa, and visited the Forbidden City in Beijing. (If you want to ponder the characteristics of an authoritarian culture, this palace to twenty-four Chinese emperors over a period of five centuries is a good place to start.) While on vacation in the Maldives, I got a look at the incredible variety of lifestyles available there.

In addition to getting out of the hotel, it's important to get out of the filter bubble of our algorithmic-driven society. Websites like Facebook and Google and personalized news feeds deliberately customize information to your current likes and dislikes, which means you are exposed to less material that challenges your status quo thinking. I make it a point to check in with information sources and media venues from different places and perspectives, especially those that don't align with my views. One easy way to do that is to visit the online Drudge Report, which has links to dozens of news and opinion sites around the world. Read books and articles, nonfiction and fiction.

Reading is like walking for the brain. Reading improves mental health, opens the mind, educates, entertains, and provides insight into people you will never meet and worlds you would never otherwise visit. For example, I would recommend Adam Grant's book, *Give and Take: Why Helping Others Drives Our Success*, particularly for his thoughts about how people interact by encouraging or challenging one another. He writes: "Every time we interact with another person at work, we have a choice to make: do we try to claim as much value as we can, or contribute value without worrying about what we receive in return?" Grant concludes that people who give more than take end up as the most successful, in many ways.

. . .

If I had to pick one activity that has promoted my learning and stretched me in multiple ways, it has been my service as a board director on companies unlike my own. I hasten to say that board service of almost any kind, and any level, is incredibly valuable. It can be a school board, a community organization, a not-for-profit, the committee of a sports league, a hospital board, the board of a local charity, a special committee of an educational establishment at a college or university. They will all test you. They all are looking for good, committed, engaged people.

My first board assignment came in April 1996, when I was running Blockbuster Europe. A headhunter called to ask if I might be interested in joining the board of directors of Limelight Group PLC—a maker and retailer of kitchen, bathroom, bedroom, and conservatory goods—based in the United Kingdom. I had never before considered board service. I was very busy at the time. But I was also intrigued. I like trying things I have never done before. I did a bit of due diligence and found that Limelight was getting ready to go public. That would be another first for me. I agreed to join the board and served for three years, but that turned out to be the beginning of a twenty-two year stretch of continuous board service on seven different public company boards, including those of Bombay, Lorillard, and Office Depot. In those assignments, I gained experience in issues and activities that I would not otherwise have participated in, including a merger and an activist investor intervention.

Board protocol and approaches vary in different organizations and cultures, but all boards can contribute significantly to an organization. In my service on public, private, and not-for-profit boards, I have not only learned an amazing amount, I have also had some fascinating experiences. I've tangled with activist investors and negotiated cultural differences in the U.S., the U.K., Japan, and Italy. I have twice served as lead independent director. I have chaired a slew of committees.

At Limelight, I had to ask a lot of questions before I could begin to make a contribution as a board director. Limelight was a small conglomerate, a kind of mini-Grand Met, with a focus on off-price kitchens. Although the company was relatively small and focused, we still had to contend with issues familiar to much larger companies and different types of organizations.

> *Should we acquire more brands in the kitchen space?*
> *What is our value proposition?*
> *Should we put more emphasis on our other product areas, such as bedrooms?*
> *Should we move into different adjacent product areas? Should we expand geographically?*
> *If so, should we test our approach in Ireland first?*
> *Or should we move into continental Europe instead?*

My board service contributed significantly to my understanding of the creation and value of the challenge culture. A well-configured board will comprise people with a broad range of skills and experiences, probably from disciplines and professions not directly related to the mission of the organization itself. I know what that is like because on two boards I have been the one and only CEO of a public company. I was able to bring a perspective about growth, finance, organization structure, and regulation that no other director offered. At Dunkin', we invited Carl Sparks to join the board in 2013 because he had deep expertise in digital marketing, thanks to his work with Expedia and Travelocity. When he came onboard, we were in the midst of a big push toward the launch of our DD Perks mobile app rewards program. Carl's participation proved invaluable. As we've seen, outsiders and fresh voices are one of the most reliable sources of status quo questioning.

That's the role boards should play in a challenge culture: they should be the challengers in chief. But many boards see their role differently. They think of the CEO as their servant; he or she is employed at their will, even their whim. Like any you're-fired culture, that environment has a squirrely effect on many a CEO. He or she begins to manipulate, dissemble, strategize, and play silly games designed to gain advantage with or over the board. For example, the CEO will misrepresent the budget in presentations to the board. He details the line items in the $100 million budget but does not mention the $2 million private contingency fund he has tucked away. Like any misrepresentation, this kind of game playing means that the board and the management team are operating with different numbers and different assumptions. And if the discrepancy ever becomes evident, it erodes trust.

In my two decades of board service, the job has gotten significantly more difficult. The stereotype of the old boys, rubber-stamp board may not have disappeared completely, but it is clearly on the way out, especially for public companies. Today, board service requires much more than showing up twice a year for some nice meals, pleasing presentations, and a few pro forma votes on foregone proposals. Not only does board service require a good deal of preparation, but boards find themselves being much more visible and accountable for their actions and decisions. I should add that compensation, too, has dramatically increased over the years. Although the median fee for a director of a private company is a modest $34,000, the median pay for directors of Fortune 500 companies is $240,000. At Regeneron Pharmaceuticals, the total board compensation in 2016 was $18,561,936, with a median pay of $2,061,064, according to a report by Equilar, a provider of board data.

. . .

I have been extremely fortunate with, and reliant on, the Dunkin' board of directors. When I joined in 2009, the board was composed of nine directors, three each from three private equity owners, Thomas H. Lee Partners, Carlyle Group, and Bain Capital. We met six times a year; we had a phone call every two weeks. I prepared like a madman for our meetings because I knew I would be challenged up and down, backward and forward, on any and every aspect of the business. Decision making was simple. If the three private equity firms were divided on an issue, I would make the final decision. They operated out of trust and respect, and I loved their involvement.

After we went public in 2011, I am extremely proud (that may be an understatement!) that the senior representatives from the private equity firms did not leave the board. Although the firms themselves exited their investments in 2012, the three individuals—Mark Nunnelly, Sandra Horbach, and Tony DiNovi—stayed with Dunkin' Brands.

In the nine years I've been with the company, our board has made a major contribution to the success of the organization. The directors have collectively and individually been a remarkable source of knowledge, counsel, questioning, discourse, and support. We have always acted as one team, which is very different from many organizations where there is a real divide between management and the board. Ours is not a confrontational or a you're-fired culture. The board and management act together to work toward success for all of our stakeholders, and key for success is total transparency.

. . .

It is my view that we are lucky to be here on earth. And because we're here for such a short time, we should enjoy it. We should maximize our experiences. And we should do what we want to do, within civil bounds, of course, with respect for the laws and customs of the world.

I have been exceptionally fortunate in my life. I have a great wife, who questions virtually every move I make, in the nicest possible way. I've got great kids who in their own way challenge me hard. I work for two of the greatest brands in the world, and I've been successful enough in my career that I can afford to go where I want to go and do what I want to do. But, even at sixty-eight, I have no desire to sit back and do nothing. I believe in the value of hard work; it's a major tenet of my ethos.

I also strongly believe in the importance of having fun, spending time with your friends and family, engaging in sports, and trying out new endeavors outside the business. Just like naps, all those things bring refreshment and revitalization. As Churchill put it, "Nature had not intended mankind to work from eight in the morning until midnight," without refreshment. A nap. A soccer game. A walk. A meal with people you care about. These are the things that, in Churchill's words, "renew all the vital forces."

The more refreshed you are, the more vital your forces are, the more able you will be to take on new challenges in new realms. That's what I discovered when I took on one of the craziest ventures of my life: purchasing a professional soccer team.

CHAPTER NINE

The Negative Normative

Lessons from the Football Pitch

don't know if I wanted to buy the English soccer team Leyton Orient Football Club (LOFC) because I loved it so much or because I was so distressed by how it was being managed.

Both, probably. I have been a loyal supporter of the O's, as fans call the club, since I was a kid, but I was greatly saddened by what had happened to it in recent years.

You've probably heard the term *normative* (often used by management consultants), which essentially means a positive standard that can be applied to other situations. The methods of the Dunkin' challenge culture, for example, are normatives that can be picked up and successfully adapted by other organizations that are very different from Dunkin'.

Well, another way to look at a normative is in the negative, a standard that can be applied in many situations but to detrimental, rather than positive, effect. That is what I believed the Leyton Orient culture had become: the exact opposite of the challenge culture. To the outsider, their organization looked closed, nontransparent, and hierarchical, characterized by confrontation, threat, fear, and distrust. In my view, it was a you're-fired culture. No wonder that in a period of less than three years, the O's performance had fallen through the floor, and the club had been booted out of the league it had played in for more than a century and dropped into the basement of English football.

Let me give you a bit of background on Leyton Orient and my relationship with the club. If you pay even the slightest bit of attention to English football, you are probably dimly aware of the Football Association Challenge Cup, known as the FA Cup, and the winningest club, Arsenal. But there are many football clubs in Great Britain, several in London alone.

Fans tend to be fiercely loyal to their club. For me, it is and has always been Leyton Orient. I can trace the roots of my passion to 1959, the year I went mad for football. I played, not very well, at my school, Buckhurst Hill County High. I followed all the local pro teams, including Leyton Orient, West Ham United, Tottenham Hotspur, and Arsenal, although I didn't really have a favorite. I devoured every word of the football news in the *Daily Telegraph*, the *Daily Mail*, and the now-defunct tabloid *Daily Sketch*. I gobbled up a comic strip called *Roy of the Rovers*, which featured the exploits of a fictional football team, the Melchester Rovers, and its star striker, Roy Race. I faithfully followed Roy and the Rovers as they battled their way to a league championship and then went on to win the FA cup. Heady stuff, I can tell you.

As mad as I was for football, I had never attended a professional game. I hadn't even seen one on television because they weren't broadcast live at the time. In October, a friend of the family invited me to a Leyton Orient game versus Sunderland. It would be my first time at a professional match, and I was incredibly excited to see the real thing. The O's weren't the winningest club at the time, but there was a lot of lively action surrounding them. Pop culture stars sometimes showed up at the games, including singer Shirley Bassey (who sang the theme songs for three James Bond movies) and American singer Pat Boone. Big-name British businesspeople sat on the board of directors, among them the media mogul Sir Lew Grade. The club's crest, its coat of arms, was cool. It featured two brilliant red wyverns, mythical dragon-like creatures, facing each other, their talons clutching a football.

The big day arrived, and we went along to the Brisbane Road stadium in the East London district of Leyton. It was even better than I could have imagined. I loved everything about the game, the team, the action, the players, the fans, the food. We played Sunderland to a draw, 1–1. I was hooked and so began a lifelong love affair with the club.

Like most football fans, I found out all I could about the club. I learned it had been formed in 1881 as the Glyn Cricket Club and only added a football section in 1888, the same year it took the name Orient, for the obvious reason that one of the players worked for the Orient Steamship Company. The club moved to the East London district of Leyton in 1937 and subsequently became known as Leyton Orient. Many of the club's players fought in the World Wars, and team supporters still make pilgrimages to the fields of northern France to honor those who lost their lives in battles there.

Over the decades, the club had its ups and downs in the standings. Football in the U.K. is organized very differently from professional sports in the United States. There is essentially a pyramid of leagues in England, Scotland, Wales, and Ireland. In England, the Premier League is at the top of the pyramid and includes such marquee-name clubs as Liverpool, Chelsea, Manchester United, and City. Then comes the English Football League, which consists of three divisions—the Championship, League One, and League Two—each of which has twenty-four clubs. At the bottom is the National League, with two tiers. Some clubs are professional, some are semiprofessional.

What is particularly noteworthy about this multilevel professional football system in the U.K. is that clubs move up or down from league to league, based on their results, moves which are known as promotion (up) and relegation (down). There is nothing like it in American professional sports. It would be like the Boston Red Sox getting kicked out of Major League Baseball and demoted to Triple A ball after a losing season. Unthinkable. Impossible.

Early in my fandom, the O's achieved a league promotion, much to my delight. In the very last game of the 1961–1962 season, our star striker, Malcolm Graham, scored two magnificent goals against Bury. The win catapulted the O's up to the top division of the English Football League. Our grandest achievement there was to pull off a dramatic win over Manchester United early in the season, but the glory did not last. At the end of the year, we were relegated back to our former level.

However, British fans do not waver in their club loyalty during these ups and downs. I was an O's guy through and through and have been for fifty-eight years now. Although there were disappointments, there were moments of triumph, too. In 1969–1970, we were champions of our division. In 1972, we reached the fifth round of the FA cup, and in 1978 we made it to the semifinal, a very big deal.

More relevant to the discussion of the challenge culture were the ups and downs of Leyton Orient management and the club's financial health. Over the years, the club had seen more than its fair share of changes in leadership. It had often struggled to make ends meet, and the owners regularly committed their own funds to support the club. A loss-making season was nothing unusual, and more than once the club came to the brink of extinction.

One of those near-death moments came in 1986 when the club was in the midst of one of its chronic financial crises. At that point, a relatively unknown figure, Tony Wood, stepped forward to purchase the club. Wood was a longtime O's fan and had made a fortune in the coffee business, based in Rwanda, where he lived. During his tenure, the O's avoided another financial breaking point but regularly ran up losses. A typical remedy was to sell the better players at the highest possible price to improve the balance sheet.

In April 1994, Rwanda was suddenly engulfed in civil strife and mass slaughter. The coffee market collapsed; Wood lost everything and resigned as chair. Money was so tight that fans kicked in £76,000 to pay off the most pressing debts. Wood put the club up for sale. Asking price: £5. In 1995, a well-known British sports entrepreneur and promoter, Barry Hearn, stepped in to save the day. Like me, Barry was a longtime O's supporter, having attended his first game at age eleven, and he brought a steady hand to the organization and gradually righted the ship. Barry came up with the £5, took on the role of chairman, and then invested a substantial amount of his own funds. There followed nineteen years of relative stability and success, with the club achieving promotion from League Two to League One in 2005.

Now we come to the crux of the story. In the 2013–2014 season, Leyton Orient reached the League One playoffs, and suddenly we were staring at the possibility of promotion to the Championship level, a higher tier of the English Football League. The deciding game came against Rotherham United at the famous Wembley Stadium at the end of May 2014. At the time, I was in Puerto Rico with the family, but I listened to the game live on the Internet, pacing around my hotel room screaming encouragement to my team four thousand miles away. We led 2–0 at halftime. O's fans around the world held their breath. In the second half, Rotherham scored two goals, and at the end of 120 minutes, the score was tied at 2–2. We went into extra time and it came down to a penalty shoot-out. We ultimately succumbed, 4–3.

In a TV interview after the loss, Barry Hearn was philosophical. Yes, he felt "gutted," he said, and had a "sense of numbness." Even so, he declared that the club was still "the mighty Orient," and he vowed that the organization would "rub ourselves down and start again next year."

That's not what happened. In June, Hearn announced that he was in talks to sell the club to Francesco Becchetti, an Italian businessman, and by July the £4 million deal was done. Barry was named honorary president and retained ownership of the club's home ground on Brisbane Road. To me, as a fan, it seemed that this could be a positive move. Becchetti was rich. He was supposedly eager for the O's to make the upward move it had just barely missed. He would carry on where Barry had left off.

That's not how it went down, and I do mean down.

Yes, Becchetti invested many millions of pounds, but the club sank in the standings rather than rose. By May 2015, not even a full year after Becchetti came on the scene, Leyton Orient was relegated from League One to League Two. Becchetti's response was to sack the manager and bring in a new one. That's not an unusual move in a professional sports team, or a business for that matter, but it turned out to be the first in a string of *thirteen* managers Becchetti hired and fired in a period of three years. Talk about a you're-fired culture.

Things went from bad to worse. Many of the pro players left the team, were kicked out, or sat on the sidelines with mysterious injuries. The team was made up of young, inexperienced players with no cohesion as a team. Loyal O's fans turned against Becchetti. Game attendance dropped. The club fell behind on tax payments. Wages went unpaid. They narrowly avoided a court-ordered winding-down order, akin to bankruptcy. Creditors lined up wanting to be paid. Fans protested outside the stadium. During a game, Becchetti actually kicked one of his assistant managers and was banned from the football pitch for six matches. Becchetti claimed it was all in good fun, but people started to wonder who this mysterious Becchetti really was and why he had purchased the team in the first place.

By the end of 2016, the club found itself in an extremely parlous, even existentially challenged, condition. It faced the disastrous possibility that it would suffer another relegation, this time dropping out of the English Football League altogether and falling into the nowhere land of the National League. This had never happened. It would be a disgrace, a disaster, a horror.

In March 2017, Becchetti was ordered by the High Court to pay back taxes by June 12 or sell the club. As the news emerged, Barry Hearn went public with his disgust. He said he regretted selling the club to Becchetti. Although he had hoped Becchetti's investments would enable the club to make improvements,

Hearn said, "It doesn't make any difference how much money you put in if you don't achieve anything from it." Indeed, Hearn said, Becchetti's thirty-one-month reign had been a "catalogue of disasters." He announced his resignation as honorary president.

In April 2017, the long-dreaded relegation happened. After 111 seasons, my childhood dream team dropped into the National League. People who cared about the club went crazy. On April 29, at a game against Colchester United, hundreds of fans swarmed onto the field screaming "Becchetti Out!" and holding red banners with protest slogans aloft, and streaming red smoke into the air. The media called for Becchetti's head. The *Daily Mail* howled: "Francesco Becchetti is turning Leyton Orient into rubbish." (He had reportedly made his fortune in the waste removal industry.) The *Express* asked, "How has Francesco Becchetti been allowed to get away with this?"

By then, the answer to that question had become painfully obvious: Becchetti had created a culture of fear and confrontation that made productive and positive challenge virtually impossible. Becchetti ruled from the top. He isolated himself. He communicated very little. Some of his managers had no direct contact with the big boss. Managers who did not meet his expectations or questioned him were fired. He ignored players who did not adhere to his ways. He sowed fear, engaged in confrontation, did not care for dialogue, threatened and executed dismissal, would not tolerate challenging up, and cared little for purposeful questioning.

Throughout Becchetti's tenure, I had watched the club closely, feeling increasing despair at its performance and rising disdain for Becchetti's approach to management. As early as December 2015, not long after Becchetti took control, I began contemplating some kind of personal involvement. But I wasn't sure the timing was right. Besides, I had heard horror stories from friends who had owned football clubs: when things go wrong, the fans turn on the owners, and it can get ugly. One of them had been deluged with twenty-five thousand angry emails when his club dropped out of the Premier League. I decided to hold off.

Then, in late 2016, I learned that a consortium had been formed with the intention of buying the club. Perfect. I got in touch with them and expressed my interest. I was duly vetted and somehow managed to pass their "no asshole" rule. I was in. Just as we began negotiating with Becchetti, the potential relegation to the National League looked more likely. That spooked some of the partners. They concluded it would be too onerous a challenge to climb out of the National League. The consortium fell apart.

Now I was on my own. I did not want to give up on my own version of *Roy of the Rovers*. I decided to put together a new group and quickly brought together several friends and colleagues who were willing to invest, but we didn't have enough committed capital to ensure long-term sustainability for the club. Then we had the good fortune to connect with Kent Teague, an ex-Microsoft executive, who had been looking for a sports club to get involved with. He had even cast his eye on Leyton Orient. It only took a couple of phone calls for Kent to come on board. Pretty soon he was staying at my house, fully engaged in the initiative. We called ourselves Eagle Investments 2017 Limited.

I began to see the purchase as an amazing, once-in-a-lifetime opportunity. Not only could I play a role in saving an organization of great meaning to me, but it was also a chance to build a challenge culture from the ground up—a managerial experiment, if you will. It would be a test of whether the positive normative could replace the negative one.

But by now it was May. The new season would begin in early August. The other clubs were already gearing up, staffing their organizations, acquiring players, putting their teams together, promoting their schedule.

We decided we would have to move forward as if the deal would be successfully completed. We would conduct our negotiations with Becchetti and, at the same time, start planning for the future.

One of my favorite management maxims is "To fail to plan is to plan to fail" or, as it is sometimes put, "If you fail to plan, you are planning to fail." I took that truth to heart early in my career, and I believe it is a normative, applicable in just about every aspect of life. If you're going to make a sea voyage, for example, planning is an essential activity with potential life-or-death consequences. You have to plan your route, lay in supplies and equipment, assess potential hazards, do preventive maintenance, and recruit your crew. You do not stroll down to the pier one morning, jump aboard ship, cast off, and head across the Atlantic. Planning is one of those fundamental but undervalued management practices.

So, for ten weeks, our consortium team members convened on a conference call every morning at 5:30 A.M. U.S. Eastern Standard Time to review our progress on both fronts: the status of the negotiations and our management plans.

Since we had little direct experience in managing a professional sports organization, we looked to other sports teams for models and normatives. Being a Boston-area resident, I had long studied the success of the New England Patriots football team (American style) and the Boston Red Sox baseball organization. Both had been brilliantly managed and achieved remarkable results in the incredibly volatile world of high-level professional sports.

The Patriots, in particular, have demonstrated how important it is to create a stable management team that can embrace and benefit from questioning and dialogue. It originated with Patriots owner Robert Kraft, who bought the team in 1994, fulfilling a lifelong dream of owning a professional sports franchise. In 2000, Kraft hired Bill Belichick as head coach, and the same year Tom Brady joined the team. Kraft planned for long-term success and created a zone of safety for the staff and coach that enabled them to question the status quo and constantly make adjustments and improvements. The Bill Belichick–Tom Brady combination is the longest-lasting and most successful coach-quarterback relationship in NFL history. The list of team accomplishments is staggering: fourteen AFC East division titles, eleven trips to the championship game, and seven Super Bowl appearances, with five wins.

Both Kraft and Belichick encourage challenge, but it looks a little different in the sporting environment than it does in a corporate setting. Challenge is encouraged but within a clear set of boundaries. One of these is that coaches and players, including the quarterback, keep their criticisms and contrarian ideas inside and do not express them to the press or other outsiders.

At Leyton Orient, by contrast, everybody seemed to be going public with their complaints. The Leyton Orient Fan Trust, a supporter organization, was critical of Becchetti. Fans had shown their displeasure on the home ground. The players were dissing management to the press.

Another of the tenets of the Patriots' version of the challenge culture is that no one is above or immune to the values of the team. This is the sporting version of the civil dialogue. On the field, Patriot players rarely engage in illegal behavior, rarely confront or argue with their opponents, rarely get into physical altercations. (They have been accused of many infractions, however, including the infamous incident involving alleged manipulation of footballs that blew up into what became known as the Deflategate scandal and resulted in quarterback Tom Brady's four-game suspension.)

The contrast of the Patriots to Leyton Orient made the importance of management stability abundantly clear to me. Unstable management—with constant turnover and changes of strategy—heightens fear, reduces clarity, and makes challenge either pointless or dangerous.

So, as part of our planning, we talked about the long-range goals for the team leadership, the kinds of human values we wanted to advocate and support, and the systems and practices we wanted to put in place to modernize operations. We thought of LOFC as a pluralistic organization and considered the contributions and expectations of the many constituencies: investors, managers, players, fans, the soccer system, and, indeed, the wider society. We knew that the Becchetti management team had alienated the all-important fan group—just as I found the franchisees had been alienated when I joined Dunkin'—and so we made plans to reach out to them in many ways, from social media to my favorite activity: walking around the ground, meeting and talking with people who cared as much about the club as I did.

The negotiations were tough. Becchetti was mercurial and sometimes hard to reach. His listening skills, on a scale of one to ten, came in at about minus five. The discussions screeched to a halt more than once, only to pick up again. Conducting due diligence on the elusive Italian billionaire proved tricky.

We persevered. At last, on June 22, 2017, we announced that we had concluded the deal. Out flew the official statements. "I have been a passionate Leyton Orient supporter for my entire life," read mine. "I feel a great sense of responsibility to the players, the staff, the fans and the community." And that was true.

Becchetti put forward his perspective. "I invested a great deal in the club in good faith and have delivered the club to Nigel Travis and his consortium without any debts to the banks, without arrears for taxes and salaries and in a normal situation with its suppliers. This is a position from which it can grow," he stated. Then came a bit of an apology, or at least an explanation of why things hadn't gone better. "Over the last two years, I have, unfortunately, not been able to dedicate myself to following the club as closely as I would have wanted." In conclusion, Becchetti went on to offer his "sincere best wishes to the fans and to the club for a bright future, full of success."

The positive response to the change of management from the fans, the media, and even other clubs was remarkable and gratifying. "Francesco Becchetti's three-year reign of terror is finally over for Leyton Orient," ran the headline in the *Daily Mail* online edition. Some fans were said to be posting the date of the sale on the walls of their homes to remind them of the day they "got their club back." It probably helped that they felt that a true fan was now in charge.

By the time the deal was done, it was late June 2017, and we had to instantly switch gears from planning to execution. Thank God for all that proactive work! We immediately turned our attention to the essential task of building a management team. We started with two key appointments: Martin Ling as director of football and Marshall Taylor, a member of our consortium, as acting CEO. Martin had excellent people skills and also operational expertise as a former manager of the club. His task was daunting because he had to hire a head coach, an entire coaching staff, and assemble the right mix of players.

Martin's strategy was similar to that described in the book *The Captain Class*. The author, Sam Walker, the founding editor of the *Wall Street Journal*'s sports section, did a rigorous study over a number of years of the characteristics of successful teams in several sports. He came to the conclusion that winning teams relied, above all, on a strong captain—not just a few brilliant stars. But it is not always possible to know who that person will be. So Martin retained talented young players and brought in experienced veterans who could help develop the youngsters and be a positive influence on the field and in the dressing room. Who would emerge as captain? The mix looked promising.

We also attracted a strong board of directors, composed of three Americans and three Brits, with diverse styles and a range of hard skills in management, finance, law, and media. I invited my eldest son, David, to join the board, not as an act of nepotism but because he brings a wealth of media and TV experience, knowledge that has become important in the sports industry, which is now essentially part of the entertainment business— and I must say, because I am immensely proud of and impressed by his achievements. Rich Emmett, our Dunkin' counsel, came on board and proved once again the value of the smart, quiet questioner. Matt Porter has a unique perspective because he was CEO at Leyton Orient before the Becchetti regime, before things went really downhill, so he can challenge us on our assumptions about what went wrong. Marshall Taylor is an entrepreneur and executive who learned the inner workings of the club's operations during his brief stint as interim CEO.

What's particularly interesting to me is that all the directors—successful and assertive people—are all attentive listeners.

They may have even sharpened their listening skills during the process of buying the club because all of our meetings were on conference phone calls. The lack of visual cues, combined with the constant strain of having to follow a conversation of several voices and of varying sound quality, required that the participants pay close attention.

Our challenge-culture roles—as sparring partners, emotional consiglieres, quiet questioners, constant challengers—were starting to take shape. It was all helped by the participation of Kent Teague, who is the best at practicing "managing by walking around." His skills truly helped us gain feedback and encourage fan engagement.

We're now working out the parameters of civil dialogue. The American directors, for example, have learned to respect the traditions of English football. The English have come to understand just how much the Americans love their sport called American football. Everybody has accepted the importance of questioning the status quo, especially the many entrenched and outdated systems and practices of this venerated sport. Why don't we sell printable tickets online? Why is the food offering so limited at the stadium? How can we use the stadium for money-making and charitable events when the team is not using it? Can we live stream the games worldwide? How can we mobilize O's fans in the U.S. and other countries around the world?

As of this writing, we are still in the process of building a future for the O's. It is no easy thing to climb out of the National League. We are doing it by adapting the challenge culture approach to the environment of the sports industry. And as we do that, I continue to learn about how the tenets of the challenge culture directly apply or must be tweaked to different situations, organizations, industries, and, perhaps above all, countries.

CHAPTER TEN

Global Expressions

*Stroopwafels, Pork Floss, and
Lager for Breakfast*

I am a big fan of the Netflix TV series *The Crown*. Not only does it cover a period of history during which I lived in England (I remember Prime Minister Harold Macmillan very well indeed), it provides some fascinating insight into the ways challenge is and must be made in different cultures.

The series is particularly strong in portraying the interactions between Queen Elizabeth II, her courtiers, and the government leaders of the day. (Elizabeth was crowned in 1952 and still reigns.) Elizabeth, of course, had complete authority over her own people at court, including her private secretaries, Allan "Tommy" Lascelles and his successor Michael Adeane. As portrayed in the show (and the portrait seems to have been fairly accurate), Tommy had clearly mastered the art of honest, direct, civil pushback—impressive for anyone but even more so considering he was dealing with so daunting a figure as the monarch of the United Kingdom, Canada, Australia, and New Zealand. Tommy was able to present to Elizabeth the hardest facts and the most deeply unpleasant truths—such as the entanglement of the Duke of Windsor (who had abdicated as king) with Hitler and the Nazis before and during World War II—and do so directly, calmly, and always with a sense of shared purpose: to find an effective course of action that will benefit all. (In this case, Tommy's revelations led the queen to deny the duke's request to hold a position in the English government.)

The queen had far less sway with the elected political leaders, including the prime minister. Interestingly enough, she was not always as skilled at challenging them as her staff members were at challenging her. She seemed caught between an old idea that deference to the Crown should be required of all her subjects and the emerging, modern notion that the sovereign should be more open to comment and change.

This tension is nicely dramatized in Elizabeth's relationship with Anthony Eden, prime minister from 1955 to 1957. The world was thrown into crisis in 1956 when Egypt nationalized the all-important international shipping lane, the Suez Canal, which slices through Egypt and connects the Mediterranean Sea to the Red Sea. Eden came to Elizabeth to gain support for Great Britain to join allies in mounting a military invasion of Egypt. As the scene plays out in *The Crown*, Elizabeth expressed her opposition to the invasion subtly and through inference, while still ensuring Eden of her trust in him personally. She did not directly challenge the proposed action, nor did she ask many questions about it. As a result, the invasion was authorized, but the UN stepped in at the last minute to prevent it going forward. It all ended badly, and Eden was ultimately forced to resign. Elizabeth wrestled with her conscience. Did she push back forcefully enough?

For me, the most dramatic instance of essential and successful challenge in *The Crown* was a sequence that takes place in 1957. A newspaper editor, Lord Altrincham, has published an article critical of Queen Elizabeth and her court as being stuffy, outdated, and out of touch with the common person. As dramatized in the show, Altrincham claimed that his comments were meant to be constructive and that his goal was to serve the monarchy. That may have been true, but he stepped well outside what many English considered to be the bounds of civil discourse when he had the audacity to criticize Elizabeth. She came across as a "priggish school girl," he wrote, whose speaking style was a "pain in the neck."

Outrage throughout England and shock and horror at court! Altrincham was summoned to Buckingham Palace and, at least in the version presented by *The Crown*, had a personal audience with Elizabeth herself. (The meeting was hush-hush, and there is some debate whether the queen or just her secretary was in attendance.) Anyway, in the TV encounter, Elizabeth is understandably frosty with Altrincham, but she nevertheless demonstrates all the best qualities of the challenge culture. (Perhaps she picked up good habits from her secretaries.) She asks questions of her challenger. She listens to his answers. She does not try to put him down or punish him in any way. She does not impugn his character. And, in the end, she takes on his recommendations—the first was that she should televise her annual Christmas message to the nation—much to the long-term benefit of the monarchy. "I very much hope," she said in the broadcast, checking her notes on the desk beside her, "that this new medium will make my Christmas message more personal and direct." And so it did.

What's delightful about *The Crown* for me is to observe this dramatization of a very specific context of challenge and to think about how different it is from the kind we practice in business in the United States. In *The Crown*, the voices are muted. The accents are plummy. There are never personal attacks. The speakers touch on controversial matters with great delicacy. Manners rule. But within all that pomp and process, there is the steel of hard questioning and rigorous debate and an intense search for solutions.

My point is that challenge looks very different from culture to culture, and in order to be effective in challenging the status quo, any organization that operates globally has to understand that. It took me some time to learn that lesson.

. . .

My first international assignment came in 1977 when I was a junior personnel manager with Massey Ferguson, the farm equipment company. Soon after I joined, we purchased a manufacturing operation in Copenhagen. I was sent over from London to introduce myself and get to know the people. I showed up in the morning and was given a tour of the facility. As I walked around, I was gobsmacked (another of those favorite British phrases, meaning "shocked") to see that more than one employee had a glass of lager on the desk. A few even had a bottle of liquor that I had never seen before. Looking closely, I could see it was called Gammel Dansk, a curvy bottle with a red wax seal containing a dark, intense-looking liquor. This was definitely not what I was used to in England. At Rolls-Royce, I would not expect to see factory guys sipping a pint at the workbench. I really didn't know how to handle it or what to say. Did this mean that drinking on the job was acceptable in Denmark? Or was it only this plant? What about safety? Did we have intoxicated guys operating machinery?

The situation was completely out of my ken, almost unfathomable. Of course, businesspeople drink in England, often at lunch, but this seemed different and totally unacceptable. As I soon learned, thanks to the wise counsel of one of my colleagues, the situation was not quite as rogue as I assumed it to be. Denmark is a beer-loving country. There is no age limit for drinking, although there is for buying. Sipping a beer during the day was seen as no big thing. And Gammel Dansk is one of those herby-spicy concoctions known as bitters, like Fernet-Branca or Peychaud's Bitters. It's considered a digestif, a healthy potion designed to soothe the stomach, not to get intoxicated.

OK, but even so. The Copenhagen company was now part of Massey Ferguson, a global corporation with headquarters (at the time) in Ontario, Canada, and the drinking of alcohol in any company facility was taboo. So, despite the local traditions and long practice of tolerance, we put a ban on drinking alcohol at the Copenhagen operation. Surprisingly enough, the ban did not raise a stink. In fact, I remember there was almost no reaction at all. Perhaps everyone knew the practice had long outworn its welcome, and the status quo was due for a change and welcomed the new approach.

There were a number of lessons for me in that experience. The first is the obvious one: behaviors and customers vary a good deal throughout the world. The second is the more important: your assumptions about local practices will be based on your own cultural background. Like my rather inaccurate assumption about Gammel Dansk, you may be getting things wrong. Just read the marketing slogan on the bottle: "Enjoyable in the morning, after a day's work, when hunting or fishing, or as an apéritif." Totally harmless!

Businesses have long contended with the issue of how to adjust and adapt products to local markets around the world, but that is the relatively easy part. Dunkin', for example, can add a different topping to a donut to appeal to local tastes without a great deal of difficulty. Baskin-Robbins flavors taste the same in every country.

It's much more difficult to create change in a corporate culture when you have not been brought up in it or spent a considerable amount of time with it. It's very easy for the incumbents to dismiss ideas for change as a lack of awareness or a misunderstanding of how things really work in that culture. At the Massey Ferguson facility in Copenhagen, for example, it was my responsibility to appoint a general manager. I asked my HR colleagues for advice and counsel, expecting that they would advise me on the necessary qualifications and skills. Instead, I got a lesson in cultural attitudes and prevailing stereotypes.

"Well, it can't be a German," one manager told me.

"Why not?" I asked.

He looked at me as if I were completely daft.

"World War II," he scoffed, with no further explanation.

Another colleague spoke up. "It can't be a Swede, either," he said.

"Why?" I asked.

Another look of disbelief. "Because they allowed Nazi soldiers to travel through Sweden during the war, of course."

Of course.

That was an eye-opener for me. This was something far greater than a personal, ad hominem attack against a particular German or individual Swede, it was a sweeping cultural stereotype that applied to an entire national group! It was a form of thinking bias that could only get in the way of purposeful, shared engagement. In the end, we hired a Norwegian—his country had remained neutral and had been occupied by the Nazis throughout World War II—and he proved very successful.

There was more. At our facilities in France, I found there was no regular, consistent process for performance appraisals. When I tried to institute the method we used in other Massey Ferguson offices, I discovered that the lack of a process was not a matter of incompetence or understaffing. It was a cultural bias. To the French, at least in that operation, all such performance evaluations methods were manifestations of the "Anglo Saxon approach to life." All that comparing, striving, competing, winning, losing. They would have none of it.

And it was not just Massey Ferguson. Later, working in the video rental industry at Blockbuster, I was amazed to learn what people in different cultures viewed as acceptable content. In Europe, for example, it seemed that nobody raised an eyebrow about explicit sex scenes but were offended by the violence we are so used to in American-made media.

Since that first assignment with Massey, I have always had international responsibility. Over the years, I have overseen offices around the world, as well as manufacturing projects in Iran, Libya, and Poland. Today, Dunkin' operates nearly nine thousand restaurants in sixty-nine countries, and I have visited thirty-one of them.

I strongly believe that my forty-odd years of international management have made me more skilled at creating and operating in a challenge culture because I have learned to assume nothing about how an interaction will go.

Everything you expect to be done in the way you are accustomed to is subject to a geographic or cultural twist. From serving drinks with ice (the American preference) to the preferred way to run a meeting (adhere rigidly to the agenda in Europe), you have to examine your own assumptions about what is normal and what is not. This point really hit me when I came to work in the U.S. for the first time and had to deal with such uniquely American concepts as "employment at will" (that is, management can fire you at any time) and limited health-care benefits.

How does this pertain to questioning, pushback, and challenge? Like Tommy Lascelles advising Queen Elizabeth, challenge will be made differently in different cultures. Many countries work strictly through hierarchies. The chain of command starts at the top, and there is no way that can be changed. Authority must be respected. Individual dignity must be preserved. So, direct challenge simply will not work. To make change, you will need to work through channels or find indirect ways to pose your questions.

In an article for *Harvard Business Review*, three academics tell an instructive story about a Western entrepreneur, a German customer, and a Chinese plant manager. The German customer contracted with the entrepreneur to supply a large quantity of bicycles. The entrepreneur subcontracted with a Chinese manufacturer to produce them. When the bikes were ready, the entrepreneur inspected them at the plant and was alarmed at what he found: the bikes rattled. If the entrepreneur had been dealing with a manufacturer in the West, he probably would have had it out with the plant manager, told him to fix the bikes, and then checked them again before the bikes were shipped. In China, however, that would have been seen as confrontation, not a challenge—an affront to the manager's position, expertise, and pride. The manager might even have taken revenge by shipping the bikes as they were. So, the entrepreneur chose a nonconfrontational path. He suggested to the manager that they take a couple of bikes for a test ride through the countryside. When they were done, the entrepreneur mentioned that his bike seemed to have been rattling a bit. The manager looked carefully at the bike and said nothing. The entrepreneur could not be sure his message had gotten through, but he soon learned that his unstated, but implied, question had indeed been heard. The bikes had been fixed, and the German customer had accepted the shipment.

· · ·

Cultural issues have certainly played a role in the development of our Dunkin' Brands businesses outside the United States, which have sometimes struggled and sometimes taken off. The Baskin-Robbins ice-cream business in South Korea, for example, has been highly successful, largely because we were aware of the practices that were different in Korea than in the U.S.—particularly regarding franchisee relationships—and also because certain aspects of the culture are similar, such as an ability to move fast and innovate.

We initially entered the South Korean market in 1985 through a joint-venture between Baskin-Robbins and a local, privately owned conglomerate called SPC Group. The new enterprise, known as BR Korea, quickly gained popularity as a supplier of exotic, premium ice cream in a country more used to flavored ices and popsicles in traditional flavors like red bean. In 1993, BR Korea launched Dunkin' Donuts restaurants, and they, too, gained widespread market acceptance. Today, we have a combined total of some 1,800 Dunkin' Brands points of presence in South Korea.

Partnering with SPC required a very different approach than working with franchisees in the U.S. SPC is a large, well-known, and respected company in Korea with a long history of its own. SPC was founded as a bakery in 1945, five years before Dunkin' was born, by the entrepreneur Hur Chang-Sung. In the early

1960s, Mr. Hur introduced a cream-filled pastry to his line of breads, and it became wildly popular. Just as Bill Rosenberg had done with his donuts, Mr. Hur's company sold its cream buns from food trucks and carts, building a particularly solid business with factory workers. Mr. Hur was also a technology innovator in large-scale baking and developed a highly efficient oven that dramatically reduced fuel costs and boosted profits.

Unlike Bill Rosenberg and Dunkin' who sold the company in 1990, Mr. Hur retained full control of his company and, in 1981, passed leadership on to his son, Hur Young-In. Mr. Hur proved to be a big-thinking entrepreneur in his father's mode and also, like his father, maintained strict hierarchical, top-down control. He proceeded to build and expand the business, by adding new brands to the SPC portfolio in Korea and elsewhere, including Paris Baguette, a bakery café, Jamba Juice, and New York's Shake Shack.

Today, SPC is a significant corporate presence with expansive operations. The company produces ice cream in its own plant in the central Eumseung region of South Korea and runs a large-scale coffee bean roasting center. In 2004, the company opened an enormous bakery facility, one of the biggest in Asia, where it produces dough, bread, vegetable and meat products, coffee, ice cream, and rice cakes. In 2014, the Paris Baguette chain, which operates thousands of outlets in South Korea, opened its first bakery café in the heart of Paris, the home of the baguette. SPC has also built a presence in China and aims to have three thousand shops worldwide by 2020. Mr. Hur's success and ambition have earned him the nickname South Korea's Franchise King.

Like Queen Elizabeth II, one would not presume to approach Mr. Hur with a direct confrontation or thorny question, especially in a public setting or without advance notice and preparation. Heated dialogue would never be acceptable. We at Dunkin' accepted that what Mr. Hur says goes at SPC. We learned that we could comment and suggest and politely discuss, but ultimately, we must appear to be playing only an advisory role.

. . .

We have not always been so fortunate in our international business development, partly because Dunkin' has been slow to adapt products and management styles to account for country differences. We have sometimes been unwilling to challenge our own practices and have doggedly stuck to an American status quo and tried to impose it on international markets.

Let me backtrack again for a moment. Dunkin' Donuts made its first small expansionary step in 1960, with a first shop in Canada, and has continued to reach out to new markets over the years since then. The expansion has been largely opportunistic and driven by the availability of interested investors and partners in promising markets, which has meant that we did not need to really understand the markets beyond our relationships with investors.

This may seem strangely unplanned but, based on my experience, is not unusual. Burger King, Blockbuster, and Papa John's all grew through opportunistic development. At Dunkin', corporate staff assisted in development and provided support services but had no overarching, long-term corporate strategy for the global Dunkin' Brands. Dunkin' received its royalty payments, and local operations were largely under the control of local management. We seized opportunities as they arose, rather than targeting key markets and adapting our offering to them.

We did not spend a lot of time in the field, listening, engaging, questioning, and learning how to challenge and engage in useful dialogue. No wonder Dunkin' had an inconsistent track record, with bright spots in specific markets, stops and starts in others, and ups and downs over time.

While Dunkin' built its presence in a piecemeal fashion, international growth went differently for Baskin-Robbins. It began its overseas expansion in the early 1970s in Canada and South Korea and went on to build a position of great strength in other markets, as well. In the Middle East, for example, Baskin is huge, the largest quick service restaurant business in the region, bar none, larger even than McDonald's there. In Japan, Baskin is also a big name, with some 87 percent of the ice-cream market.

What accounts for the relative success of Baskin in comparison to Dunkin'? Ice cream is, in a sense, an internationally understood language, and it is largely seen as an original American product. Ice cream is marketed as a source of happiness and leisure time and has few of the more serious cultural associations that coffee does. Ice cream, therefore, has a powerful appeal to people of all descriptions, and its surefire flavors—like chocolate, vanilla, and strawberry—need no translation or explanation.

Ice cream is also a delightfully flexible food. The ice and cream can be blended with a huge variety of ingredients to customize it for local tastes. Baskin-Robbins offers Green Tea in China, Spicy Guava in India, and BeaverTails in Canada (a local brand of fried dough ribboned into cinnamon-caramel ice cream). And the flavor names can be adapted to local languages and references, without changing the recipe itself.

With Baskin's remarkable success in some markets and with Dunkin's continued, if relatively inconsistent pace of acceptance, by 2017, we had achieved a large global presence, with over twenty thousand points of distribution for both brands in sixty-nine countries.

. . .

Starting in 2014, we began to rethink our approach to international markets and experiment with ways to challenge the Dunkin' status quo. We decided to take the modeling approach—by developing new expressions for a localizable Dunkin' shop and testing them in key focused markets in Europe, the Middle East, and South America. A good example is the Amsterdam expansion we initiated in 2016.

In late 2015, we appointed a new president, Bill Mitchell, to lead our international operations. Previously, Bill had been with Baskin, and during his five-year tenure, from October 2010 to December 2015, he and his team had achieved a dramatic turnaround—five years of consecutive sales growth and a huge leap in profitability for Baskin business owners. Before joining Baskin, Bill had been president of global operations for Papa John's, with responsibility for 3,400 restaurants in twenty-nine countries, including in China, the Middle East, Europe, North Africa, and Latin America.

We charged Bill and his team with finding a new way forward for international development, especially for Dunkin' Donuts. In the beginning of 2016, a couple of months into the job, they began with the questioning essential to the challenge culture but which had been lacking in our international operations.

They asked tough questions about the very heart and soul of the business: the status quo of our coffee, our food, and our in-store experience. They visited stores in several regions, talked with operators and staff and customers, and asked simple, open-ended questions: How does Dunkin' coffee rank in this area? Who offers the best donuts? The answers were not comforting. After two months on the road, no one had said that Dunkin' donuts were the best. Coffee taste ranked low in comparison to competitors.

The team decided to build on the input they had received in their discovery process to create a new model for Dunkin' development and store operations. It would include directions for coffee and food offerings, concepts for store layout and design, and guidelines for the restaurant experience. It would be a kind of development template that could be used around the world to ensure consistency of the Dunkin' Brands but that also would have enough flexibility so it could be adapted and customized to local conditions.

We decided to try out the model in Amsterdam. It was an ideal test market because we had not had a store in the Netherlands since 2000. We could have started in Germany, where we have seventy restaurants and where a transformation would likely have generated more revenue more quickly. But a trial there could also have been more difficult and the transformation more time-consuming precisely because it would have required redoing existing outlets. Plus, to open a new model restaurant in the middle of a well-established market like Germany might be seen as a direct challenge to the incumbents, almost a confrontation.

The Netherlands, by contrast, offered a green field, and Amsterdam was a kind of playground in which we could try new things freely, without risk of offending anyone or competing with existing shops. And because the Netherlands is a small, densely populated, well-connected country, if things went well, word of the new American-based coffee and bakery restaurant would travel fast. There were suitable investors, with experience in retail and restaurants, eager to get involved. Because the infrastructure and services were good, multiunit networks could eventually be built out without undue complication.

There was another very important reason for choosing Amsterdam: the people there care a lot about coffee and baked goods. The Dutch have been drinking coffee since the middle of the seventeenth century and pioneered the European coffee trade in Indonesia. Today, the Netherlands has the highest per capita consumption of coffee of any country on earth. The Dutch are also known for a ravenous sweet tooth, and Amsterdam has what might be called a sophisticated cookie culture. The grocery store shelves are lined with baked goods, including cookies, breads, and pies.

The love of coffee and bakery items has been ritualized throughout the Netherlands. There is the 11:00 A.M. coffee and cookie break and then postlunch coffee. At 4:00 P.M., as the day winds down, tea or coffee is taken again, often with baked goods. After dinner, more coffee and a sweet. And at any time of day or night, Amsterdammers are likely to stop at a café for an espresso and the cookie they call *soppen*, Dutch for "to dunk."

Given all this, if we could find a way to translate the Dunkin' Brands in a way that the Dutch responded to, that could be a huge win. But it would necessarily mean challenging our long-established homegrown ideas of what makes for a good cup of coffee, a satisfying bakery treat, and an appealing savory snack.

. . .

Coffee first.

To localize, we had to challenge our flavor profile. We had been doggedly pushing our American-style, medium-roast drip-brewed coffee to European consumers who had been in love with espresso and espresso-based coffee drinks for more than two centuries. They saw American-style drip coffee as weak and flavorless.

So, we questioned everything about our approach to coffee, starting with the bean. Flavor is key, of course, but so is sustainability. We chose to partner with the Rainforest Alliance, a globally recognized standard of sustainability, and, as always, we utilized only high-quality 100 percent Arabica beans.

With the dark-roasted Arabica bean, we could legitimately herald the Amsterdam model as the European expression of the coffee-forward strategy we were following in the U.S. market. To get the message across, we would have to steep our partners, employees, and customers in the whole coffee story: provenance, sustainability, premium value, and the Dunkin' commitment to the coffee experience—which would be delivered through training for employees and through in-store signage and graphics for customers.

On to baked goods. In Europe, consumers expect what we call three-dimensionality in their bakery goods. They want complexity, structural interest, subtle flavors, and elaborate toppings, and given their long traditions with food, they want to enjoy favorite tastes and local ingredients. In America, we have our traditional favorites, of course, including the chocolate chip cookie and the brownie, but we are also deeply attached to our mass-produced favorites, particularly Oreo cookies, which have no particular local identities. We are less concerned with artistry, fine detail, subtlety of color, and complex taste blends.

So, for the Amsterdam model, we challenged ourselves to create an American take on the *stroopwafel*. Our variation was a glazed donut, topped with half a stroopwafel cookie, semimelted into a dark-chocolate icing, and crisscrossed with caramel drizzles.

The Amsterdam developers also created a dark-chocolate-topped glazed donut that could be decorated with a variety of local emblems in colored icing. One features a ruby red tulip. Another is adorned with the elements of the Amsterdam flag, the symbol of the capital city: a crimson red field shot through with two bold black stripes each inset with three silver X's. This is a donut you will not find in a Boston store. Yet.

A Dunkin' restaurant thrives on variety and seasonality, as well as customization. So, for the Amsterdam model, the international team developed an offering schedule, known as a planogram, to keep up interest in donuts throughout the year. It lays out the in-store arrangement of donuts and bakery items, as well as the rotation of different styles and flavors, for an entire eighteen-month period.

The other major food offering at Dunkin' European shops had been the sandwich. This practice, too, was based on the American assumption that a made-to-order sandwich is what customers want, but this is not how Europeans think of the sandwich. It is a lunchtime exception rather than the norm. They think of it as a quick-grab, easy alternative to the more customary and elaborate sit-down meal. Because they want convenience and choice, they would rather have their sandwiches ready made, simple to access, and easy to buy but still a little more elaborate and complex than the typical American version. Sandwich making is also an expensive proposition for a Dunkin' shop. A sandwich station takes up a lot of internal real estate, and it involves significant labor resources in taking the order and preparing and packaging the sandwiches. Because of the cost of ingredients and labor involved, sandwiches had proved to be less profitable for European Dunkin' shops than coffee beverages and bakery items.

For the Amsterdam model, we decided to offer a limited menu of ready-made sandwiches, prepared that day with fresh ingredients and displayed in a refrigerated case for easy selection and purchase. You could grab them and go, or we'd heat them up for you. On offer: salmon with cream cheese, caprese, Andalusian chicken, Mediterranean veggies.

We also rethought the look and feel of the interior and exterior of the restaurants, including colors, textures, materials, construction features, and lighting. We worked with a Mexican designer who specified woods, tiles, millwork, and fabrics to add detail and a sense of Old World architectural styling to the space but also left room for localization. In Amsterdam, we featured colorful ceramic tile in the Delft tradition. In other locales, such as Guatemala, locally woven fabric could be a highlight.

We further developed three store sizes or expressions: small, limited, and full. The small expression would be a compact twenty square meters or just over two hundred square feet, offering an extensive coffee menu and a selection of bakery items but no sandwiches. The limited expression would be coffee-forward, with the full range of coffee specialty drinks and an "explosive" bakery, offering the full planogram of donuts, sandwiches, and savories. The full expression would be the largest store, which would offer the most complete coffee and menu selection with plenty of comfortable and nicely lit seating areas.

This range of store expressions would be essential to our expansion in Europe and other regions. By tailoring to the market, owners could reduce costs and increase profitability. As a result, we believed, the owners would be encouraged (and have access to the capital) to open new shops, thus driving organic growth in the market. This might take longer than a massive corporate plan of fast-track expansion but would be more deeply rooted, better thought through, and far more sustainable in the long run.

The first Amsterdam Dunkin', located at 147 Nieuwendijk, not far from the central train station, opened on Thursday, March 23, 2017. People lined up outside the shop from early that morning. A few even spent the night on the street so they could be the first customers to test out the new Amsterdam expression of this venerable American brand. (They may also have been tempted by the offer of free donuts to the first hundred customers through the door.) According to one news report, at least two young customers found the wait worthwhile. One of them described Dunkin' as the "caviar among donuts."

. . .

As of this writing, ten stores are operating successfully in Amsterdam. The stroopwafel donut has been a huge hit and is far and away the best-selling bakery item. They sell plenty of espresso-based beverages, lots of donuts and ready-made sandwiches, and the dark-roast drip coffee is holding its own.

The modeling approach, while directed by the home office, was developed with lots of local input and was designed to reflect the needs, tastes, and customs of the country market. When you look at the Amsterdam model, you know you're in a Dunkin', but you also know it belongs in the Netherlands.

The influence and modeling approach we tested in the Netherlands has reaped gains in other locations, including in other European cities such as Munich, as well as other countries, including South Korea and Chile. In South Korea we have successfully affected innovation through a similar kind of suggestion. In 2017, we proposed to SPC an online ice-cream cake ordering initiative for the Baskin-Robbins brand. It was a proposal supported by a business case, which had a model to follow, but the proposal was hardly a dictate and had plenty of room for discussion and refinement. Not only did our Korean counterparts get onboard, they developed and executed with amazing speed and effectiveness. Within ninety days of the go-ahead, we had an online cake-ordering site up and running.

Education, communication, and information sharing are key to making the challenge culture work in different cultures, perhaps even more important when dealing across cultures than with those within a single geography. For example, we learned early on that country managers were starved for connection with one another and were fascinated by the challenges others faced. They wanted to ask questions and learn from one another on specific issues without having to debate or come to a decision of some kind: they just wanted to share experiences. So the international team put together a committee of twelve leaders in key geographies. These leaders participate in quarterly sessions to discuss how things are going, with particular emphasis on the people side of the business.

The international team also holds regional meetings throughout the world. Their Southeast Asia get-together in 2017 attracted more attendees than in any other such recent event. When I visit these events, I conduct face-to-face meetings and group conversations. These essential meetings are worth their weight in gold, as the time I spend with attendees is appreciated and my own knowledge level rises appreciably. The international team members continue their nonstop travels to locations around the world: connecting with franchisees and investors, touring restaurants, and attending local training sessions, where the attendance by local franchisees is often 100 percent.

We have also learned that many of the techniques and practices that work in one locality can be exported, sometimes with minor tweaks, for use in other markets. In each geography, a key staff member is known as the Dunkin' Donuts finishing manager, the expert responsible for all aspects of localization. To facilitate the sharing of ideas, we've developed a mobile application that contains information contributed from finishing managers around the world. They can check the solutions from across the Dunkin' countries and learn what their colleagues are doing and what the results have been.

The modeling approach has been working so well that, thanks to the success of the Amsterdam model, franchisees in the Netherlands and elsewhere are asking: How soon can *we* implement the new model? The influence is even coming full circle. The American development team was so impressed by the Amsterdam model, they decided to test aspects of it in the United States.

But, as I said, international development is a long road precisely because it requires shaking up the status quo in cultures that have long histories and deeply rooted customs and practices. This is why it's so important for leaders to travel extensively and to engage with their colleagues and customers in local markets. Listen to them. Socialize with them. Be yourself with them. Allow yourself to make blunders, and seek help when you need it. I have traveled extensively for forty years. The more I travel, the more I understand a country's culture and how people there engage in challenge.

And the better you understand a culture, the more clearly you will recognize the potential roadblocks that exist in doing business in specific countries. McDonald's had to try three times before succeeding in France; it was only after a decade of presence in China that Starbucks turned a profit. So accept that you must work to get buy-in for change initiatives and that it will take longer to achieve in some markets than in others. Sometimes good things happen on their own, and we have multiple examples around the world. In Saudi Arabia our Dunkin' model is really successful, and our role was just to be supportive of the changes made by the local franchisee.

We still have a long way to go, but today, the Dunkin' brand is slowly taking on a more global identity. In Russia, you can buy a cranberry-filled donut. In India, a big seller is the Big Joy Paneer Delight, a patty of paneer cheese on a bed of fresh greens, ladled with a zesty sauce, and tucked into a soft bun. At a Dunkin' shop in Beijing, you can order your favorite coffee drink along with a donut topped with a fluffy savory-sweet concoction of dried, tenderized, shredded pork known as porkfloss. A "fresh salty taste of exploration" is how Dunkin' franchisees promote it. Not only is the product customized to local preferences in China, the payment method is also different—over 70 percent of purchases there are made through a digital app such as Alipay or WeChat.

It's certainly not the Dunkin' status quo we're used to, and that's a good thing.

CHAPTER ELEVEN

Overcommunicate

On Blenders, Strategy, and Alligators

C ommunication in a challenge culture is a messy process as people pose questions, engage in discourse, explore ideas, disagree, define shared purpose, and seek solutions to problems.

We like to think that messages can be perfectly honed, that people will completely comprehend them, that directives will instantly lead to intended action, that everybody will get (and read) the memo.

The reality, of course, is different. Communication is an exchange, a sharing, a delivery, and a receipt of something: information, ideas, emotions, opinions. No matter what the form of expression (a conversation, a video, a piece of writing), it will be imperfect and open to many interpretations.

The only way to overcome the imperfections of exchange is to *overcommunicate*. Communicate a lot. More than you think is required. More often than you might think is really necessary. Communicate through many different expressions. Communicate with groups and individuals. With anybody and everybody. Anywhere and at any time.

At Dunkin', we make sure there are formal, embedded, and regularized mechanisms that facilitate communication and that we also have ways to communicate in informal and ad hoc ways when that makes sense. This may sound rather obvious. Don't all organizations have communications departments? Don't they all maintain websites and have regular get-togethers? In my experience, internal communications often gets short shrift in comparison to external communications. Department or staff meetings are held on a regular schedule and proceed by agenda. Rarely does senior management connect informally with people outside their immediate staff. CEOs issue pro forma statements about performance and results and send out formal comments about important developing issues, but there is little room in such communications for questioning, push-back, and dialogue.

. . .

At Dunkin', we have a special communications situation be-cause of our organizational structure, which includes the fran-chisees—independent businesspeople who are not physically located in company facilities. They are, if you will, outside in-siders. They are insiders because they run Dunkin' shops and are the frontline of the business, but they are also outsiders, too, because they are not employees of the corporation. In the past they had often felt more like outsiders than insiders, and we have taken many steps to address that problem through constant communication.

I am always intrigued that people outside the business find the nature of franchising interesting. They are not aware of how franchising works or what the nature of the relationship be-tween the brand and the restaurant owners is. They tend to think in stereotypes about the franchisees—that they are mom-and-pop shopkeepers or uninvolved investors. In fact, the fran-chisees are sophisticated businesspeople who play an essential role in managing the company and building the brand. As such, communication is paramount and that is why we operate with a formalized structure that provides lots of opportunity for questioning and dialogue between corporate people and franchisees, and between and among franchises themselves.

The Advisory Council System, which has been in place since about 1975, has three tiers: The District Advisory Council (DAC) operates at the local level and every franchisee in the district, which is simply a geographical area, is a de facto member of this group. Each DAC selects one of its members, through a general election, to represent it on the Regional Advisory Council (RAC). There are five regions and thus five RACs. The Brand Advisory Council (BAC) is made up of twenty-six representatives elected from the regional councils. The Dunkin' CEO serves as cochair of the BAC, with a franchisee, and members of Dunkin' corporate staff attend all the BAC meetings. The Advisory Council System also appoints various subcommittees to manage specific issues that need further exploration, discussion, and proposals for action.

So, we have a DAC, a RAC, and a BAC. Although the system has existed at Dunkin' for more than three decades, it has not always been positioned as a forum for shared influence and civil debate. During the period of almost manic growth that preceded my tenure, for example, relations between corporate and franchisees frayed, and the advisory system could sometimes look like a coliseum for confrontation.

When I arrived, as noted earlier, Dunkin' Brands had more lawsuits pending against it than most other quick service restaurant operations. That's one indicator of the prevailing mood at the time. I heard loud and clear that the tense relationship was having a negative impact on the performance of our business. When it became known that I wanted to change the culture from one of discord and rancor to one of purposeful questioning, civil dialogue, and productive challenge, others came on board and helped set the tone.

The Advisory Council System became an important channel for productive communication, for issues large and small, routine and anomalous.

Consider, for example, the case of the Island Oasis blender.

At a get-together of the Brand Advisory Council in August 2015, the corporate staff recommended to the franchisees the acquisition of this new and wonderful machine known as the Island Oasis blender. It was an industrial-strength blender that would enable our Dunkin' restaurants to produce a wide range of iced beverages, smoothies, and other blended drinks very quickly and efficiently. At the meeting, we presented the capabilities of the machine, its potential to increase top-line revenue, and the expected amortization schedule and profitability. We said that we believed the machine would benefit our customers and be a moneymaker for franchisees.

But the Oasis machine wasn't cheap. Corporate proposed that each store install three blenders, at a cost of $1,800 per store.

Yikes. If corporate had been footing the bill, there might have been no argument or discussion, but the franchisees would be bearing the cost. For multiple restaurant owners, that could amount to a big ticket. If one owner had, say, three hundred stores, that would mean a tab of more than a half million bucks.

So at the BAC meeting, the matter of the Oasis Island Blender, which seemed to me like a pretty obvious boon to the business, sparked a massive debate. We went over the financials in detail. The franchisees did not like the sound of the upfront capital investment. There were also ongoing operational issues for them to consider and pay for.

What would it cost to install and maintain the blenders?
What about training and safety?
And what about the bigger issue of strategy?
Did the Oasis machine signal a shift of emphasis from hot beverages to cold?

The questioning got intense and the dialogue more heated than we expected. Why did a blender create such turmoil?

At the time, my BAC cochair was a franchisee named Jim Allen. This is a tricky position because the franchisee represents his compatriots, but he is also the chief ambassador to and engager with corporate.

Jim was very skilled at the job, and I got to know him well in the four years we cochaired the BAC together. Jim is a dyed-in-the-wool, up-by-the-bootstraps American business guy. In 1986, when Jim was fifteen, his grandmother "grabbed him by the ear," as he puts it, and told him he'd better get his act together. His first job was cleaning toilets at a Dunkin' in Worcester, Massachusetts. Jim kept at it, learned how to be a baker, moved up to assistant manager, and then store manager. In 2001, at age thirty, Jim purchased four stores, with a bit of financial help from his father-in-law. At the time of the BAC meeting, Jim owned more than fifty stores in Massachusetts and Florida and had built a management organization with seven hundred employees. In an industry where more and more owners buy stores as investments but do not get deeply involved in the day-to-day operations, Jim stands out. At age forty-eight, he's been in the Dunkin' system for more than thirty years, his entire working life.

Not only has Jim followed a different professional path than I have, he is personally very different from me. I'm fairly liberal politically. He's conservative. He was raised Catholic and says grace before every meal. Soccer is my religion. Jim swears like a trooper. I swear more like a coach.

But, as different as we are, we got along extremely well. He played a role that I would call the loyal opposition, to borrow a British phrase. He would speak out for the franchisee position but always with the good of the brand and the company in mind and at heart. Most important, Jim and I were completely in sync on the issue of challenge and the importance of questioning and engaging in civil dialogue. Jim is particularly good at probing for truth and for making explicit those moments when an insight surfaces.

It was Jim who helped guide the Oasis conversation away from finances and onto a deeper, underlying issue. We had been really getting into the weeds on the details of financing the machines and the payback period, and there were, admittedly, some areas of uncertainty. Finally, Jim piped up. "Nigel," he said, "it's very obvious to all of us in the room that what you're trying to do is distract us with the numbers, like you always do." He said it in a way that sounded funny. He wasn't dissing me. "But, look, I think there is a lot more to this issue than the math. As you know, I'm not totally with you on the numbers, but I am getting a sense there's something else involved here that you may not understand."

I didn't know what he was referring to, but plenty of other people in the room seemed to.

"Nigel," Jim said, with great seriousness, "does the Turbo-Chef oven ring a bell with you?"

I could feel the atmosphere in the room change instantly. "No, tell me about it."

Turns out that before the Island Oasis blender there was the TurboChef oven. About ten years earlier, before I came onboard, Dunkin' corporate had proposed the adoption of a new oven known as the TurboChef. Its primary purpose was to make hash browns for the breakfast menu, and it, like the blender, involved a significant capital expense on the part of the franchisees. They had not been thrilled at that prospect, nor were they convinced by the business case. In fact, corporate had not made much of a business argument for the TurboChef. Instead, they pushed and pressured the program ahead, with the grumbling participation of the franchisees. The oven eventually proved its worth, but the process left a bad taste in the mouths of the franchisees. It seemed like another example of the confrontational culture of the time, where questioning was not standard operating procedure.

Back to the blender. "As you know, Nigel," Jim said, "I'm not very good at math." Everybody laughed at this. Jim is exceptionally good with numbers, as he's proved throughout his career. "So I'm having a hard time following your logic here on the financials. I wonder if we should take a step back. Table the decision for now. Dig a little deeper into the profitability and ROI [return on investment] scenarios."

I could have declined the request, cut off the discussion, and refused further questions. It was within corporate's purview to require the purchase of equipment, but buy-in is essential and the use of force or direct order does not create buy-in and may even cause rebellion. And Jim's challenge went to the heart of this corporate-franchisee relationship. Although he didn't say it in so many words, he was getting to the heart of the matter and making it explicit:

Does Nigel really believe in this business of questioning and challenge?
Would corporate force the matter?
Was this conversation just for show, or did it have real meaning?

"OK!" I said. "I get it. Let's table the blender for now. We'll take some time. We'll put together some more forecasts. Then we'll have another session. We'll go through all the concerns. We'll look at all the numbers."

That's what we did. The franchisees eventually supported the Island Oasis blender, and I believe it was largely because we had built trust through the process. It had been transparent. We heard the stated concerns, and we surfaced the underlying emotions. Thanks in part to Jim, the discussion didn't go off the rails. The new machine rolled out in the summer of 2015 and paid for itself within eighteen months.

Some might say that we had overcommunicated. Two meetings about a blender? But seemingly minor issues often link to major concerns. Only through a lot of communication will they make themselves evident.

· · ·

Sometimes formal channels don't suffice, especially when an urgent issue comes up that really can't wait for the next scheduled event.

That's what happened in early 2017.

It started in February, when, out of the blue, the quick service restaurant industry exploded into turmoil. First, the restaurant conglomerate Restaurant Brands purchased Popeye's Louisiana Kitchen for $1.8 billion. Then the Brazilian private equity firm 3G Capital made a huge, bold, debt-financed bid for Unilever, the Dutch food giant. Although Unilever didn't have any quick service restaurant brands, they were a big player in the larger food industry—owners of a long list of food brands, including Knorr, Lipton, and Hellman's—and could decide to make a move in our direction at any time.

So, there was instantly a huge amount of buzz. Everybody in the quick service restaurant industry was talking. Dunkin' Brands employees and Dunkin' Donuts franchisees, in particular, began to wonder, worry, speculate, too. Would Dunkin' get swept up in the mayhem? Would we be a target for purchase or takeover? After all, Dunkin' Brands is an independent, publicly traded company, with systemwide sales of about $11 billion for Dunkin' alone and corporate profits approaching half a billion. Would some larger company, or a private equity investor, see us as a nice fit for their portfolio?

That spring, the action heated up some more. Unilever rejected the 3G bid, but another private equity firm, the Luxembourg-based JAB, shook up the coffee and bakery sector. JAB and partners already owned Peet's Coffee & Tea, Keurig Green Mountain (a Dunkin' partner), Caribou Coffee, Einstein Bagels, and the donut maker Krispy Kreme. In April, JAB announced the purchase of Panera Bread for $7.5 billion. And then came the real whopper: Amazon's purchase of Whole Foods in July for $13.4 billion.

It seemed as if everything was in play. And we expected there was more to come. After all, the consolidation and reconfiguration had actually started back in 2010 when 3G purchased Burger King for $1.56 billion. In 2012, the company took Burger King back into public trading, and then in 2014, Burger King took over the Canadian QSR chain, Tim Horton's, at a cost of about $14 billion. Next, 3G picked up Kraft and Heinz, merging them in one entity. 3G made billions on the Burger King deal.

Well, we had no plans to merge, make an acquisition, or seek to be acquired. We had no announcement to make. Management could have put out a statement to that effect, but I felt that we needed to really hash this out. I could feel the tension rising among the corporate staff and the franchisees. We had already lived through a period of private ownership, and nobody was eager to try it again right away. I started to hear talk that maybe Dunkin' should beat any prospective acquirer to the punch. Maybe we should purchase another company—be the acquirer, not the acquired?

This is the kind of speculative topic that comes up in businesses all the time. Often, management doesn't want to talk because they haven't formed a strategy yet or don't want to give anything away. Or, if they do have a plan, they are legally bound *not* to talk, as is the case during a period of due diligence.

But people do want to talk about it. So, with no meetings within the Advisory Council System on the immediate horizon, I decided it was time for a quick boat trip.

For off-agenda items like this, I find it's useful to take the communication to an off-site location, and my favorite venue is my boat. It's a conference room, except it can cruise at 32 knots. Conversation aboard a boat has a special quality: everybody is removed from their normal situation. Blue ocean ideas seem to be encouraged. But it doesn't have to be a boat; almost any off-site location will do.

I invited about eight franchisees to go out on the water for a few hours and talk about the issue. They weren't official reps of the franchisees but rather an almost random mix of disparate voices. I did not have a fixed point of view. I genuinely wanted to hear opinions and ideas, ask questions, and check on everybody's state.

Everybody had an opinion. And nobody wasted time expressing their views.

"Nigel," said one franchisee passionately—I'll call him Jackson—"We have to move fast. We should go out and buy somebody immediately. Now. Right away. Before the window closes."

"OK," I said. "Who would we buy?"

He knew exactly who. He named a privately held West Coast boutique coffee shop company.

"Really? Why would we buy them?" I asked. "They compete with Dunkin'."

"No, no, no, they don't compete with us," Jackson told me, as if I knew very little about the coffee shop business. "They operate on a much higher level than we do. They're a boutique. High end. That's exactly why we should buy them."

"But they'd be competing in your territory, wouldn't they?"

"Yeah, but no problem."

"Do you have any data on them?" I asked. Because they were privately held, the necessary information, including financials, would be harder to come by.

"No," Jackson admitted, "but I have a pretty good feel for their operation."

"OK," I said. "Interesting idea."

"No, it's a crap idea," said another of the franchisee-mariners. "We shouldn't buy another coffee company. What about buying a pizza company? You know pizza, Nigel. We could broaden our food offering, just like that!"

"What! Are you crazy?" Jackson could not believe that anyone would suggest pizza.

"Why would we want to get into pizza?" I asked.

"It would give us a better handle on another day part," he said. "Bring in a whole new set of customers for lunch and dinner and late night."

On it went. My role in this seaborne communication was to listen, facilitate, restate, probe, ask questions.

The upshot? This group ended up with no strong conviction about whether we should sell or what we might buy. They didn't really want to take any action. They just wanted to talk and be heard. So, we didn't come to a conclusion or take an action. And that might be considered by some as a waste of an hour or two. But what would have happened if we had *not* had the discussion? The talk would have continued. Rumors would have spread. Social media chatter would have intensified. People would have been distracted.

Instead, this group of eight communicated through their networks, and gradually the nervous noise died down throughout the organization. I'm convinced that the boat ride—as informal and inconclusive as it was—had a calming and positive effect.

. . .

Sometimes the formal and the impromptu communication approaches come productively together. The great benefit of having a built-in structure and the skills for off-the-cuff conversation is that you can respond to special situations and deal with issues of much greater importance than whether to buy a blender.

That was the situation in late 2015, when our comps—comparative sales year-on-year for individual stores—hit a wall. Such plateaus in performance happen to most companies, often in cycles of five to ten years, but we felt that something more fundamental was going on, beyond the normal ebb and flow of sales growth. We came to the conclusion that the issue was nothing less than the Dunkin' Brands image and market positioning.

I strongly believed that some kind of reset was required. However, I did not want to approach it like a typical top-down five-year planning initiative in which the leadership team brings in a consultant to develop a strategy, agrees on it with the board, and finally presents it as a fait accompli to the company and the franchisee network. No, I wanted to dig deep into the issue and come up with solutions through dialogue, and for that, we needed to get the franchisees involved in a very meaningful way. We wanted to learn what the franchisees thought about our current situation and to see if they supported developing a new direction.

This was an initiative for which the coffee chat format and Advisory Council System were ideally suited. Starting in October, we conducted a series of get-togethers with franchisees around the country, all of them focused on the issue of the brand reset. The franchisees got incredibly engaged in this discussion.

Why wouldn't they? Corporate was looking to them to help set the strategic direction of the corporation. How often does that happen?

One exercise involved mapping the landscape of our industry and positioning Dunkin' in relation to our competitors. I have rarely seen a group of people throw themselves into a group engagement with such intensity. They were literally jumping to their feet and running to the flip charts to make their contributions.

On the left side of the industry map, we ended up grouping a set of competitors that we defined as the purveyors of cheap coffee. These included quick service restaurants like McDonald's, who see coffee as a commodity to drive traffic, and the C-stores, as we call convenience stores. These included Cumberland Farms and 7-Eleven, gas stations, and combination convenience stores and gas stations like Wawa, where you can get a latte, a salad, a snack, and a tank of gas. On the opposite side of the industry map, we put the higher-end coffee houses that provide cushy in-store environments and charge steeper prices than Dunkin'. These places include Starbucks, The Coffee Bean & Tea Leaf, Peet's, and several more. Many of these operate only at a local level, not nationally or globally, as Dunkin' does.

The exercise was conducted in the spirit of a great insight that is often attributed to Steve Jobs: "You can't look at the competition and say you're going to do it better. You have to look at the competition and say you're going to do it differently."

What ultimately emerged from this period of questioning and dialogue was a new brand strategy that we called lean right—meaning that Dunkin' should move toward the higher-end, experiential area of the spectrum but do it in our own way. (No political leanings were implied, though it did help everyone to remember it!) And that meant a focus on coffee and beverages, with fewer food products, and an experience of efficiency and convenience for customers on the go, rather than in-store dining.

It became a kind of internal rallying cry. Even if people had their quibbles with the lean-right approach, everyone understood it and knew how it had originated. They had their chance to make comments and suggestions, and they had, for the most part, grabbed the strategy with both hands.

To me that was another indicator that the challenge culture was really taking root: people who had thought of themselves as adversaries for years could now think of one another as players in an important game but one in which both sides could win.

. . .

Elon Musk, founder of Tesla, is with me on the importance of overcommunication.

Some years ago, Musk circulated a memo to all Tesla employees with the subject line: *Communication Within Tesla*. He writes that there are different "schools of thought" when it comes to information flow within a company. The first is that information should be routed through the hierarchical chain of command. Musk argues that this approach gives the manager power but does not serve the company well. It is, he says, "dumb," and leads to cumbersome and inefficient communication. Musk is so adamant on this issue that he goes so far as to issue a warning: "Any manager who allows this to happen, let alone encourages it, will soon find themselves working at another company. No kidding."

To improve communication, Musk writes that any Tesla employee should talk to or write email to anyone in the company who can help solve a problem that will be beneficial for the entire company. He urges people to talk to their manager's manager, any VP in any department, even to Musk directly. No permission necessary. He goes further, saying that employees should consider themselves *"obligated"* [my italics] to work this way until they achieve the result that they think is right for the company. The purpose of this unfettered talk is not to increase the amount of chatter but rather to ensure "ultra-fast" execution. That is the only way for Tesla to compete with bigger companies—"with intelligence and agility."

Anybody can talk to anybody.

Not only does the anybody-to-anybody approach speed up communication and facilitate decision making, it opens up opportunities for dialogue and challenge among diverse participants. As Musk put it, "We are all in the same boat."

That's why we overcommunicate. We engage in communication that runs the gamut, from relatively formal, built-in channels (such as earnings day or weekly management meetings or my weekly voice mail to all staff) and our internal social media channel to unplanned, off-the-cuff chats (e.g., office walkarounds), in a variety of formats, from big gatherings to dashed-off texts.

As with other aspects of the challenge culture, it's important to be explicit about your communication habits, to make it clear that you are deliberately communicating and why. Communication is important in times of uncertainty, such as that period of industry consolidation, but it becomes even more critical in times of crisis and big change.

This was most recently demonstrated to me during the process of purchasing the Leyton Orient Football Club. As negotiations got underway, the media, the Leyton Orient Fans' Trust (LOFT), and indeed the entire football culture was in a lather about what was going on. Of course, this was a situation where we could not divulge the details for fear of jeopardizing the deal.

But we knew that, when the deal was done, we would need to overcommunicate, so we prepared. As soon as the documents were signed, we went into overcommunication mode. I prepared a video expressing my delight at the deal, recognizing my partners in the consortium, thanking the leaders of the organization, and reaching out to the fans for their encouragement and support. I did a raft of interviews with media outlets.

I went for an interview with our LOFC media and communications manager at the time, Charlie Long, in the trophy room at the Leyton Orient football ground on Brisbane Road.

"How does it feel to sit here as club chairman?" Charlie asked.

Before answering that question, we engaged in a bit of banter about trophies and the glory days, and then I reviewed all the communicating I was doing. This was deliberate and a key point worth mentioning about overcommunication: not only do you need to communicate constantly, you want to communicate about your communication. You want people to know how much attention you're paying, how much listening you're doing, who you're talking to, what you heard, and what it means to you.

Overcommunication is sometimes metacommunication. Communication about communication.

I told Charlie about my meeting with Barry Hearn, who we had reinstated as honorary chairman, about my talk with leaders of the local council, Waltham Forest, and my chat with members of the Fans' Trust. I thanked everybody who had been involved in the sale and transition of the club. The communication went on and on, with radio, video, the print press. It had to be immediate, it had to be open, it had to be with multiple audiences, and it had to be open to question and discussion.

(About six months into his tenure with us, Charlie took a job with the Chelsea Football Club, one of the legendary leaders of European soccer. I was over the moon with his success because it signaled that Leyton Orient was now seen as a worthy training ground for exceptional talent.)

· · ·

Of course, there are risks to overcommunication. There are traps and dangers and things can go wrong. (My interview with Fox News about the immigration issue is just one example.) That is why I have been through endless media training courses, and I keep freshening up my skills. I've seen what can happen if you don't.

When I was at Blockbuster, Karen Raskopf decided we should go through a media training course, conducted by a high-profile journalist who would put us through a live simulation of crisis communications. We all duly reported to a conference room at

Heathrow. The journalist was indeed expert at his job because he had been on the other side of the fence, hounding senior executives for comment about sensitive issues of the day.

Our trainer told us that our imaginary company was in a serious strike situation. He briefed us on the details and then told us that we were to exit the room and that, outside, we would be confronted with a pack of ravenous journalists, eager for comment about this made-up strike taking place on our watch. We were instructed on how to navigate through the journalists, how to stick to our talking points, and how to gracefully leave the scene.

One of my Italian colleagues at the time was famous for his garrulous nature. He loved to talk. He enjoyed engaging with the press. He naturally assumed that everyone considered him to be a man of goodwill and impeccable honestly. He was utterly unprepared for such an aggressive set of questioners. Every comment he made provided them with a new opening to grill him further. Every sentence he uttered seemed to turn into a paragraph. Every point he made got him deeper and deeper into a morass of confusion and uncertainty. While the rest of us navigated successfully through the throng of journalists, we left our colleague to talk his way through the fray. He could not extricate himself for at least five minutes.

Media skills are important, especially today when there is so much exposure, so many channels, so much coverage. By media skills, I mean more than just the ability to talk successfully with members of the press. I mean the ability to communicate with different audiences, formally or informally. Everybody, no matter what role they play in a company, will at some point have to make a presentation, give a talk, make a pitch, do some training. A lot of us will face skeptical or downright unfriendly audiences. Many of us will find ourselves on TV or on a big stage. How we perform makes a big difference to the business and how it is perceived by the media, partners, analysts, regulators, customers, and potential employees. We are all de facto spokespeople for our company.

Social media has made it even more of an imperative that we get in the conversation; avoiding it is virtually impossible. If you don't talk, everybody else will carry on the conversation around and for you. You are almost always better off being in the dialogue. If you stay out of the conversation, you create a vacuum, and it will quickly be filled by others.

. . .

There are other elements of communication that greatly facilitate exchange and meaningful discourse and one that is sometimes ignored is humanity and humility. Perhaps the most effective way for managers and leaders to really get people to engage is to allow themselves to be human beings, to admit their weaknesses, reveal their faults, and let others know them as complete and complicated people.

The very simplest way to start the process is to ask that people call you by your first name. Everybody calls me Nigel, inside the company and out. Using first names gets rid of barriers. If I am Mr. Travis or the CEO, I am immediately set apart. It sounds remote and detached. I am not big on titles because they have such a distancing effect. Too many people have a title bestowed upon them without doing much to earn it. And if you have to call somebody by a title, it might as well be Your Majesty or Your Grace. It suggests inequality. It discourages challenge. It makes questioning impertinent.

While I was still living in the U.K., I became chair in 1988 of the London Borough of Hillingdon's Technical and Vocational Education Initiative. At the first meeting, I was shocked by the way people addressed one another. Sir and madam. The royal we. The honorable minister. And so on. I was having none of that. I mandated the use of first names only. It made an incredible difference. The meeting was no longer a series of statements and pronouncements and reports, with the occasional sideways reference to a previous statement. The use of first names went a long way to promoting straightforward questioning and open dialogue.

As far as admitting weaknesses goes, I have plenty of those and have been known to share them. One of the formative experiences of my life came in adolescence. For some reason—I didn't know why then and I still don't know why today—my voice broke very late. If I had to pick two or three things that were important in my life, that was one of them. When I was fourteen or fifteen and my voice still hadn't broken, while all my friends' voices had dropped in pitch, I simply didn't want to talk to anyone with my little squeaky voice.

I'll never forget one moment. I used to answer the phone at my dad's business. One day I picked up a call from a man who asked if my dad was in. I said no, he was out at the moment. The guy said, "Oh, don't worry about it madam. I'll call back later." Mortified. Horrified. Ashamed. Embarrassed. I literally would not go back into Dad's shop for a year after that. I didn't want to have to speak.

Then, at last, my voice broke, and the world magically opened up. I had gone through a bad struggle, and I was suddenly released from it. It gave me a new burst of energy as well as tremendous empathy for people who have differences that I still feel to this day.

I will also tell ridiculous stories about myself and don't mind when others pick them up and spread them around. For example, there's the alligator story. Many years ago I was alone at our vacation home in Naples, Florida. One Sunday I put in my earbuds, cranked up the music, and went for a run. It was raining, but I ended up going farther than usual, probably five miles. Near the end of the run, I came to a wooden bridge that crossed a creek. I was getting tired and the boards were uneven. I snagged my toe on one of them, went down flat on my front, skidded across the boards, shot under the railing, flew off the edge of the bridge, and plunged four feet into a disgusting, mucky canal. My first thought was, "Alligators!" I thrashed to my feet, scrambled out of the stream and somehow made my way home. I stripped off all my running gear, chucked it away, looked at my battered and bruised body, and had one thought: thank God no one saw that.

Of course, word got out. I must have told somebody, but I don't remember who or why, and pretty soon everybody in the company knew. People thought it was one of the most amusing stories they had ever heard, and now the story is part of corporate folklore. Did you hear about the time Nigel flew off the bridge and was almost eaten by alligators? You talk differently to a person when you can picture him in muddy running shorts with blood running down his legs and a look of fear on his face. You're not so reluctant to question him or to push back.

I recently met a young man who was working at General Motors. We talked about my book, and he asked me how much time I spend with people. I said, "A lot." He said that is what he had assumed. He told me that his boss had criticized him for spending too much time interacting with his employees. As a result, he had decided to leave the company, and I told him I thought he was right to do so.

. . .

Let me close this chapter with a word about the risk of overcommunication.

First, people may think you talk too much. I will quote one of my revered colleagues who has a standard line about me and communications. "If you want to communicate something throughout the organization quickly and efficiently," he likes to say, "the best way to do it is tell Nigel and make sure he knows it's completely confidential."

Second, you may fear that you will say something stupid. Well, you probably will. As Megyn Kelly, the on-air newscaster and talk show host, put it: "If you're going to be on the air several hours a week on live television, you're going to say stupid shit. That's just the reality."

Those are risks and they have their downsides. On the whole, however, I think the benefits of communicating early and often, with everyone, in any direction, far outweigh them.

CHAPTER TWELVE

Cycles within Cycles

Freak-Outs, Slow Laps, Anticipation,
and the Belichick Reset

T he challenge culture does not always purr along
smoothly and at a steady pace. It progresses in cycles.
There are periods of intense, all-consuming challenge,
such as the Dunkin' IPO. There are times when challenge is focused on a specific issue or initiative, such as the Lean Right
strategy development. There are pockets of challenge, like the
Island Oasis blender debate. There are scraps of everyday challenge, which we saw in my debate with Paul Twohig at that
early leadership team meeting or the discussion about acquisition on my boat.

And then, yes, there are stretches of time when challenge
is really not necessary. Things cruise along smoothly. As Barry
Gibbons, my ex-boss at Burger King, liked to say, "Sometimes
you have to let yourself take a slow lap. You don't have to run a
four-minute mile every mile you run."

I have to keep reminding myself of that because it is my
nature to be restless with the status quo, no matter how good
it is. But I have learned that people need periods of stasis, me
included. Initiatives need sufficient time to operate in normal,

everyday mode to realize their full potential. Too much challenge, or challenge at the wrong time, can mean disruption and chaos and may actually harm performance.

Here's an example, in microcosm, from Leyton Orient. We brought in a new coach, Steve Davis, in July of 2017 after our relegation from League Two at the end of the season. We knew Steve faced a tough challenge—basically rebuilding the club from the ground up—but we had high hopes for him and the team. Unfortunately, as the season progressed, our winning record was dismal. We won only five out of nineteen games.

Steve became so frustrated with his lack of results and so anxious to win that, as I saw it, he lost trust in his strategies. I will not forget one game where this became obvious. Steve had developed a game plan and practiced it with the team. The players understood their roles and the formation of the team on the pitch. But, early in the match, the formation clearly wasn't working. Rather than stick with it for a little while longer or make some minor adjustments, Steve called for a different formation, and substituted players. That didn't work. The players looked uncomfortable in their roles and didn't seem to know how to execute. Our opponent was dominating. Steve then called for yet another formation. By the end of the game, which we lost, Steve had tried four or five completely different formations. The players looked confused, frustrated, angry, and demoralized. Eventually, it became clear to us that we needed to work with a different coach who had experience at team building. The issue was about much more than field formations or game strategies.

My point is that people in a challenge culture, especially leaders, have to be aware of where they are in the cycle of challenge. Are you facing a long period of challenge ahead? Are you dealing with a one-off issue? Can you focus on smooth running for a while? Is it necessary to reassess where you are and make some adjustments?

Three or four times each year, I sense that things are a bit out of balance and that we're at some kind of articulation point in the challenge cycle. As I've said many times in this book, I strive for a balance in my life, among my many personal interests and work activities. Balance is, in fact, a favorite word of mine. It doesn't necessarily suggest that all parts of my life have or should get equal attention but rather that they have an appropriate amount of weight at the time.

The trick is to become sensitive to these moments of imbalance. For me, they sometimes come to the surface in response to an outside event that holds a mirror up to my situation so I see it more clearly. You will not be surprised when I reveal that I am particularly sensitive to the revelatory power of a sporting event.

. . .

I remember one of those moments very well. It happened Monday, September 18, 2017. I woke up from a sound sleep with the New England Patriots on my mind. I live outside Boston, so the Pats are my home team, although, I must confess, they are not the team I regularly root for. (That would be the Miami Dolphins, the first team I followed when I came to live in Florida in 1989.) However, I have tremendous respect and admiration for the Patriots organization, its management and coaching, and its incredible success over a period of more than a decade.

The Patriots had beaten the New Orleans Saints 36–20 that Sunday, in the second game of the season, but they had lost the season opener the Sunday before that. In fact, they had been routed, losing 42–27 to the Kansas City Chiefs. That lopsided defeat had thrown New England fans into a wobble of outrage and introspection. This was the team that was supposed to open the new season with a win and keep on winning. The beloved Patriots had, after all, won their fifth Super Bowl that January, in a game that sportscasters called epic. No New England fan will soon forget how quarterback Tom Brady and his squad came back from twenty-five points down to win, overcoming the largest deficit and achieving the biggest comeback in Super Bowl history. The Patriots were hailed as the greatest NFL franchise of the century.

So, fans were not expecting the Patriots to lose by fifteen points to Kansas City in the opening game of the new season. And they didn't lose by a little or as the result of some factor beyond their control, such as weather conditions or a bad call from a ref. No, they lost and lost catastrophically. The Pats gave up more points and allowed more yards against them (537) than in any game in the Belichick era, which began in 2000.

After that game I had to wonder, like all Pats fans, what happened? The team's loss made me feel strangely uneasy. If the Patriots' winning formula could so quickly be made obsolete, what about ours?

Belichick was typically vague about what caused the loss. "Bad defense," he said. "Bad coaching. Bad playing. Bad football."

But a week later, the Patriots had bounced back. They beat New Orleans by sixteen points. To me, they had proved once again that, during the period of Bob Kraft's ownership and Bill Belichick's coaching, the Patriots had created a culture of winning that embraces and thrives on constant change. They had mastered the ability to look hard at their mistakes and upsets (rather than ignoring or explaining them away), to analyze their situation with clear eyes, to anticipate what might be awaiting them in terms of competition and challenges, and then to make successful adjustments, large and small.

When things were out of balance, as they clearly were in the Chiefs debacle, the Patriots didn't tolerate them, ignore them, or try to rationalize them. They fixed them. In the game against the Saints, for example, they changed the structure of the defensive lineup (going from 3-4 to 4-3) and gave two young players bigger roles. They successfully brought into the active playbook an offensive tactic they had rarely used known as the jet sweep, also called the end around. In this play, the quarterback hands off the ball to a running back who sprints along parallel to the line of scrimmage, giving the offensive blockers time to form a wall in front of him. He can then either pass the ball to a receiver or turn up field and run as the blockers push aside the defenders.

It is truly remarkable, and almost unprecedented, how the Patriots have been able to look at themselves, challenge their own status quo, look ahead, and keep on winning. Not only do they do it game after game, they often do it *within* the game, by adjusting their strategy and formation at halftime—taking into account the opponent's strategy and their own performance in the first half. (This is just what happened in a December game against the Buffalo Bills. In the first half, their running game produced only field goals; in the second half, they went with an aggressive passing strategy that gave them the win.)

But it can take a jolt, like the Patriot's season opening loss to the Chiefs, to catalyze a moment of reconsideration. As Brady put it, the team lost because they did not have a sense of urgency. They did not have, as he put it, that "winning attitude that you need to bring every day." Instead, said Brady, "We had it handed to us on our own field. It's a terrible feeling, and the only people that can do something about it are in that locker room."

The need for a reset is clearer in a football game than it is in a business situation because there are fewer factors involved and the score keeping is so clear-cut. So comparisons between sports teams and business performance have their limitations. But that is the value of such metaphors: they remove some of the clutter and complexity and that can bring clarity. The simple lesson is that in business, as in football, challenge comes in cycles. Sometimes the team itself is fundamentally challenged, as Leyton Orient was in 2017–2018. Sometimes it's the team on a particular game day, as the Patriots were challenged in the 2017 Super Bowl. Sometimes it's within a single drive or pivotal play. But they are always facing challenge.

What about Barry Gibbons and his admonition about taking a "slow lap" now and again? I'd argue that, today, those occasions are few and far between, and the amount of time that you can afford to coast is very short. It seems that Bill Belichick, for example, *never* allows a slow lap. He has been accused of "running up the score" to crush opponents, and he has been criticized for leaving Tom Brady in the game, even in the final minutes of the game when the Patriots are assured of a win.

When a reporter criticized Belichick for leaving Brady in a game against the Dolphins, the coach, obviously irritated, barked, "It's easy for you to sit there and say the game's out of hand," by which he meant that it would be impossible for the other team to win. "If you watch games in the National Football League," he said rather rudely, considering that the reporter covered the NFL regularly, "a lot can change in a hurry." Belichick made it clear that he would only rest easy when he was absolutely sure the game could not be lost. "The only time I think the game is in hand," he told the reporter, "is when they're not going to have enough possessions to get the number of points that they need."

There is no analogous time in business. We can never really assume that the game is "in hand." Just ask the fabled list of companies that were once the big winners and were quickly toppled, from Polaroid to Enron.

. . .

I had the Patriots model on my mind when I arrived at the office that Monday in September because the Dunkin' business had just been dealt an unexpected blow. Irma, one of the most powerful hurricanes ever to hit the U.S. mainland, had swept through Florida, causing flooding, power outages, disruption, death, and billions of dollars of damage. Now another massive storm, Hurricane Maria, was headed for Puerto Rico and possibly a landfall on the mainland.

The restaurant business is remarkably sensitive to weather conditions. Customers venture out less in bad weather and make fewer stops when they do, so Dunkin' restaurant traffic usually suffers. Severe storms can affect a restaurant's ability to function normally because of damage or power outages or equipment failure, disrupted shipments of coffee or bakery items, or short staffing because employees can't get to work. Irma had already had a serious negative impact on our comp store sales in Florida, and Maria could likely make matters worse.

My antennae went up. My sense of balance felt off. We were approaching the end of the third quarter. I would be providing the board with an update in a few days, followed by the third quarter earnings announcement. I concluded that our performance for the quarter did not meet the list of expectations we had set at the start of the quarter (I do this every quarter and ask, "What do we want to see written in our next earnings call?") and, what's more, that we could be looking at a tough year-end.

I immediately sent a note to my senior team members asking them for a week-by-week assessment of comps for the rest of the year. I wanted to know their analysis of our status and what they saw ahead. A few hours later we got together to discuss where we were. I put out a rather aggressive challenge to them, saying that we weren't where we needed to be. I asked for their thoughts and ideas for a reset. It turned out to be a highly productive meeting. We made improvements to the calendar of events and activities that we believed could boost sales and make up for lost revenue. We debated some of the assessments that our franchisees had provided and resolved to go back to them with new targets. We developed some new initiatives for moving the brand forward.

Later that day, we turned to a very different issue: a proposal for Dunkin' to make a major acquisition. (This is a perennial discussion.) This one would run completely contrary to the approach we had agreed to and followed for several years: being an asset-light company. The acquisition we were considering would require us to rethink that policy. It would take us out of our current comfort zone, disrupt the status quo, and affect our balance but, once accomplished, might put us in a better position for the future.

I had opened up the issue of an acquisition just a few weeks earlier. First, I had had some informal, exploratory talks with a few board directors. Getting some encouragement from them, I made a detailed presentation to the full board, which prompted a particularly intense debate. Some directors expressed great enthusiasm for the acquisition idea, while others vehemently rejected it. In the end, the board agreed that the proposal had sufficient merit that we should form a subcommittee to look into it further. I could easily have populated the committee with directors who supported the idea, since they had made their views evident. In the spirit of the challenge culture, however, I invited several dissenters to serve.

When the subcommittee met a week later, one of the directors started off by saying, "I'm very surprised Nigel asked me to join this committee after all the stuff I said about the acquisition plan to him, when we talked one-on-one." Another of the directors spoke up. "That's what a CEO is supposed to do," he said, "create a balance of views. I'd be disappointed if Nigel didn't do that." We went on to a productive session and agreed on a number of actions we would take to move the idea along.

By the end of the day that Monday in September, which had started with a sense of imbalance brought on by the Patriots, I felt that Dunkin' was taking steps to regain our balance but that it would have a slightly different look and feel than it had in the past. Most of all, I felt encouraged that we had this strong culture and a process in place that enabled us to deal with upsets, constantly challenge the status quo, analyze what might affect balance when it seemed in jeopardy, and together develop solutions for future success.

· · ·

What a company wants, of course, is to manage these cycles of challenge to achieve long-term sustainability, just as the Patriots have by making adjustments in anticipation of future conditions and also by managing resets quickly when they suffer a setback. That is how they have managed to rack up such an impressive set of wins to become one of the most successful football teams in NFL history. Since Belichick became head coach in 2000, their record is 201 regular season wins and seventy-one losses, fourteen AFC East titles, seven AFC championship wins, and five Super Bowl victories. In the ten-year period, 2006–2015, the Patriots were by far the winningest team in the NFL. As Fox sports analysts put it: "New England has been the NFL's best team over the past decade, and no one else even comes close."

But when the Krafts purchased the team in 1994, the situation was very different. In the decade prior, the Patriots had the worst win-loss record in the NFL, the lowest season ticket base in the NFL, the lowest average attendance per game, and the lowest sponsorship number in the NFL.

They were last in almost everything.

How did they turn the club around? They built a challenge culture that has many similarities to the kind of culture we have worked to create at Dunkin', one that can deal with disruptions and pressures.

One of these pressures, of course, is the demand for short-term results. Over the years, I have had a chance to get to know Robert Kraft and his son Jonathan and learn a bit about how the Patriots operate. As Jonathan, president of the Patriots organization, put it to me: "People are always focused on the short term in pro sports. Because of the spotlight of the fans and the media and the second-guessing, it's very hard for an organization, especially the coach or general manager, to think about putting in a long-term strategy to consistently be competitive. The demands of the moment and the season at hand are always too great."

What's particularly intriguing about the Patriots and the NFL is that, unlike other major league sports, football teams operate with a salary cap and very strict rules regarding player movement from team to team. That means that an NFL organization cannot simply go out and buy their way to a star-studded team. "You're not competing on the size of your wallet," as Jonathan put it. "You're competing based on being able to formulate a strategy, execute it, and stick to it." That resonates with me. Although Dunkin' is successful and has resources, we are not in league with the Googles of the world (or even the New York Yankees), organizations with billions of dollars of cash available to deploy in hiring or any other corporate initiative they wish to pursue. We have to be careful, focused, and strategic with how we allocate our resources.

Over the years, the Patriots built an organization in which questioning and challenge are accepted and valued. Especially in the off-season, when they're putting the team together, there is a tremendous amount of debate within the management team. "Anybody who has invested time and energy into researching the available players has the right to say anything," Jonathan told me. The Patriots are known to be ruthless about questioning the specific value of a player to the team and determining what position and role that player will take on. If they do not see the right value in the player, or the potential to develop it, they will remove or trade him. The Patriot system is so effective that—with the exception of a single player, Tom Brady—everybody can be swapped in and out.

There are limits to challenge, however. Questioning and dialogue do not extend to the playing field. This is similar to what happens at Dunkin'. When it comes to how to bake a donut or prepare a latte or take an order, the standards have been set and the practices defined. The customer wants consistency and quality every time they visit a Dunkin'. There can be no discussion behind the counter, while the customer watches, about how much coffee to pour into a cup.

In the Patriots organization, the challenge does continue, however, throughout the season on the business side of things. "Ideas percolate up from anybody," Jonathan told me. "As long as they make the challenge respectfully, if somebody thinks we're doing something that isn't right in serving any one of our constituencies—the season ticket holder, a sponsor, a media partner, a fan—they can absolutely speak up. We'd like to think our culture encourages and celebrates that."

The Patriots constantly work to "elevate the brand," Jonathan said. Once the customer knows what "a brand stands for and that it is constantly being pushed forward and innovated," he said, then you can invest in new initiatives, such as technological solutions that have the potential to take the loyalty and service to a whole new level.

It is a process, Jonathan said, and it involves resets and reevaluation on both the football and corporate sides. The Patriots find themselves constantly challenging and reinventing things they have developed years earlier: "If you don't challenge the status quo, and either validate that what you're doing is still right, given the way the world has evolved, or determine that it isn't right and figure out where it's all going, then eventually you're going to fall back. No one's afraid of challenging the status quo in any element of this organization, for just that reason."

The Krafts have been around the business long enough to know how fragile success in pro sports can be. The Boston Celtics, for example, had an amazing run in the 1980s with stars Larry Bird, Kevin McHale, and Robert Parish. The Celtics tickets sold out, season after season. "There was supposedly a lifetime waiting list" for season tickets, Jonathan remembered. Then, three years after Bird retired, the Boston Garden (now the TD Garden) was half empty at game time. The Patriots, by contrast, "have sold every ticket for every game that's ever been played since we've owned the team. And we have a very, very, very long paid waiting list." Let me repeat that: the Patriots have an unbroken sellout streak, starting in 1994, with the very first game played under Kraft ownership, and continuing as of this writing, in early 2018.

But sustainability is never guaranteed, and even the mighty Patriots look ahead and think about what could cause their demise. "We want to stay ahead of the curve," Jonathan said. "And that's because we're scared and we're paranoid about going back to the way things were when we bought the team."

. . .

Which brings me to the issue of anticipation. It's typical for a company to look ahead and assume its current success will continue on its sunny path. That is the dominant thinking bias, after all: to assume that everything will turn out OK. It is certainly the preferred mind-set for American business leaders. I myself am relentlessly positive and optimistic. I am also aware of the dangers that lurk everywhere, which is one reason I want skeptics on my team: they help me test my sunny predictions.

For us at Dunkin', such an upbeat view might be justified, at least based on past performance. We've had our ups and downs since going public, but the trajectory and results have been remarkably positive. We've built an effective management team that has constantly been renewed over time and improved corporate operations significantly. We've improved franchisee relationships, welcomed new owners into the fold, and opened nearly three thousand new restaurants in just over five years. We've plunged into the digital, mobile, online world to make the guest experience more convenient, fun, efficient, and appealing to a broad range of customers. With our loyalty program and big data analysis capabilities, we are building a digital ecosystem that brings new benefits to customers and enables us to customize our offerings and gain long-term loyalty. We are well on our way to building out the Dunkin' Brands system in geographies throughout the world, from California to China. And we have delivered healthy profits to franchisees and shareholders.

It feels nice to be able to toot one's own horn about successes, but it's equally valuable to spend time pondering what a more troublesome future might look like, just as the Patriots' management does. Contemplating the negative, too, is part of successful anticipation. As any CFO or stock analyst will caution you: past performance is no guarantee of future results.

Perhaps it was my experience at Blockbuster that made me realize that planning should not always assume happy outcomes or beneficial trends. That company's eventual collapse made me realize just how important it is to consider how the future might develop in ways that could disrupt the company, throw the business off-balance, or lead to a serious bump in the road.

That is why we regularly engage in a group exercise of anticipation that we call "define your demise." We try to imagine and explore all the ways that the business could face serious, even existential, challenges.

In this exercise, we consider well-known threats, such as a weather catastrophe or the nightmare scenario of a food safety crisis, a security breach, or a terrorist incident, to make sure the relevant plans and systems we have in place are current and robust. But those don't take much imagination to conjure up. It's the out-of-left-field disruptors that are harder to see, the weak signals that are tougher to pick up on the radar screen, the incursions from adjacent industries that are difficult to imagine.

We try to challenge ourselves by looking at a wide range of information and analysis, particularly as it relates to the changing needs of customers and likely advances in technology. What emerging trends or activities might eventually affect us and how might we respond? What categories of development might somehow impact what we do?

Here are just a few potential disruptors:

Delivery: drones, personal aircraft, robots, autonomous vehicles. Home delivery disrupted the pizza parlor business. Netflix delivery of DVDs by mail disrupted Blockbuster and contributed to its demise. Could drones hover outside workplaces and dispense hot coffee? Could self-driving vehicles deliver coffee and bakery orders to homes and offices? Will customers be sending their personal drones to pick up orders through Dunkin's On-the-Go Mobile Ordering app? Should we be considering the impact of new mobility systems on our business?

Security: fingerprint and facial recognition. As we gather large quantities of data about our customers, could we become a target for hacking? Retailers are already testing various forms of identification, including face recognition. What benefit, if any, would that bring to us and our customers?

Coffee alternatives. Americans do not have the coffee tradition that Europeans do, and coffee was not always the huge and profitable business it is today. Could Americans turn to a different beverage that rivals the wonderfulness of coffee? Could caffeine become obsolete? Could coffee be challenged? Could America ever *stop* running on Dunkin'?

Demographics. What does the aging of America's population mean to us? How will consumption patterns change? Should we be considering different beverage and menu offerings? How can we continue to attract new, young customers to ensure a vibrant and sustained customer community?

Global disruption, political events, economic downturn, tight capital. What if we experience another economic trial as serious as the one starting in 2009? What if we go to war? What effect will Brexit have on our business in Europe? What if the availability of capital for development dries up? What if the supply of coffee beans or other essential ingredients is seriously disrupted?

Coffee utility. What if, by contrast to the emergence of a coffee alternative, coffee becomes recognized as America's essential drink and is made available on tap? Apartment complexes, schools and universities, office buildings, and residential communities would tout their on-tap coffee as a benefit. No need to leave your home or brew your own: always-on coffee.

Public transportation. What if transportation systems fundamentally change or improve? What if people stop driving? Drive-through ordering and pickup today accounts for 64 percent of the business at Dunkin' outlets that have that capability. How would that affect our current businesses and the selection of future locations?

Amazon attack. If Amazon can move into the grocery business, can coffee shops and bakeries be far behind?

These what-ifs could be seen as far-fetched and not worth wasting time thinking about, but that is, of course, exactly how disruption happens. At Blockbuster, we clearly saw the rise of

DVD delivery, vending, and online streaming, but even when those signals grew strong, they could not drown out the soothing mantra of the status quo:

Nothing can ever replace the in-store video buying and renting experience.
    Until something did.

. . .

In the execution of day-to-day business, anticipation can lead to very near-term and practical actions—as opposed to distant possibilities of the kind we ponder in the define-your-demise sessions. These often require reconsidering a decision or action that we ourselves have initiated but that no longer achieves the balance we're seeking and that does not fit our vision of the future. This can require questioning, altering, and even reversing a decision that was made for very good reasons, and such changes of direction can go against the management grain, for fear of being seen as second-guessers or flip-floppers.

But no aspect of the status quo should be immune from consideration and reconsideration. For example, in 2016, we reexamined the decision we had made in 2009 regarding company ownership of Dunkin' shops and decided that it was time for a different approach.

Earlier in the book, I told the story about how I pushed the need for company-owned stores when I was interviewing for the CEO job in 2008. Let me add a bit more detail to the story. I had taken a close look at the company's status and thought hard about its future, always with the fate of Blockbuster in the back of my mind. I felt a keen sense of imbalance about what I learned. I saw that, as competition grew more intense on all sides, we needed to reset the Dunkin' brand and, to do that, the corporate leadership needed to chart the course and lead the way for the franchisees. But that was not happening, largely because of the strategy of the ownership at the time. They were more focused on system build-out and short-term profitability than on long-term sustainability and building brand strength.

I believed that one effective way to provide leadership, especially in an organization like ours that is changed through influence rather than command and control, was to operate company-owned stores where new concepts could be tried, proved, and demonstrated. In other words, we would offer models to be emulated, just like the international team would later do with the Amsterdam expansion. At the time, however, Dunkin' was 100 percent franchisee owned. There were no company-owned stores.

However, there was one factor that probably turned the tide: the planned IPO. If the board had simply wanted to sit on their investment and milk it as a cash cow, they probably would not have approved an investment in company-owned stores. But to make Dunkin' an attractive investment opportunity for shareholders, it had to be seen as a company with committed leadership, a powerful brand, great operations, and plans for a bright future.

I was hired, and in the questioning I did in the period after I started, it became clear that the need for company-owned stores was even greater than I had realized. Several franchisees explained to me that the corporate operations managers, who were the closest and most vital link between Dunkin' corporate and the franchised stores, did not have the skills required to translate new company initiatives into workable on-the-ground practices. They lacked executional expertise and what the franchisees called operational feel. They were good at coming up with fine-sounding schemes but were not so good at making them work in practice. This would be a stumbling block in our efforts to reset the brand.

So, we agreed to get some company stores up and running as quickly as possible. Over the next eighteen months, the rotten state of the economy provided us with the opportunity to bring a number of existing stores into the company fold. One franchisee who owned restaurants in Las Vegas and in Buffalo went bankrupt, and we acquired them. We were also able to buy stores in Dallas and Atlanta.

Although these stores helped us in building the brand in the South, we knew they wouldn't be as useful as models in the Northeast, the stronghold of the Dunkin' Donuts brand. But there were no faltering franchises there. In fact, a Dunkin' shop in the Northeast is considered to be "gold dust," an almost surefire ticket to wealth creation. The data bear this out. In the restaurant industry, the value of a restaurant when it is being sold varies considerably, but a reasonable average would be seventy-five to eighty cents on the dollar of sales of a store. In the Northeast, the average for a Dunkin' Donuts store is usually above $1.30 and could go as high as $1.40. That is based on the fact that a Dunkin' operation can generate profits almost twice the industry average, so franchisees tend not to sell. They prefer to expand and build their businesses rather than cash out.

Sure enough, there were no franchisees who wanted to sell any of their Northeast stores to the company. What's more, they argued that they, not the corporation, should have the opportunity to buy any stores—or develop any new sites—that became available in the region. They did not want to think of themselves as competing with the company, and with company-owned stores, for business. (I should add that most companies in the quick service restaurant business do own some outlets. McDonald's, Burger King, Papa John's, and Sonic, for example, all own between 10 and 20 percent of their units.)

The dialogue between management and franchisees on this issue was, as you might imagine, heated and prolonged, and in the end, we went ahead and opened several new company outlets. The franchisees understood why we were doing it, although they didn't particularly like it. However, because we had made our purpose clear, we were able to move forward without alignment but also without antagonism.

The move proved prescient. In order to successfully go public, we needed to improve our operations significantly, and having company models was instrumental in implementing many of the improvements I've mentioned, from new product introductions to online ordering. Most important, it helped our operations managers sharpen their skills in execution and restaurant feel.

Now we come to the reset. In 2016, we had achieved the goals we had set for operating company-owned stores. By paving the way in Las Vegas, Dallas, and Atlanta, we had demonstrated the potential of those markets and a strong group of franchisees were willing to buy in. By modeling new practices in the Northeast, we had sharpened up our operations throughout the system. Now I anticipated that—with improved operational corporate skill and better engagement with the franchisees— we could effectively test new products and systems in selected franchise stores and that this would further strengthen the relationship between corporate and franchisees. Company-owned stores might now become a barrier rather than a pathway.

By the end of 2016 we had sold all our company stores, and it is working well. Will we revisit that decision sometime in the future? Almost certainly.

Organizations of every type, for profit and not for profit, need to develop the ability to reconsider and reset because conditions change and processes become moribund. The Greater Boston Food Bank (GBFB), for example, has fine-tuned this skill under the leadership of Catherine D'Amato, president and CEO. (My wife, Joanna, sits on the board of directors.) Founded in 1974, the GBFB now delivers sixty million pounds of food every year to feed more than 140,000 people every month. The organization, which began with modest funding and ambitions, is now the leading hunger-relief agency in New England and one of the largest in the country. It is a true success story.

Why? Precisely because the organization, following Catherine's lead, goes through a process of challenge and reinvention in all of its activities. For example, they pay close attention to the nuts and bolts of the supply chain, which enables them to source food and deliver it effectively to places of greatest need. They constantly look for ways to remove barriers to make the process as frictionless as possible. They have also rethought and redefined their mission. It is no longer just about providing food to people who are hungry. They see food as a form of medicine and, accordingly, have developed partnerships with healthcare providers to customize their offerings so as to help improve health outcomes—such as the mitigation of type 2 diabetes.

Anticipation has many such short-term and practical benefits.

For example, long before Hurricanes Irma and Maria hit Florida in 2017, I had seen the intense impact that weather events can have on the business. I was at Burger King in 1992 when Hurricane Andrew struck and damaged our Miami headquarters badly enough that we had to vacate for two years while it was restored to operation. I have witnessed the effects of several other hurricanes, as well as other disasters, including several plane crashes.

Every such calamity delivers a lesson, and I have learned to expect, and plan for, the worst. That anticipation paid off during Hurricane Irma, which made U.S. landfall in the fall of 2017. At the height of the storm, we had to close over nine hundred stores. But the team had anticipated the possible effects and responded fast. We provided donuts, coffee, water, and ice cream to shelters. Our franchisees found places for employees and others to stay for the duration of the storm. They distributed free food and coffee to first responders. They donated funds to relief agencies. We would not have been able to respond so quickly and well if we had not applied what we had learned in the past and anticipated what could happen in the future. I saw an exceptional example of this kind of resilience when I visited the Four Seasons Resort in Kuda Haraa in the Maldives in 2017. The resort—like most of the facilities in the islands, which are located in the Indian Ocean about seven hundred miles from the southern tip of India—was devastated by the effects of an undersea earthquake in December of 2004. While the resort was rebuilding and getting back on its feet, management did not let any employees go, even though there were no guests to serve. Rather, they sent many staff members to locations around the world for further training. The end result was that the employees became tremendously loyal to the management, the resort, and the company. From devastation came renewed commitment and deep engagement.

. . .

Perhaps it is just my nature to be aware of these cycles of challenge and to try to anticipate what might come next. The family joke is that, when we're on vacation, I'm always planning the next one. Perhaps I am more willing to dwell on the issue of demise than other senior leaders are and more convinced about the importance of anticipation. But I believe the capacity to face adversity and achieve a reset, cycle after cycle, is essential for the long-term health of a company and also for the society in which the company operates.

The Social Value of Challenge

S omething quite disturbing can happen to senior leaders, managers, and indeed any employee who lives and
works in a traditional, hierarchical culture, especially
(but not exclusively) that of a large company. They become so
used to living in the bubble of their isolated culture, so accustomed to people agreeing with them, and so focused on their
internal issues that they actually lose some of their ability to em-
pathize with other people and their capacity to hear and accommodate views that don't fit neatly with their own.

Jerry Useem, a business researcher and author, explored this
phenomenon at length and reported on some remarkable dis-
coveries. For example, a neuroscientist who had looked into the
brains of powerful people found that they lacked capacity for
the neural process known as mirroring, which essentially enables
people to understand and feel the emotions of others.

This is sometimes known as the power paradox, a negative
effect that comes about as the result of having too much power
and authority. It is similar to a kind of brain damage that reduces
one's ability to read other people. Those with this diminished
capacity lose the ability to comprehend individual traits of other
people, especially those with whom they have little regular contact, and so fall back on stereotypes and on visions and general
conceptions of how people should behave in a company.

This is also sometimes called the hubris syndrome, another way to characterize the mental disorder caused by having held too much power for too long. John Stumpf, former CEO of Wells Fargo, has been "diagnosed" with the syndrome. According to many accounts, he did not seem remorseful about the company's abuses in his congressional hearing. Instead, he seemed unable to comprehend what was happening to him. He was completely unused to being questioned so directly and challenged so vehemently. No wonder he had been able to initiate, approve, or tolerate the kind of malpractices that got Wells Fargo into such trouble—including opening as many as three million accounts without customer knowledge or consent, charging unwarranted fees, and other infractions.

Political leaders, such as a president or national officeholder, are even more susceptible to the power paradox because they are so powerful, so isolated, so completely surrounded by people seeking favor and influence. The president who does not have a sense of shared purpose, does not answer to a higher calling, does not listen, does not have a reverence for truth seeking, and does not tolerate questioning and challenge can really go off the rails into narcissism, blame placing, revenge, delusion, and tyranny. History is full of examples of such tyrants, from Henry VIII, who almost bankrupted England to pay for his extravagant lifestyle and severed relations with the Catholic Church to accommodate his desire for a divorce, to Kim Jong-un, who in 2017 threatened nuclear war to puff up his personal status as a world leader.

In a challenge culture, where people engage and debate, where the discourse can go up, down, and sideways, the senior leaders do not enjoy that kind of unquestioned power. Indeed, the research shows that the kind of challenge practices I've been discussing can help prevent the behavior that comes from holding great power in large organizations. One of the most important of these is to have people around you, whether at work or at home, who will pose questions, make direct statements, and engage in real dialogue that can keep a leader grounded.

Researchers also believe that people in power who have had the experience of being powerless at some time in their lives are less likely to fall into the hubris trap.

Abraham Lincoln offers an example of such a leader. He was raised poor and lived a humble life before his presidency. When facing the incredible challenge of eradicating slavery, he assembled a leadership team of people who not only disagreed with him but had actually opposed him in the presidential election. He created what historian Doris Kearns Goodwin famously termed a "team of rivals."

Although I had not been aware of this research into the power paradox and the hubris syndrome until recently, I have long watched these behaviors play out and have done my best to avoid them. The very structure at Dunkin', with independent franchisees who have their own authority, and the emphasis on lots of communication through both regular channels and ad hoc engagements are important factors in keeping us on the straight and narrow. A lean headquarters operation also contributes, as does a management team with members who are expected—even obligated—to ask questions, engage in purposeful dialogue, and pose challenges.

. . .

Another important contributor in avoiding the concentration of power and the creation of cultures of fear and confrontation is inclusion. The inclusion of people of different cultural alignments, thinking styles, and genders and gender identities almost automatically improves the chances that the status quo will come into question.

We live in an era, however, in which the importance of inclusion is being challenged in many arenas. We have a White House that is whiter and more male than any in recent history and where loyalty is often more valued than questioning and where civil dialogue is hardly practiced at all. We see police departments coming in for criticism for their exclusionary promotion practices. Elite colleges and universities are struggling to achieve the kind of inclusion they want. The worlds of technology and finance are largely male dominated.

The challenge culture is always strengthened by the inclusion of diverse voices and multiple viewpoints. While I wrote this, the president was in a public battle with the NFL regarding the players who protest what they see as racial injustice by taking a knee during the playing of the National Anthem at the start of the game. The president called for such players to be fired. This provoked a response from many players and owners, including Robert Kraft, who counts himself as a friend to the president. His statement underscores the Patriots' commitment to the challenge culture. "I am deeply disappointed by the tone of the comments made by the President," Kraft wrote, appropriately enough, in a tweet. "I am proud to be associated with so many players who make such tremendous contributions in positively impacting our communities. Their efforts, both on and off the field, help bring people together and make our community stronger." He went on to say that "political leaders could learn a lot from the lessons of teamwork and the importance of working together toward a common goal" and concluded that he supported the players' right "to peacefully affect social change and raise awareness in a manner that they feel is most impactful."

Companies struggle getting inclusion right, just as sports teams, governments, police departments, and universities do. Sometimes it takes a jolt to provoke questions and spur action for change.

At Dunkin', we had just such a jolt in March 2016, at the company conference we hold each year for corporate employees and field staff. The conference is designed to provide the Dunkin' staff of about one thousand people with an overview of the business and plans for the future, as well as a chance to interact with one another and the leadership team.

After the conference, we asked for comments, and the feedback we got was an eye-opener. Many of the women respondents described their amazement at the sight of the senior management team when they went onstage to make their presentation. No women in the group. All men, most in their forties.

One female vice president for Dunkin' Donuts U.S. told me later that she saw that moment as a "stark wake-up call for a lot of people" in the company. The audience was far more diverse than the leadership group onstage. Our customers come in every conceivable human variation. But here were five guys, all of whom looked alike. How much of a challenge could they pose to each other?

That had a powerful effect on me, and we began to talk about what we could do. I took another look at an employee resource group called WIN for Women, which was established several years ago and is meant to bring together and provide support for women in the company. This is one of several employee resource groups, but it had lost a little steam over the years, and I wondered if it was really adding value to its members or to the organization. Karen Raskopf, too, had her doubts, and we talked about how WIN could be reinvigorated.

Around that time, Karen was approached by a gay employee, I'll call him Chris, who wanted to start a new employee resource group, this one for the LGBTQ community. Karen asked Chris why he thought it was necessary, since we're a relatively small company with a pretty open culture. He explained to Karen the difficulties of being gay that still exist in corporate America. "It's hard to be fully yourself," Chris said.

That struck a chord. How can you mount a challenge in an environment where you don't feel included and supported for who you truly are? How can you engage in civil dialogue if your very identity is in question or you fear your viewpoints could be dismissed based on gender identity or cultural background?

And so Chris and some colleagues put together a plan for an LGBTQ employee resource group and kicked it off soon thereafter. The impact was amazing. People throughout the company felt proud that such an employee resource group could be formed. People in the group were empowered because they suddenly had a voice they had never had before. And, for management, the groups proved to be an invaluable resource because we could go to them to discuss specific issues and test ideas that might affect people—employees and customers—who identify as they do. Their contributions fortified the challenge culture at Dunkin' by building another mechanism for dialogue—and horizontal challenge—into the organization.

The WIN for Women group, too, took on new energy. More women attended, and to our surprise and delight, many men turned out as well. We brought in provocative, even controversial, speakers. At one session, the guest was Nicole Lapin, the broadcaster, businessperson, and author of the book *Boss Bitch*. She was challenging in every way, in her thinking and in the way she expressed her ideas. The major benefit of these sessions was that they sharpened the focus on the challenges women face, not just for those who attended but also for the whole company—word spread quickly.

In addition to encouraging the employee resource groups, I started holding women-only Coffee Chats. The goal was to identify issues that women were dealing with and, in particular, the barriers—real or perceived—that women in our organization felt were preventing them from progressing. These sessions gave me a much better understanding of the range and quality of talent in our organization. They also made me aware that policy changes were needed to help make women more successful. It was the Coffee Chat discussion that I discussed earlier, for example, that led to improvements in the family leave policy.

One of the most important issues for women in corporate America is their presence in the leadership ranks. It's hugely important for women throughout an organization, especially younger women and those just joining, to see women occupying positions at the highest levels in the company. "You can't be what you can't see," as Sherrill Kaplan has said to me many times. You need to relate to people in leadership, and if you don't see anyone who looks like you or acts like you in leadership, then you say to yourself, "Maybe this isn't the place for me, long term."

The issue of the balance of women leaders is chronic in American business. *Harvard Business Review* reported the dramatic findings of a study that looked at female leadership around the world and in a range of industries. "In 2017 women make up 25 percent of senior executives in the thousands of companies covered by the survey. That hasn't changed much in the past 13 years." That's a global average; the U.S. came in at 23 percent in 2017. In 31 percent of U.S. companies, there are no women senior leaders at all. Financial services rate at the bottom of the list of industries, with women comprising just 16 percent of executives. Travel, tourism, and leisure rates far higher than any other sector, at 37 percent female leadership.

Over the last several years, we at Dunkin' Brands have worked hard to improve our performance at bringing women into leadership positions. In our succession planning and management development meetings, we have constantly looked to identify women who are already in the organization who could be candidates for senior management positions.

For us, the effort has been made more difficult than perhaps it should be because of our position in the great corporate food chain. Many companies are looking to bring more women into leadership roles and are happy to poach great candidates when they find them. We had two very strong women candidates for senior leadership roles, both of whom were hired away to take bigger roles in larger companies. They were outstanding performers, but given the relatively small size of our company, they decided they could not pass up these significant opportunities. (One of them, as I mentioned earlier, went on to head up human resources for Nordstrom.)

One's stated commitment to supporting women in leadership roles can at times be put to a very real and highly visible test. That happened in 2017, when our chief financial officer, Paul Carbone, left Dunkin' to take a much-wanted general management position as chief operating officer with another company in an industry he knew well from previous experience.

We had already identified Paul's likely replacement, Kate Jaspon, but assumed that Paul would not be leaving his position for several years and Kate would have sufficient time to be groomed and to ready herself for the job. As it happened, we had little notice of Paul's departure. The board unanimously agreed to move Kate into the position of acting CFO.

There was risk involved, as there would be with any successor of a successful and long-serving senior executive, especially one in need of a bit more seasoning. The central challenge was not a matter of Kate's competence or expertise but her own capacity to see herself in such an important leadership role, especially in a challenge culture where she would be expected to question and be questioned, engage in dialogue, and offer challenge when she felt it was required.

This is a well-documented issue for women who take on leadership roles. In her book *Lean In*, Sheryl Sandberg, COO of Facebook, talks about how women think about the risks involved in taking on new and unexpected assignments and how they may weigh the benefits and difficulties differently than men do. This was a major topic of discussion at the Women's Foodservice Forum that I mentioned earlier and an issue that Ellen Brennan, the wingsuiter, and I talked about at length onstage.

As a group of researchers put it, for many women, coming to "see oneself, and to be seen by others, as a leader" is a "fragile process." The threats do not come from the mere act of promotion, the acquisition of new skills, or adapting your behaviors to the new role. "It involves a fundamental identity shift," they wrote. The problem then is that companies "inadvertently undermine this process when they advise women to proactively seek leadership roles without also addressing policies and practices that communicate a mismatch between how women are seen and the qualities and experiences people tend to associate with leaders."

We knew that we could not simply thrust Kate into such a key position without a good deal of support. Two board members with relevant experience stepped up to act as her mentors, and we secured a third mentor from outside the company. I also worked with some of Kate's colleagues to identify ways they could work with her as she moved into the role, by helping her think through tough decisions, as needed, and providing encouragement and support.

It would have been easy to avoid taking a risk on Kate. We could have made it clear she would be taking the position on an interim basis and conducted a search for candidates outside the company. But I truly believe that the stability of the management team, the sense of commitment to people within the company, and the unity of purpose in helping a new person succeed contribute to the challenge culture. A global company, operating in a complex, fast-changing world, requires diversity of viewpoints and thinking.

It worked with Kate, and within two months, we removed the word *acting* from her title. Eight months in I am so pleased we made the move, and the board members are delighted with what she is doing. Kate joined Karen Raskopf on our senior leadership team. We have plenty of work to do when it comes to inclusion. But at least now, when our management team goes onstage to make a presentation, women in the audience *can* see what they could become as a senior leader.

. . .

The issue of succession brings up another characteristic that I believe is key to creating a strong, sustainable challenge culture: stability. As we've discussed, people will be more likely to speak up in an environment that is stable, where the values are understood, and the guidelines of behavior are clear and consistently observed over a significant period of time. In other words, a place where they feel reasonably safe and that the risks of questioning and making a challenge are relatively minor. (Is any place completely safe or totally risk-free?)

Such stability comes largely from the leadership team and from its consistent performance over time. We have seen over and over again how constant disruption in the management ranks creates turmoil and uncertainty. Will the new person understand how the challenge culture works? Will they expect to be questioned? Will they be interested in dialogue? These questions can only be answered in real situations of the kind I've discussed.

When I joined Dunkin', I knew that I would have to change a number of people precisely because they didn't fit with the challenge culture I envisioned. But I did not do a purge of the kind we did at Burger King. Instead, I made changes in a gradual way so that the organization wasn't destabilized, and over time I established a core group of people who have remained with me for a number of years. As I've said, even three representatives of the private equity owners remain on the board six years after the IPO.

Stability of the culture makes it easier to adapt to the inevitable changes to the makeup of the management team that do naturally occur over a period of years. During the time I was working on this book, for example, we lost three senior members of the leadership team—my sparring partner Paul Carbone, who took a more senior position at another company, and two others who retired.

I was delighted because it's always good to see your people getting on in the world, and I'm happy with the record that Dunkin' has in that regard. But what makes me even happier is that their departures did not destabilize our organization. That's partly because the culture is now so established that it transcends individuals. And it is partly because several core members of the original team are still in place, including Rich Emmett, Karen Raskopf, and Scott Murphy, who brilliantly helped transform the Dunkin' culture he joined in 2004 through his focus on data and fact-based decision making.

So, a great benefit of stability is that people can leave and others can join, both from outside and from within the ranks, without undue disruption. However, what I have found is that each new person who moves into a leadership role embraces the idea of the challenge culture differently. This requires that others on the team, including the CEO, make an effort to understand the new person's style and how he or she will interpret and practice the tenets of the culture. Everybody has to pay attention and adjust his or her style as needed.

This was true when Kate replaced Paul in the CFO position. She very definitely does not operate in the Carbone mode, always walking right up to the edge of confrontation without crossing the line. Kate challenges in her own quieter way. Nor can I expect that I will have another Paul Twohig who so thoroughly understood my approach and was so adept at knowing when and how much to challenge. Nor, for that matter, am I likely to work with another Jim Allen, who could deflate the tension from a situation with humor and cheek. The new players will play differently, bringing their unique talents and approaches to the enterprise. And, in a reciprocal process, they will affect the culture, just as the culture affects them.

This is a positive development because it means that the stability does not become stiffness. The challenge culture must be, by definition, flexible and resilient, capable of adjusting through one cycle after another. As I was finishing this book, we came to the ultimate proof of the stability and resilience of our culture. David Hoffmann, who came on board as president of Dunkin' Donuts U.S. and Canada in October 2016, moved into the CEO role and I continue as chairman. No doubt Dave will make adjustments and changes as time goes along, but the fundamental values and practices of the challenge culture remain as strong as ever.

. . .

A company with a sturdy challenge culture is able to adapt to external changes in cultural and social conditions and demands, as well as to its own internal shifts. There is no question that the quick service industry, for example, will continue to be under pressure to respond and adapt to evolving social issues.

One of these is employment, the very issue that got me into a muddle with Fox News. The quick service restaurant industry often comes in for criticism as a sector characterized by low-paying dead-end jobs. Burger flipping and coffee pouring are favorite euphemisms for the supposedly terrible fate that awaits the unskilled or struggling worker.

Let me offer a bit of perspective on this stereotype. The restaurant and food service sector contributes nearly $2 trillion to the economy annually and is the second-largest private sector employer in the U.S., providing 14.4 million jobs in 2016, or about 10 percent of the U.S. workforce. If you look at the franchising business separately, it, too, is a huge job-creation machine—in fact, it creates more jobs than any other business bar none. Franchisees generate approximately 250,000 new jobs each year, and franchising has been growing at twice the rate of nonfranchises for six straight years. The 790,000 franchise businesses in the United States account for about nine million total jobs.

But what about the low-level workers: the coffee servers and donut makers and sandwich toasters? I see the quick service industry, and Dunkin' in particular, as a key part of a de facto training system for millions of Americans in a country that offers very little in the way of practical, vocational education. In fact, a significant percentage of Americans get their start in a fast-food or quick service restaurant job or have worked in one at some time during their careers. There is a long list of well-known and very successful people who have worked in the industry, the most famous of whom is Barack Obama, whose first job was scooping ice cream at a Baskin-Robbins in Honolulu, Hawaii.

In a Dunkin' Donuts restaurant, a Baskin-Robbins shop, or any number of other quick service venues, employees can learn the basic, essential skills of working in a business—or any kind of organization or endeavor, for that matter. Punctuality. Responsibility. Safety. Managing customers. Managing yourself. Communication. Teamwork. As Obama put it, "My first summer job wasn't exactly glamorous, but it taught me some valuable lessons. Responsibility. Hard work. Balancing a job with friends, family, and school."

People who master these essential skills are not doomed to a life of drudgery and low-end pay. You can start at the very bottom, as franchisee Jim Allen did, and quickly move up through the organization. Jim ended up running a multimillion-dollar operation. Along the way you provide employment, offer training, contribute to your community, and create wealth for yourself and many others. As Obama wrote, "I'll never forget that job—or the people who gave me that opportunity—and how they helped me get to where I am today."

I should add another quality that is fundamental to success in the challenge culture: persistence. I don't mean aggressiveness; I mean being extremely consistent in your requirements and making sure that people, including yourself, are held accountable—and, above all, not giving up easily or too soon.

In early 2017, for example, we had an opportunity to build our business in Germany when a franchisee who had long dominated the market ran into financial trouble. As we've seen, Dunkin' has had its struggles in Europe, and with the Amsterdam expression, we are just beginning to improve our performance there. So I felt that Germany, with its increasing love of coffee, might be a good next market for us to expand into, if we could change the ownership structure and develop a workable plan for consolidating our operations there to facilitate growth.

When this opportunity arose, I added Germany to the agenda for our weekly leadership team meeting. At each meeting, I would ask the responsible leaders, especially the executive John Varughese, who oversaw the German market, to report on their activities with regard to advancing Dunkin' in that region. It stayed on the agenda for months, without much to show for the efforts. Finally, Karen Raskopf did her challenge thing. "Nigel," she said, "why do we have to keep Germany on the agenda every single week? Everybody is extremely bored with the subject. We're getting nowhere, and most of us have nothing to do with the issue and can do nothing about it."

"Well, if we don't keep talking about and debating the right approach, we will certainly not be able to do anything about it," I replied. "If we keep at it, I'm confident we can find a way."

Karen sighed. Germany appeared on the agenda the following week and many weeks after that, for a total of some eight months. We kept looking at different options for consolidation, both within Germany and outside. I kept asking John to report on how things were going. We finally hit upon a solution. A very successful franchisee from Saudi Arabia expressed interest in the market. He had a deep understanding of the business and possessed the resources to build a significant presence in Germany. We did the deal, and just nine months later, the Saudi franchisee leads the German market.

Not long after Germany was removed as a regular agenda item, John said to me, "Thanks for persisting on this. The pressure of having to report weekly definitely made us work hard to achieve it." It was the combination of my persistence in asking questions and John's persistence in seeking solutions that brought us success.

. . .

One final point: I truly believe that a challenge culture enables a company like ours to be a worthy part of the fabric of people's everyday lives and to make a valuable, positive contribution to the society as a whole.

For starters, we at Dunkin' Brands get the satisfaction of providing millions of people with the coffees and teas, donuts and sandwiches, ice creams and shakes they love and rely on to keep them running every day.

We are also the keepers and builders of an iconic brand. As Paul Twohig often said, we want to propagate love for the brand. And that love is a real thing. In New England, where Dunkin' got its start, people cherish their Dunkin' memories. One longtime customer, Leonard Blanchette, recalled how he and his older sisters would sometimes skip Catholic Mass and go to Dunkin' instead. One Sunday when they came home, their mother asked which priest had officiated. Leonard's sister said, "Father Dunkin'." Dunkin' is one of those brands, now seventy years in the making, that helps define who we are and what we value.

Dunkin' also contributes to society through service and sharing activities. We have found that one of our most effective and satisfying initiatives is the work we do through the company's charity, the Joy in Childhood Foundation. Established in 2006, the goal of the foundation is to focus on helping kids—particularly those facing hunger and sickness—find joy in their daily lives. Through the generosity of franchisees, employees, vendors, and others, the Joy in Childhood Foundation raises funds to support partnerships with children's hospitals, food banks, and nonprofit organizations directly committed to serving sick and hungry kids. In 2015, some 1,500 Dunkin' Donuts and Baskin-Robbins franchisees, crew members, and corporate employees volunteered more than four thousand hours to provide hundreds of thousands of meals to kids and families in communities across the country.

And with this book I hope that we can add a new layer of meaning and a new source of value to the Dunkin' Brands. We are a company of relatively modest size, and we harbor no grand ambitions beyond those I have talked about in this book: to meet customers' needs, to build great franchises, to constantly improve our operations, to create and share wealth, to strengthen the brand, and to contribute to the communities we serve.

To that list of ambitions, however, I will add one more: to make a contribution to the practice of management and leadership. Through our modeling of the challenge culture concept at Dunkin', and through the discussion in this book, I'd like to think that we can help organizations open themselves up to the power of questioning, the excitement of civil dialogue, and the benefits of productive challenge.

As I write this, we are at a moment of national and global imbalance, a time during which we are looking back at past decisions, reconsidering the status quo, and trying to develop a new vision of the future. It is certainly a period of questioning. My belief is that it can lead to a positive reset. If we can avoid trashing anyone or anything, the questioning will produce new solutions and the challenge will ultimately make us all stronger.

America was, after all, founded as a challenge culture. We have a duty and a responsibility to keep it going.

A Checklist for Creating a Challenge Culture

Here are some questions you might ask as you think about your culture and whether it encourages questioning, dialogue, and challenge.

1. Do people in your company fear they will be fired if they challenge the status quo or question ideas or plans too forcefully or too often? Do you live in a you're-fired or confrontational culture?

2. What defines a culture that is *not* what you want yours to be?

3. What are the constituencies that influence your business and how do they define success? Can these differences be aligned? Do they need to be?

4. Have you defined and distributed the ground rules for civil dialogue in your organization?

5. What qualitative skills are most important to your culture and business? How do you foster and encourage them (e.g.,

questioning, listening, debate, challenge, being interviewed, public speaking)?

6. Do you value listening? Do you practice listening skills? Do you take notes during dialogues?

7. Have you established channels and venues that provide regular opportunities for people to pose questions and make challenges to others at every level, including their bosses?

8. Are your people able to challenge their peers and colleagues? How?

9. Does the core management team consist of people who will challenge and question each other? Do they have a diversity of viewpoints and backgrounds?

10. Do you have an emotional consigliere? A sparring partner?

11. What role does HR play in your organization? Does it help create the challenge culture?

12. Do you, and the members of your team, personally live and model the characteristics of the challenge culture?

13. What have you learned about your culture from other industries, organizations, or activities?

14. Have you anticipated your organization's potential demise?

Acknowledgments

My thanks and appreciation go to:

My wife, Joanna, whose dedication to the task was nonstop.

My young children, Ian and Brooke.

My parents, Roland and Joan Travis, who gave me an entrepreneurial spirit, and my brother Malcolm.

My oldest son, David, and his wife Karen.

Karen Raskopf, who challenged me nonstop.

My outstanding collaborator John Butman, who taught me many important lessons regarding the English language.

My literary agent, Zoë Pagnamenta, who guided me through the whole process.

John Mahaney, whose management of the process at PublicAffairs was perfect and very clear.

Ruth O'Quin, who has been my dedicated assistant for fifteen years in three cities.

Kent Teague, without whom we could not have saved Leyton Orient.

Rich Emmett, Mark Goldstein, Paul Twohig, John Costello, Bill Mitchell, Nicole Lapin, Scott Murphy, Sherrill Kaplan.

The Dunkin' Brands board of directors, especially Sandra Horbach and Linda Boff, both of whom read the book and provided detailed comments.

Nick Shepherd, Chris Wyatt, George McAllen, Kate and Brian Jaspon.

Significant mentors in my career, David Haenlein, David Tagg, Barry Gibbons, and John Antioco.

Jim Allen, Clayton Turnbull, and many Dunkin' and Baskin franchisees.

Thank you all!

Notes

Chapter Two
Leaders Must Model: Paul Takes a Stand

32   **The company engaged in a variety of dubious practices . . . :** Michael Corkery, "Wells Fargo Fined $185 Million for Fraudulently Opening Accounts," *New York Times,* September 8, 2016, www.nytimes .com/2016/09/09/business/dealbook/wells-fargo-fined-for-years-of -harm-to-customers.html.

32   **"The whispers among employees . . . ":** Emily Glazer, "Wells Fargo Bankers, Chasing Bonuses, Overcharged Hundreds of Clients," *Wall Street Journal,* November 27, 2017, www.wsj.com/articles/wells-fargo-bankers -chasing-bonuses-overcharged-hundreds-of-clients-1511830230.

32   **employees said they felt intense pressure:** Bess Levin, "6 Ways Wells Fargo Made Its Employees' Lives a Living Hell," *Vanity Fair,* April 10, 2017, www.vanityfair.com/news/2017/04/wells-fargo-john-stumpf-carrie -tolstedt.

33   **Just a few of the questions they threw at him:** Jeffrey Sonnenfeld, "How Wells Fargo's CEO Could Have Avoided His Senate Belly Flop," *Fortune,* September 23, 2016, http://fortune.com/2016/09/23/ wells-fargo-ceo-stumpf-senate/.

34   **activist investors made public demands:** Josh Black, "The Activist Investing Annual Review 2017," Harvard Law School Forum on Corporate Governance and Finacial Regulation, February 21, 2017. https://corpgov.law.harvard.edu/2017/02/21/the-activist-investing -annual-review-2017/.

34   **Samsung rushed its Galaxy Note 7:** Paul Mozur, "Galaxy Note & Fires Caused by Battery and Design Flaws, Samsung Says," *New York*

Times, January 22, 2017, www.nytimes.com/2017/01/22/business/sam-sung-galaxy-note-7-battery-fires-report.html.

35   **"unusual secrecy":** Alina Selyukh and Elise Hu, "In Samsung's Messy Phone Recall, Lack of Transparency Takes Center Stage," NPR on-line, October 18, 2016, www.npr.org/sections/alltechconsidered/2016/10/18/497949435/in-samsung-s-messy-phone-recall-lack-of-transparency-takes-center-stage.

36   **Schein reports that:** Edgar H. Schein, *Humble Inquiry: The Gentle Art of Asking Instead of Telling,* Kindle ed. (San Francisco: Berrett-Koehler, 2013), 59.

36   **Maxfield describes how:** David Maxfield, "How a Culture of Silence Eats Away at Your Company," Harvard Business Review, December 7, 2016, https://hbr.org/2016/12/how-a-culture-of-silence-eats-away-at-your-company.

37   **expressed in a 2017 book:** Ray Dalio, *Principles: Life and Work* (New York: Simon and Schuster, 2017).

37   **Dalio announced that he would step aside:** Alexandra Stevenson and Matthew Goldstein, "Bridgewater Associates, World's Biggest Hedge Fund, Shakes Up Leadership," *New York Times,* March 1, 2017, www.nytimes.com/2017/03/01/business/dealbook/ray-dalio-bridgewater-hedge-fund.html.

38   **Bower decided to ditch the approach:** Elizabeth Haas Edersheim, *McKinsey's Marvin Bower: Vision, Leadership, and the Creation of Management Consulting,* Kindle ed. (Hoboken, NJ: Wiley, 2006), 50.

38   **"walked out thinking this . . . ":** Warren Berger, *A More Beautiful Question: The Power of Inquiry to Spark Breakthrough Ideas,* Kindle ed. (New York: Bloomsbury, 2014), 2.

Chapter Three
Overcoming Challenge Aversion:
The Difference Between Dad, Socrates, and Blockbuster

45   **if we start with the "wrong questions":** Simon Sinek, *Start with Why: How Great Leaders Inspire Everyone to Take Action,* Kindle ed. (New York: Portfolio/Penguin, 2009), 1.

46   **Socrates, in the search for truth:** *Theaetetus,* 150b–d.

51   **"You can take the man out of Wal-Mart . . . ":** Patricia Sellers, "Wal-Mart's Big Man Puts Blockbuster on Fast Forward," *Fortune,* November 25, 1996, http://archive.fortune.com/magazines/fortune/fortune_archive/1996/11/25/218687/index.htm.

53   **he quit after just thirteen months:** David Altaner, "Blockbuster Looking for New CEO," *Orlando Sun-Sentinel,* March 23, 1997.

54   **Hastings saw his health club membership:** From an interview with Hastings in "Out of Africa, Onto the Web," *New York Times,* December 17, 2006, www.nytimes.com/2006/12/17/jobs/17boss.html.

54   **Hastings later said:** Cited in Wikipedia: Gina Keating, *Netflixed: The Epic Battle for America's Eyeballs* (New York: Portfolio/Penguin, 2012).

Chapter Four
Developing People for Challenge:
Why Allen Sheppard Kept a "Light Grip on the Throat"

69   **"I expect people to counterpunch . . . ":** "Lord Sheppard of Didgemere—Obituary," *Telegraph,* April 2, 2015, www.telegraph.co.uk /news/obituaries/11509443/Lord-Sheppard-of-Didgemere-business man-obituary.html; Allen died in 2015 at age eighty-two.

78   **89 percent of the executives polled:** Kate Davidson, "Employers Find 'Soft Skills' Like Critical Thinking in Short Supply," *Wall Street Journal,* August 30, 2016.

Chapter Five
Setting the Rules of Engagement:
How We Launched K-Cups

83   **"This was raw and angry politics . . . ":** Gerard Baker, "A Memorable, Riveting, Nasty Debate—but Will It Change the Direction of the Race?" *Wall Street Journal,* October 9, 2016, www.wsj.com/livecoverage /hillary-clinton-and-donald-trump-second-debate-2016.

Chapter Six
Ask Me Anything: Sixty Coffee Chats and Counting

106   **"Pray give us the essential facts . . . ":** From A. Conan Doyle's story "The Five Orange Pips."

114   **"thinking without thinking":** Malcolm Gladwell, *Blink: The Power of Thinking Without Thinking* (New York: Little, Brown, 2005).

115   **Goleman's purpose:** Daniel Goleman, *Emotional Intelligence: Why It Can Matter More than IQ* (New York: Bantam Books, 1995), xi.

116   **"If one were to attempt . . . ":** Raymond S. Nickerson, "Confirmation Bias: A Ubiquitous Phenomenon in Many Guises," *Review of General Psychology* 2, no. 2 (1998): 175–220, //psy2.ucsd.edu/~mckenzie/nickerson ConfirmationBias.pdf.

120   **"That means if you're a team member . . . ":** Roger Schwarz, "5 Ways Meetings Get Off Track, and How to Prevent Each One," *Harvard Business Review,* May 3, 2016, https://hbr.org/2016/05/5-ways-meetings -get-off-track-and-how-to-prevent-each-one.

Chapter Eight
The Personal Nudge:
Jumping Off Cliffs When You're Not Really in the Mood

147   **it's easier to think:** Ernest Hemingway, *A Moveable Feast* (New York: Vintage, 2000).

147   **you should walk at a normal pace:** Marily Oppezzo and Daniel L. Schwartz, "Give Your Ideas Some Legs: The Positive Effect of Walking on Creative Thinking," *Journal of Experimental Psychology: Learning, Memory, and Cognition* 40, no. 4 (2014): 1142–1152.

149   **You do not wake up feeling groggy:** Sara C. Mednick, *Take a Nap! Change Your Life,* with Mark Ehrman (New York: Workman, 2006); Michelle Carr, "How to Dream Like Salvador Dali," *Psychology_Today,* February 20, 2015; Salvador Dali, *50 Secrets of Magic Craftsmanship* (Victoria, BC: Dead Authors Society, 2017), 36–37.

150   **"Don't think you will be doing less work . . . ":** Jane E. Brody, "New Respect for the Nap, A Pause That Refreshes," *New York Times,* January 4, 2000, www.nytimes.com/2000/01/04/health/personal-health -new-respect-for-the-nap-a-pause-that-refreshes.html.

151   **"Every time we interact . . . ":** Adam Grant, *Give and Take: Why Helping Others Drives Our Success* (New York: Viking, 2013), p. 4.

156   **"Nature had not intended mankind . . . ":** Matt McFarland, "Why You Should Be Proud to Sleep on the Job," *Washington Post,* March 5, 2014, www.washingtonpost.com/news/innovations/wp/2014/03/05/why -you-should-be-proud-to-sleep-on-the-job/.

Chapter Nine
The Negative Normative:
Lessons from the Football Pitch

163   **"catalogue of disasters":** "Exclusive Interview: Selling Leyton Orient 'an absolute disaster'—Barry Hearn Launches Scathing Attack on Francesco Becchetti," *Telegraph* (London), March 1, 2017.

167   **"Francesco Becchetti's three-year reign . . . ":** Kieran Gill, "Dunkin' Donuts Chief Executive Nigel Travis Completes Leyton Orient Takeover as Francesco Becchetti's Disastrous Three-Year Reign Ends," *MailOnline,* June

22, 2017, www.dailymail.co.uk/sport/football/article-4629734/Nigel
-Travis-completes-Leyton-Orient-takeover.html.

Chapter Ten
Global Expressions:
Stroopwafels, Pork Floss, and Lager for Breakfast

177   **In an article for *Harvard Business Review*:** Jeanne Brett, Kristin Beh-
far, and Jeffrey Sanchez-Burks, "How to Argue Across Cultures," *Harvard
Business Review,* December 4, 2013.

187   **"caviar among donuts":** Janene Pieters, "Dunkin' Donuts Eyes 160
Netherlands Store Locations," *NL Times,* March 23, 2017.

Chapter Eleven
Overcommunicate: On Blenders, Strategy,
and Alligators

203   *Communication Within Tesla:* Justin Bariso, "This Email from Elon Musk
to Tesla Employees Describes What Great Communication Looks Like,"
Inc., August 30, 2017.

203   **"with intelligence and agility":** Bariso, "This Email from Elon Musk."

203   **"If you're going to be on the air . . . ":** Lloyd Grove, "Megyn Kelly:
'Roger Ailes Tried to Grab Me Three Times. I Had to Shove Him Off
Me'," *Daily Beast,* November 29, 2017, www.thedailybeast.com/megyn
-kelly-roger-ailes-tried-to-grab-me-three-times-i-had-to-shove-him
-off-me.

Chapter Twelve
Cycles within Cycles: Freak-Outs, Slow Laps,
Anticipation, and the Belichick Reset

213   **greatest NFL franchise:** Ryan Wilson, "SuperBowl 2017: Tom Brady
Leads Epic Comeback, Patriots Stun Falcons in OT," *USA Today,* February 5, 2017.

215   **"We had it handed to us . . . ":** Lorenzo Reyes, "Tom Brady Calls
Out Patriots' Effort After Chiefs' Historic Outburst," *USA TODAY,* September 8, 2017, www.usatoday.com/story/sports/nfl/patriots/2017/09/08
/new-england-patriots-kansas-city-chiefs-tom-brady-tyreek-hill
-alex-smith/644794001/.

216   **"The only time I think . . . ":** John Breech, "Bill Belichick Scoffs
at Idea that He Should've Pulled Tom Brady in Blowout," CBS Sports

website, November 27, 2017, www.cbssports.com/nfl/news/watch-bill
-belichick-scoffs-at-idea-that-he-shouldve-pulled-tom-brady-in-blow
out/.

219   **"New England has been the NFL's . . . ":** Brett Pollakoff, "Every
NFL Team's 10-Year Record, Ranked from 32 to 1," Fox Sports website,
January 5, 2017, www.foxsports.com/nfl/gallery/every-nfl-teams-10-year
-record-ranked-32-1-010417.

Conclusion: The Social Value of Challenge

231   **Jerry Useem, a business researcher:** Jerry Useem, "Power Causes
Brain Damage," *Atlantic,* July/August 2017.

237   **The issue of the balance:** Sarah Carmichael Green, "Lots of Companies Still Have No Senior Executives Who Are Women," *Harvard Business
Review,* March 8, 2017.

238   **"It involves a fundamental identity shift":** Herminia Ibarra, Robin
J. Ely, and Deborah M. Kolb, "Women Rising, The Unseen Barriers,"
Harvard Business Review, September 2013.

243   **"I'll never forget that job . . . ":** Richard Feloni, "Barack Obama Ex-
plains What he Learned from Scooping Ice Cream as a 16 year old," *Business Insider,* February 26, 2016, www.businessinsider.com/barack-obama
-lessons-from-first-job-scooping-ice-cream-2016-2.

244   **"Father Dunkin'":** Francis Storrs, "Dunkin's Run: A Love Story,"
Boston Magazine, September 2010.

Index

Roger D. Pelissier

NIGEL TRAVIS, the chairman of Dunkin' Brands, was the company's chief executive officer from 2009 to 2018. From 2005 through 2008, Nigel served as president and CEO of Papa John's, the pizza chain. Prior to Papa John's, Nigel was with Blockbuster, Inc., from 1994 to 2004, where he served in increasing roles of responsibility, including president and chief operating officer. Nigel has served on the boards of numerous nonprofit organizations and also is part owner and chairman of Leyton Orient FC in London. Nigel's distinctive human-centered perspective on leadership and management, now viewed as essential in today's complex and diverse global organizations, took root early in his career when he was a human resource manager.

PublicAffairs is a publishing house founded in 1997. It is a tribute to the standards, values, and flair of three persons who have served as mentors to countless reporters, writers, editors, and book people of all kinds, including me.

I. F. STONE, proprietor of *I. F. Stone's Weekly*, combined a commitment to the First Amendment with entrepreneurial zeal and reporting skill and became one of the great independent journalists in American history. At the age of eighty, Izzy published *The Trial of Socrates*, which was a national bestseller. He wrote the book after he taught himself ancient Greek.

BENJAMIN C. BRADLEE was for nearly thirty years the charismatic editorial leader of *The Washington Post*. It was Ben who gave the *Post* the range and courage to pursue such historic issues as Watergate. He supported his reporters with a tenacity that made them fearless and it is no accident that so many became authors of influential, best-selling books.

ROBERT L. BERNSTEIN, the chief executive of Random House for more than a quarter century, guided one of the nation's premier publishing houses. Bob was personally responsible for many books of political dissent and argument that challenged tyranny around the globe. He is also the founder and longtime chair of Human Rights Watch, one of the most respected human rights organizations in the world.

· · ·

For fifty years, the banner of Public Affairs Press was carried by its owner Morris B. Schnapper, who published Gandhi, Nasser, Toynbee, Truman, and about 1,500 other authors. In 1983, Schnapper was described by *The Washington Post* as "a redoubtable gadfly." His legacy will endure in the books to come.

Peter Osnos, *Founder*